Our Common Bonds

Chicago Studies in American Politics

A series edited by Susan Herbst, Lawrence R. Jacobs, Adam J. Berinsky, and Frances Lee; Benjamin I. Page, editor emeritus

ALSO IN THE SERIES:

Additional series titles follow index.

Our Common Bonds

Using What Americans Share to Help Bridge the Partisan Divide

MATTHEW LEVENDUSKY

The University of Chicago Press
Chicago and London

The University of Chicago Press, Chicago 60637
The University of Chicago Press, Ltd., London
© 2023 by The University of Chicago

Published 2023
Printed in the United States of America

32 31 30 29 28 27 26 25 24 23   1 2 3 4 5

ISBN-13: 978-0-226-82468-0 (cloth)
ISBN-13: 978-0-226-82470-3 (paper)
ISBN-13: 978-0-226-82469-7 (e-book)
DOI: https://doi.org/10.7208/chicago/9780226824697.001.0001

Library of Congress Cataloging-in-Publication Data

Names: Levendusky, Matthew, author.
Title: Our common bonds : using what Americans share to help bridge the
    partisan divide / Matthew Levendusky.
Other titles: Chicago studies in American politics.
Description: Chicago : The University of Chicago Press, 2023. | Series: Chicago
    studies in American politics | Includes bibliographical references and index.
Identifiers: LCCN 2022034820 | ISBN 9780226824680 (cloth) |
    ISBN 9780226824703 (paperback) | ISBN 9780226824697 (ebook)
Subjects: LCSH: Party affiliation—Social aspects—United States. |
    United States—Politics and government—21st century.
Classification: LCC JK2271 .L48 2023 | DDC 324.273—dc23/eng/20220816
LC record available at https://lccn.loc.gov/2022034820

Contents

Is Overcoming Division a Fantasy?

On a blustery January day, just moments after being sworn in as the forty-sixth president of the United States of America, Joe Biden delivered an address centered on "that most elusive of things in a democracy: unity." This was perhaps a slightly odd choice, as the country seemed to be more divided than ever. Just two weeks before, supporters of former President Trump had stormed the US Capitol in an attempt to block the certification of Biden's victory in the November 2020 election. January 6 marked only the second time in US history that the Capitol had been breached, but the first time that American citizens—rather than foreign troops—had been the ones doing the ransacking. Even before that insurrection, few would have characterized the United States as unified: the country was seemingly torn asunder by divides over how to address the COVID-19 pandemic and associated economic recession, as well as a centuries-overdue reckoning about the legacy of slavery and racism. Dissolution, not unity, seemed like a more appropriate topic for the moment.

Biden acknowledged that there were deep and significant challenges to be overcome. But he argued that to confront these challenges, we have to "end this uncivil war that pits red against blue, rural versus urban, conservative versus liberal." He acknowledged that this will be difficult, and that unity does not imply unanimity: "The right to dissent peaceably, within the guardrails of our Republic, is perhaps our nation's greatest strength. Yet hear me clearly: Disagreement must not lead to disunion." But he argued that if we could come together as one, we could "heal a broken land" and "write an American story of hope, not fear, of unity, not division, of light, not darkness" (Biden 2021).

Those stirring words, poetic as they were, likely seemed hopelessly naïve to most Americans. Biden himself acknowledged as much, saying that he knew his words sounded like "a foolish fantasy" to many. The public agreed with his assessment: in a poll by the Pew Research Center early in his term, of all of the issues polled, the public was the *least* confident in Biden's ability to unify the country, even when compared to major challenges like responding to the COVID-19 pandemic or reforming immigration policy (Pew Research Center 2021). This skepticism reflects the conventional wisdom about American politics: politicians in Washington, DC, are hopelessly divided and cannot come together on almost any issue, and ordinary voters are little better. Indeed, not only do voters disagree with one another, they also fundamentally dislike and distrust one another. This animosity seemingly eviscerates any calls for unity among members of the public.

Public opinion data reinforce this bleak outlook. When asked about their feelings toward the other party, 79 percent of Democrats, and 83 percent of Republicans, described those feelings as negative, rather than neutral or positive. Seventy-five percent of Democrats said that Republicans were closed-minded, and 55 percent of Republicans said that Democrats were immoral (Pew Research Center 2019c). Nearly 8 in 10 say that they "fundamentally disagree about core American values" with those in the other party (Pew Research Center 2020), and more than 70 percent think that those from the other party are "a clear and present danger to the American way of life" (UVA Center for Politics 2021). Animosity and ill will between the parties have become the norm.

Scholars term this phenomenon of partisan distrust and dissensus *affective polarization* (Iyengar, Sood, and Lelkes 2012). Such partisan animosity damages our social and economic interactions with one another, and it also poisons our politics, potentially diminishing democratic accountability and complicating the response to significant, ongoing crises, such as the coronavirus pandemic, economic inequality, and climate change. While affective polarization does not bear all of the blame for these issues, it is part of "Why Washington Won't Work," in Hetherington and Rudolph's (2015) apt phrasing. What, if anything, can be done about this partisan animosity? Is there any way to lessen it and ameliorate some of these corrosive consequences?

This book argues that we can reduce affective polarization, and it outlines a set of strategies to do so. The unity that President Biden spoke of so stirringly in his inaugural address will not be easy to achieve, and progress will be slow and halting, measured more in inches than in miles, as the months since Biden's inauguration have illustrated. But it is possible to make progress toward that goal. To be clear, the strategies I present in this book reduce affective polarization, but they do not eliminate it—this is about amelioration, not cessation. Affective polarization is a hard problem caused by a number of different factors, and, as Finkel et al. (2020, 536) note, "there are no silver bullets" that will allow us to erase it altogether. There will be cases where our divides cannot—and should not—be bridged, and some people will not be moved from disliking the other party. In a diverse and pluralistic country, there will always be some level of partisan animosity that cannot be avoided. Nevertheless, it is still possible to lower the nation's political temperature, and make our social and political interactions more constructive. This book focuses on how to do that.

My approach starts from the fact that there are many different factors that drive partisan animosity. But one important factor is that Democrats and Republicans *think* they are more dissimilar than they actually are. This is not to say that they agree on everything, or even a lot: there are real and important differences between the parties. Yet most people still exaggerate those differences, and that heightens affective polarization. Reducing those misperceptions reduces affective polarization.

How do I do that? How can I reduce this misperception that Democrats and Republicans have nothing in common? I do so by highlighting our common bonds: the things that Americans share, sometimes surprisingly, across the partisan divide. In particular, the book focuses on three sets of common bonds between Democrats and Republicans. First, partisans share a set of common identities that bind them together. Normally, Democrats and Republicans see each other as rival partisans, but in fact they possess a number of common identities, most prominent among them their identity as Americans. If I prime this shared national identity, then this changes how they see members of the other party—not as partisan rivals, but as fellow Americans—and their animus toward them will fall. This same logic applies to other shared identities as well, and I explain how various sorts of identities can also help to bridge the partisan divide.

Second, they share a set of relationships that cross party lines. While it is true that Democrats are typically friends with other Democrats, and likewise for Republicans, it is equally true that almost all Americans—more than 80 percent of us—have at least some close relationships with those from the other side of the political aisle. Some of those we know and respect—our friends, family members, neighbors, coworkers, and so forth—come from the other party. When we remember these connections, our image of the other party changes. It is no longer just partisan stereotypes and media caricatures—it contains important people in our lives. As a result of this re-envisioning of the other party, animus toward it falls.

Finally, and perhaps most surprisingly, Democrats and Republicans share some common ground with one another. This might seem odd given the popular narrative of polarization, but there are areas where both parties agree (Fiorina 2017; Hill and Tausanovitch 2015; Fowler et al. forthcoming). This is not to say that the parties agree on most things, or even many things; clearly, they do not. Nevertheless, a narrower claim is true: on some issues, common ground remains. Further, and even more importantly, partisans exaggerate—often dramatically—the divergence between the parties (Levendusky and Malhotra 2016b; Yudkin, Hawkins, and Dixon 2019). This is not just true of their issue positions; they also overestimate the degree of dissimilarity in terms of political interest, values, willingness to compromise, demographics, and many other factors. But if partisans realize that the other side is more similar to them in a variety of ways, animus will fall. I argue that can be accomplished with a civil cross-party dialogue, which functions as a powerful tool for highlighting commonalities across the partisan divide.

What unites these three distinct strategies is that they all use the ties that bind us together to lessen animosity. The media—and many political elites—emphasize what divides us, as trafficking in fear and division is often a winning strategy (if for no other reason than that negative emotions are more powerful than positive ones; see Lau 1982). But this belies what we have in common. It is certainly the case that there are important divisions between the parties, and there are fundamental disagreements in American politics, especially at the elite level. But it is equally correct that many Americans remain more centrist than extremist (Fowler et al. forthcoming), and partisans of all stripes share a set of identities and friendships. When we emphasize what ordinary Democrats and Republicans have in common, rather than what divides them, we can build bridges across the political divide. Political elites in Washington, DC, may well have irreconcilable differences, but in the wider public the divides are gaps more than chasms.

Using a variety of data sources—including large-scale national surveys, survey experiments, and a lab-in-the-field experiment—I evaluate these claims, and find that all of these methods do, in fact, lessen affective polarization and improve attitudes toward the other party. Not only that, I show that a series of downstream consequences also flow from efforts to reduce affective polarization, including reducing ideological polarization and partisan motivated reasoning more generally.

All of this demonstrates that it is possible to reduce partisan animosity, and that doing so has important consequences. But it is also worth emphasizing that sometimes partisan animosity can be a *good* thing. In a diverse and pluralistic society like the United States, there will likely always be some partisan animosity, because there are real, and important, policy differences between the parties, and the choice between them matters. The danger is when, as at the present moment, that animosity reaches a point where it damages our social and political lives. The goal here is to help reduce this more harmful polarization, and help Americans find ways to engage more constructively with one another across partisan lines. This book lays out this argument, and explains how we can take small steps as individuals that can hopefully translate into something more meaningful for our politics.

What Is Affective Polarization?

Debates over polarization in American politics are nothing new. In the mid-1980s, scholars first noticed that congressional politics had become more polarized and dysfunctional (Poole and Rosenthal 1984), a trend that that has only accelerated in the years since then (Lee and McCarty 2019). By the early 2000s, many argued that the same was true of the mass public as well, noting that issue positions in the public had grown more divided over time (Abramowitz and Saunders 2008; though, for the alternative view, see Fiorina, Abrams, and Pope 2008). This literature, however, focused almost exclusively on changes in voters' issue positions, and hence is often labeled "ideological polarization" (or issue-based polarization). In the end, the evidence suggests that this type of mass ideological polarization is limited (Hill and Tausanovitch 2015; Fiorina 2017), though voters' issue positions have become considerably more strongly related to their partisanship over time, a process known as partisan sorting (Levendusky 2009; Mason 2018).

More recently, however, a different sort of polarization has emerged. Regardless of how divided voters are on the issues, they often display high levels of animosity toward those from the other party (Iyengar, Sood, and Lelkes 2012; Mason 2015). Scholars argue that this reflects a new type of polarization: affective polarization, or "the tendency of people identifying as Republicans or Democrats to view opposing partisans negatively and copartisans positively" (Iyengar and Westwood 2015, 691).

One might wonder if affective polarization is simply another name for ideological polarization. After all, part of the reason people dislike and distrust those from the opposing party is that they disagree with them on the issues, often quite vociferously (for a lucid discussion of this point, see Fiorina 2017). It is certainly the case that those who are more ideologically extreme are also more affectively polarized (Bougher 2017), and growing ideological divisions among political elites also fuel affective polarization (Rogowski and Sutherland 2016; Webster and Abramowitz 2017).[1] But it is incorrect to conclude that ideological and affective polarization are synonymous. Many voters with moderate issue positions are quite affectively polarized. Indeed, the title of Mason's 2018 book—*Uncivil Agreement*—captures this logic: even when partisans agree on the issues, they view the other side with suspicion and hostility. As Iyengar, Sood, and Lelkes (2012, 424) note, "the evidence presented above . . . is at odds with the view that partisan affect is driven primarily by ideological affinity. Instead, the data suggest that the two . . . [are] distinct forms of polarization" (see also Lelkes 2018). While affective and ideological polarization are closely related, they are best thought of as distinct concepts both theoretically and empirically.

Similarly, one might wonder if affective polarization is just another name for strong partisanship, with high levels of animosity being another indicator of partisan strength. The answer is, once again, no. While the two are correlated (Klar, Krupnikov, and Ryan 2018; Mason 2018), they are distinct concepts. Strong partisanship is about a positive identification with one's political party (Huddy, Mason, and Aarøe 2015), whereas affective polarization is more about negativity toward the other party (Iyengar and Krupenkin 2018). Attachment to one's party and derogation of the other party are different concepts: one can strongly identify with one's own party without derogating the other, and vice versa (Bankert 2021; Groenendyk 2018; Mason 2018). Much like ideological polarization, the concept of partisan strength is distinct from (though obviously related to) affective polarization. Affective polarization is not simply old wine in new bottles.

HOW DO WE KNOW AFFECTIVE POLARIZATION WHEN WE SEE IT?

But how do scholars measure affective polarization, and how has it changed over time? In later chapters I will have more to say about the measurement of this concept, but for now, I will note that the best data on how levels of partisan animus have changed over time come from the American National Election Study (ANES), the gold standard survey for public opinion researchers. Since 1978, the ANES has been asking the public to rate both the Democratic and the Republican Parties (along with leading politicians and various social groups) on a feeling thermometer scale. This item shows respondents a 100-degree scale (depicted visually on a thermometer) and asks them to rate each party on it. A score of 0 means the respondent feels very negatively about the party, a score of 50 means they are ambivalent toward it, and a score of 100 means they feel very positively about it. While we cannot know *why* respondents are giving a party a particular rating (is it their foreign policy? their nominee for president? their congressional leadership?), these evaluations give us a sense of their sentiment toward the party as a whole. As such,

FIGURE 1.1. Same-Party and Other-Party Feeling Thermometer Trends

Note: Same-party feeling thermometer ratings are given in black, other-party feeling thermometer ratings are in gray; the solid lines are the values for face-to-face respondents, the dashed lines are for online respondents.
Source: American National Election Study

scholars have used it as an over-time indicator of partisan animosity (Iyengar, Sood, and Lelkes 2012). Figure 1.1 plots the over-time trends in how individuals evaluate both their own party (in black) and the opposing party (in gray).

Note that in figure 1.1 there are two lines for same-party feeling thermometers, and two for other-party feeling thermometers: a solid line, running from

1978 until 2016, and a shorter dashed line, running from 2012 to 2020. These two lines represent the two different modes of administration of the ANES. Traditionally, the ANES was administered face to face, with the interviewer sitting with the respondent in their home. But in 2012 the ANES began a mode experiment where some respondents would be interviewed face to face in the traditional format, and others would be interviewed online, in preparation for a potential web-only future. That future arrived sooner than expected when the COVID-19 pandemic forced the ANES (and really all surveys) to pivot to an online-only format in 2020. As the data make clear, there are real mode effects, with the online ratings of both parties typically being somewhat lower. This difference stems from both sample selection issues (i.e., different sets of people are willing to respond online versus in a face-to-face survey; see Malhotra and Krosnick 2007) and the fact that respondents answer questions differently online than they do face to face (Homola, Jackson, and Gill 2016).

But while there are different levels across modes, the trends are the same, and are quite striking. Over time, respondents' feelings toward their own party have been relatively constant at roughly 70 degrees—people like their own party. Indeed, if we exclude 2016, there is no time trend at all in face-to-face same-party ratings (though see Groenendyk, Sances, and Zhirkov 2020). The 2016 decline is likely due to the fact that both Hillary Clinton and Donald Trump were uniquely unpopular, even among their fellow partisans. When most people think about the Democratic or Republican Parties, they think about their most prominent politicians, chief among them the presidential nominee (Jacobson 2019), so negative evaluations of Clinton and Trump shaped how people perceived the parties in 2016. If we look at the online data, the 2020 data look like the 2012 data, suggesting that 2016 was largely an aberration.[2]

To put an average same-party feeling thermometer rating of 70 degrees in perspective, consider how it compares to average ratings of other key social groups. The ANES has respondents use the feeling thermometer scale to assess many different groups of people and individuals, not just the political parties. Over the past forty years, the ANES has asked about dozens of social and political groups: different social classes, labor unions, big business, Christian fundamentalists, feminists, environmentalists, the police, and many others. During that whole time, only two groups have had an average rating higher than 70 degrees: the military and middle-class people. This is rarified company, and it underlines the point that people like their own party quite a lot.

The same cannot be said for the other party, though. In the late 1970s and early 1980s, people were relatively neutral toward the other party, with an average rating just below 50 degrees. By 2016, that had fallen dramatically to around 30 degrees, or a decline of nearly 40 percent since the item was introduced. Looking at the online data, we see a steep drop as well: in 2012, the average other-party feeling thermometer rating was 32 degrees, but that fell to only 19 degrees by 2020, a 40 percent decline in just eight short years.[3] Ratings of the other party today have the ignominious distinction of being among the lowest ratings ever assigned to any social group. Indeed, the only groups who have lower average ratings are truly stigmatized groups from the past, such as Black militants or radical students. This is much less rarified company to keep.

Over time, we have constant same-party ratings, and declining other-party ratings, so the gap in how people feel toward the parties has grown considerably. In the late 1970s, it was less than 25 degrees, but by 2016, it had risen to almost 40 degrees, and in 2020 it ballooned to 53 degrees, more than one-half of the entire scale, and more than double its value at the outset of the time series. Sentiments toward the parties have diverged sharply over the past generation. From this vantage point, it is clear that the public has affectively polarized in recent decades—people continue to like their own party, but they increasingly dislike the opposition.

WHY AFFECTIVE POLARIZATION MATTERS

But it is not simply that respondents say they dislike the other party on a survey—there are broader, real-world manifestations of affective polarization as well. Americans today report that they do not want to interact with the other party in a wide variety of ways—they do not want to be their friends (Wehner 2016) or their neighbors (Pew Research Center 2016), and they do not want to date or marry them (Huber and Malhotra 2017; Iyengar, Konitzer, and Tedin 2018; Bonos 2020). Indeed, in extreme cases, differing political views are now even being cited in divorce proceedings (Gabriel 2019; Pajer 2020). This animosity makes Americans want to spend less time with their friends and families, even on ostensibly apolitical days like Thanksgiving (Chen and Rohla 2018). It affects hiring decisions (Gift and Gift 2015), which companies people patronize (Kam and Deichert 2020; Panagopoulos et al. 2020; Mac-Farquhar 2021), and economic transactions more generally (McConnell et al. 2018). Even on clearly apolitical tasks—like solving puzzles—politics affects whom we are willing to select as a partner (Iyengar and Westwood 2015), and how much we trust other people that we do not know (Carlin and Love 2018). It affects the decisions we make about our own health care (specifically, whether to enroll in plans linked to Obamacare; see Lerman, Sadin, and Trachtman 2017), and the advice given by our health care providers (Hersh and Goldenberg 2016). Partisans discriminate against those from the other party in a variety of different settings (Deichert, Goggin, and Theodoridis 2019), and, in some settings, even perceive the other party to be less human (Martherus et al. 2021; Cassese 2021).

All of this demonstrates that affective polarization has politicized and damaged the social sphere, which is reason enough to be concerned about it. But its effects do not end there: it has also poisoned our politics in a number of important ways. First, it nationalizes elections (Abramowitz and Webster 2016), thereby weakening democratic accountability. As out-party animus increases, voters are less willing to vote for any candidate from the other party, even in down-ballot races (Rogers 2016). That means that rather than holding politicians accountable for their decisions (i.e., holding state legislative officials accountable for state-level policies and actions), voters simply treat the ballot box as a referendum on events in Washington, DC. All elections become increasingly nationalized in ways that do not benefit a highly federalized system (Hopkins 2018).[4]

Second, it helps to undermine support for core democratic norms—"the 'fundamental values' or 'rules of the game' considered essential for constitutional government" (McClosky 1964, 362), things like ensuring free and fair elections, protecting the right to free speech, limits on executive power, and so forth (see also Levitsky and Ziblatt 2018). The danger, as Simonovits, McCoy, and Littvay (2022) point out, is that people become democratic hypocrites: they support these principles when it benefits their own party, but not when it helps the opposition (see also Druckman et al. 2022a). Democrats supported Biden using executive actions to extend the eviction moratorium, even though Biden himself admitted it was unconstitutional to do so (an assessment the US Supreme Court later confirmed). Likewise, Republicans supported Trump's efforts to stonewall Congress and the Mueller investigation (again, actions of dubious legality). What are supposed to be bedrock constitutional principles become expedient political footballs for those with high levels of political animosity.

What's worse, elites know that they are unlikely to be punished for this sort of behavior. Graham and Svolik (2020) show that because of voters' dislike for the other side, and growing polarization, even when their party violates these norms, voters still support them. The price—seeing the other party gain power—is too great, so voters rationalize their way into supporting their own party. This highlights the point above about weakened accountability: if partisans overlook bad behavior, what incentive do elites have to prevent it?

Affective polarization also makes government less functional and less able to respond to crises in two related ways. First, if such crises become politicized, then affective polarization drives responses to them. When the COVID-19 crisis first emerged in the US, political elites here—unlike in most other countries around the world—politicized the issue and transformed it into a partisan debate, rather than simply a public health crisis (Lipsitz and Pop-Eleches 2020; Fowler, Kettler, and Witt 2020; Merkley et al. 2020). Unsurprisingly, the media, and then the public, picked up on this fact (Hart, Chinn, and Soroka 2020). As a result, there were pronounced divisions between Democrats and Republicans in response to the crisis, with Republicans taking the crisis less seriously, being less likely to wear a mask, socially distance from others, or engage in other protective behaviors (Allcott, Boxell, et al. 2020; Annenberg IOD Collaborative 2023). While we might worry that such survey responses simply reflect partisan cheerleading—answering a survey in a way that signals a respondent's partisanship, even if those answers are untrue (Bullock et al. 2015; Schaffner and Luks 2018)—actual behavioral data (geo-located data gathered through cell phones) confirmed that these survey responses did, in fact, reflect genuine differences in how partisans responded to the crisis (Gollwitzer et al. 2020). But as Druckman et al. (2021) show, these partisan gaps were driven largely by animus—it is those who dislike the other side the most forcefully who cause these partisan gaps to emerge (see also Druckman et al. 2022a). This is because these polarized respondents are the ones who react most strongly to these elite cues, and hence drive the parties apart. This politicization, and subsequent polarization, makes problem solving immeasurably harder than it needs to be.[5]

Second, affective polarization hollows out trust in government more generally. It is a well-known finding that Americans today trust government much less than they did sixty years ago. While this is true, there is another fact about political trust that might be even more disturbing: Democrats and Republicans alike only trust the government when their party controls it (Hetherington and Rudolph 2015). When President Biden took office from President Trump, Democratic trust increased while Republican trust fell, and the reverse happened when President Trump succeeded President Obama. This has significant consequences because trust is crucial for building programs to address large-scale social problems like economic inequality, racial injustice, and climate change (Hetherington 2004). Just at the moment when we need trust the most, we have the least of it.[6]

What Are Our Common Bonds?

Seeing this litany of pernicious consequences, a question emerges: is there any way to ameliorate them? I argue that there is: we can emphasize our common bonds, the things that tie Democrats and Republicans together across the partisan divide. In chapter 2, I outline the theoretical rationale as to why these factors help to ameliorate animus, but first, there's a more basic question: what, exactly, are these common bonds?

In this book, I focus primarily on three of them: Democrats and Republicans share a set of common identities, a set of friendships that cross party lines, and a set of shared values and issue positions. As I explain in later chapters, these bonds provide the mechanisms that can help us ameliorate the divisions that plague America. But these are far from the only ones that could be used—undoubtedly there are additional things that connect us, and future work will find even more effective ways of bridging the divide. These three are the start of the conversation, not the end of it.

A SET OF SHARED IDENTITIES

One of the most fundamental things that bind Democrats and Republicans together is that they share a set of common identities. We all have multiple identities: we are not just Democrats and Republicans; we are also Americans, parents, spouses, sports fans, music lovers, fans of particular TV shows, and so forth. How do Democrats and Republicans perceive these different identities: do they see the same ones as equally important, or do they prioritize different dimensions of their lives? Table 1.1 provides data from several different surveys that asked Americans to rate different dimensions of their identities, and breaks down the importance that they assigned to them by party.

Begin with the data from the 2018 Brigham Young University (BYU) American Family Survey (Karpowitz and Pope 2018). That survey asked respondents to rate the importance of five different identities—their identity as a spouse or partner, their identity as a parent, their partisan identity, their occupational identity, and their community identity—using a five-point Likert scale: extremely important, very important, somewhat important, not too important, and not at all important.[7] The question here is whether Democrats and Republicans prioritize different identities: for instance, perhaps Democrats see their occupational identities as extremely important, while Republicans instead prioritize their familial roles.

But the data here show similarity, not difference. Here, I look at the percentage of respondents who rate the given identity as extremely or very important, but the pattern would be very similar if I just looked at the average rating on the underlying 5-point response scale. What identities did people prioritize? Their most central identities were their most personal ones: their roles as parents and spouses, the identities that give shape to their family lives. While Republicans attached somewhat greater importance to these roles, this was largely a function of age: Democrats were somewhat younger

TABLE 1.1. Shared Identities as a Common Bond

Item	Response	Democrats (%)	Republicans (%)
2018 BYU American Family Survey			
Importance of your identity as a spouse or partner	Rated as very or extremely important	64	78
Importance of your identity as a parent	Rated as very or extremely important	64	79
Importance of your partisan identity	Rated as very or extremely important	31	33
Importance of your occupational identity	Rated as very or extremely important	39	38
Importance of your local community identity	Rated as very or extremely important	32	32
2019 Druckman and Levendusky Affective Polarization Study			
Importance of your identity as an American	Rated as very or extremely important	69	88
Importance of your gender identity	Rated as very or extremely important	70	68
Importance of your racial identity	Rated as very or extremely important	47	43
Importance of your social class identity	Rated as very or extremely important	35	31
Importance of your partisan identity	Rated as very or extremely important	41	30
2020 More in Common American Fabric Study			
I am proud to be an American	Agree	66	93
I am grateful to be an American	Agree	74	95
It is important to me to be an American	Agree	70	93
I feel a strong sense of connection to other Americans	Agree	69	87
If I could live anywhere in the world, I would still pick America	Agree	72	94
Readers Digest and More in Common American Unity Survey			
We should all be Americans first, before being a Democrat, Republican, or Independent	Strongly Agree	75	76
2021 Associated Press Poll			
A fair judicial system and the rule of law	Very or extremely important to the United States' identity as a nation	91	88
Individual liberties and freedoms as defined by the Constitution	Very or extremely important to the United States' identity as a nation	84	88
The ability of people living here to get good jobs and achieve the American dream	Very or extremely important to the United States' identity as a nation	87	83

(continued)

TABLE 1.1. (*continued*)

A democratically elected government	Very or extremely important to the United States' identity as a nation	88	79
A shared American culture and set of values	Very or extremely important to the United States' identity as a nation	63	71
A culture established by the country's early European immigrants	Very or extremely important to the United States' identity as a nation	25	36
A culture grounded in Christian religious beliefs	Very or extremely important to the United States' identity as a nation	23	62
The mixing of cultures and values from around the world	Very or extremely important to the United States' identity as a nation	77	40
Bovitz Forthright Party Cue Study			
Consider yourself a fan of any NFL team		58	58
Morning Consult			
Have a very favorable opinion of at least one team in the NBA		42	26
Have a very favorable opinion of at least one team in the NFL		38	31
Have a very favorable opinion of at least one team in the MLB		38	32
Have a very favorable opinion of at least one team in the NHL		36	33

and hence less likely to be married or to have children. But even in the Democratic Party, a super-majority still attached a great deal of importance to these roles, so it is fair to say that these identities were significant for members of both parties. This is consistent with past work showing that these sorts of personal, relational identities are central to most people (Reid and Deaux 1996).

But it is worth noting which identities are *not* important. Democrats and Republicans alike attach little importance to their partisan identities, their occupational identities, and their identities as a member of their local community (though this last one is a bit hard to interpret, as it may be very geographically heterogeneous, with stronger community identities in some places than in others). The lack of importance both parties attached to their partisan identity is noteworthy, in that it runs against the grain of the totalizing influence of partisanship, but it reinforces a long-standing result about ordinary people: for most of them, politics is not a central part of their lives (Dahl 1961; Krupnikov and Ryan 2022).

Druckman and Levendusky's (2019) data reinforce these patterns. At the end of their study, they asked respondents to rate the importance of five identities using an equivalent Likert scale. Using the same metric (the percentage of each party that rates each identity as extremely or very important), this data showed that people once again did not attach much importance at all to their partisan identities. Here, partisanship was rated similarly to social class, a consistently unimportant identity in American politics. They attached more importance to their gender identity and especially to their American identity, with the latter having the highest average importance rating.

The data from More in Common (Hawkins and Raghuram 2020) reinforces the centrality of American identity. Their study, which asked a slightly different set of questions, showed that both Democrats and Republicans saw their American identity as particularly salient. Super-majorities of both parties were proud of and grateful for their identity as Americans, felt connected to other Americans, and saw their American identity as important to them. Indeed, if they were given the chance to live somewhere else, the vast majority of both parties would choose to remain in America. The study also asked people how grateful they were for a variety of different identities: their American, racial, religious, gender, and familial (i.e., parental/spousal) identities. While members of both parties are, by and large, grateful for all of them, they were most grateful for their familial identities, followed by their American identity, consistent with the BYU data above. Another study by More in Common, done in collaboration with *Reader's Digest*, asked respondents whether they agreed that "We should be Americans first, before being a Democrat, Republican, or Independent." Three-quarters of both parties strongly agreed with the statement, and there was effectively unanimity once those who somewhat agreed with that statement were included (91 percent of Democrats, and 97 percent of Republicans, felt that way).[8] Core identities, such as American or familial identities, are more important to ordinary citizens than partisan identities.

The data so far highlight that partisans agree that American identity is important, but they do not say what they think American identity is. What are its key components? Data from the Associated Press (2021) speak to this question. They asked Americans how important they thought various things were to American identity; the data in the table shows what percentage thought each dimension was extremely or very important to it. Once again, we find considerable convergence across parties: both parties emphasized a shared culture and set of values, the ability to achieve the American dream, individual liberties and freedoms, a fair judicial system, and a democratically elected government. The core of American identity is rooted in these creedal beliefs.

To be clear, however, there was partisan disagreement about the importance of two dimensions of identity: religion (where Republicans put more
emphasis), and immigration (where Democrats put more emphasis); these
reflect long-standing divisions between the parties (Smith 1997; Schildkraut
2010). Nevertheless, there is a core set of American values—centered on our
political institutions and principles of government—that the vast majority of
Americans of both parties share.

A recent report by FixUS (a nonprofit working to improve governance
in the United States) reaffirms this shared sense of American identity. They
asked Americans how important different values were to defining America
as a nation, and there was a common set where both parties agreed. Both
parties saw free speech (83 percent of both parties see it as extremely or very
important to American identity), equal justice under the law (83 percent of
Democrats, 80 percent of Republicans), ensuring everyone has an equal opportunity to succeed (82 percent of Democrats, 81 percent of Republicans),
and working together toward the common good (77 percent of Democrats,
79 percent of Republicans) as central tenets of American identity (FixUS 2021).
Likewise, Americans share a similar set of individual values across party lines.
When asked what values were important to them as individuals, Democrats
and Republicans alike shared the same ranking: the most important value was
honesty (91 percent of both parties rated it as extremely or very important to
them), then being hard-working (85 percent of Republicans, 83 percent of
Democrats), then being independent (82 percent of Republicans, 78 percent
of Democrats; see FixUS 2020). American identity is not simply a matter of
birth or geography (as it is in many other nations); rather, it reflects a deeper
set of shared values and principles.

American identity is among our most important identities, but it is not
the only one. Another set of identities centers on our hobbies and interests.
While there is some political sorting of some of these behaviors (i.e., Republicans are more likely to listen to country music), a good deal of mainstream
entertainment and sports remains a shared bipartisan experience (Praet
et al. 2022). In particular, both Democrats and Republicans root for and cheer
on the same sports teams. As one example of this, at the close of one of my experiments (the Bovitz Forthright Friendship Study discussed in chapter 4), I
asked respondents whether they considered themselves to be a fan of any National Football League (NFL) team (I asked about the NFL because football is,
by far, the most popular professional sport in America). An identical 58 percent of both parties considered themselves a fan of some professional football
team! Paine, Enten, and Jones-Rooy (2017) found similar patterns in their data

as well: "every team in the NFL has both Democrats and Republicans in their fan base." Football remains a bipartisan activity—Democrats and Republicans cheer on the same teams sitting side by side in the stands.

But this is not just true of football: other professional sports remain similarly bipartisan. Take, for example, a poll conducted by Morning Consult (Silverman 2020). In that study, being a fan was defined as having a "very favorable" impression of at least one team in a given sports league. There were quite modest partisan differences across sports, though note that the percentages were lower here because of how they classified partisanship (they did not break out partisan leaners, so this data had a much larger share of Independents than the other data I analyzed). The largest gap was for the National Basketball Association (NBA), but that was also the sport with the largest non-White fan base, hence the larger partisan gap (given the correlation between race and partisanship in the United States). Looking across every team in every one of the major sports leagues, there were differences in the partisan composition of their fan bases (based largely on the partisan composition of the surrounding area; see Paine, Enten, and Jones-Rooy 2017), but all teams had substantial numbers of Democrats and Republicans rooting for them.

This is obviously just a subset of the types of different identities shared across party lines: Democrats and Republicans attend the same colleges and universities (and much like the above, root for the same college sports teams), watch the same movies and television shows (at least when considering mainstream, popular shows, rather than niche programs), shop at the same big box stores, and so forth. Partisanship is a powerful identity that divides us, but there are nevertheless a set of identities that can serve to bridge the partisan divide.

SHARED CROSS-PARTY FRIENDSHIPS

It is a truism that social networks and friendships are homophilous along many dimensions, and partisanship is no exception (McPherson, Smith-Lovin, and Cook 2001). But largely homophilous does not mean completely so, and friendships can and do cross party lines. Most friendships form because of some shared bond: a shared hobby, workplace, or neighborhood, and while these are correlated with partisanship, the relationship is weaker than many think (Sinclair 2012). Table 1.2 presents the data on whether friendships can indeed be bipartisan.

Take the data from the Pew Research Center (2017). Here, we see that 75 percent of Democrats, and 80 percent of Republicans, had at least some friends from the other party. To be clear, most people had more friends from

TABLE 1.2. Cross-Party Friendships as a Common Bond

Item	Response	Democrats (%)	Republicans (%)
2017 Pew Political Data			
Have at least a few friends from the other party	Yes	75	80
2008–2009 NES Panel			
One of three main political discussion partners is from the other party	Yes	34	37

their own party than from the opposing side, as one would expect. But the overwhelming share of individuals did have friendships that crossed the partisan divide, a finding that I also replicated in several original studies discussed in chapter 4. Simply put, most people's circle of friends is bipartisan.

But do people talk about politics in those friendships? After all, if people are friends with those from the other party, but then never talk about politics, such friendships are unlikely to do much to reduce partisan animosity. While the Pew data did not include this question, there are some related data that allow me to examine this. The 2008–2009 ANES panel study asked respondents to name up to three individuals with whom they had discussed politics in the past six months. Of those who named someone (i.e., they discussed politics with someone in that time frame), what percentage named at least one person from the other party? We see that roughly one-third of each party did so, suggesting that cross-party discussion does occur, even in our polarized political moment. Indeed, as Levendusky and Stecula (2021) show, there is a surprising amount of cross-party discussion in nearly all demographic groups (see their table 1 on p. 14), suggesting that it is not just limited to one subset of the population.

There is another fascinating wrinkle to this data that is worth underlining. The ANES also asks respondents how different the discussants' views were from their own. For conversation dyads that cross party lines, one might expect the answer to be that they were extremely different, but this was not the case. Among those who named a discussion partner from the other party, a majority (58 percent) said that the other person's views were moderately different, not too different, or not at all different from their own. Indeed, another study found that 60 percent of both Democrats and Republicans often or sometimes have constructive conversations with those who disagree with them (Friedman and Schleifer 2021). This underscores a point I will discuss in later in this chapter, and will return to in chapters 4 and 5: while there are many important differences between the parties, there is more common ground than it might appear at first glance, and it is possible for people to bridge the partisan divide, at least in some circumstances.

One might worry, however, that the fraction reporting a regular discussion partner from the other party is quite a bit lower than the fraction reporting at least a few friends from the other party. While true, it is important to note that the questions are really asking quite different things. It is a much lower bar to simply have a friend from the other party than it is to name someone from the other party as one of three people with whom you have discussed politics in the last six months. Indeed, from that perspective, that makes the fact that there is much cross-party discussion at all quite remarkable, and suggests that with a broader lens (i.e., how often do you have discussions with those from the other political party?), we would likely see an even higher number reported (see also Minozzi et al. 2020).

Taken together, these data suggest that friendships cross party lines, and at least some of those generate cross-party political discussions. This might seem surprising, in light of the rhetoric about political silos and the segregation between partisans. But it is worth remembering that most people do not seek out like-minded political company: instead, they form ties with others on some other grounds, and then friendships and conversations follow (Sinclair 2012; Minozzi et al. 2020). As a result, cross-party friendships, and political discussions, do in fact occur.

SHARED ISSUE POSITIONS

Another common bond between the parties is a set of shared issue positions. This might seem like a contradiction in terms: isn't American politics deeply, perhaps irrevocably, polarized? No one would deny that there are deep fissures between the parties, or that there has been considerable partisan sorting in the mass public. Nevertheless, there remains a set of issues where there is common ground and consensus between the parties (Fiorina 2017; Hill and Tausanovitch 2015), and most Americans—including most partisans—remain closer to the center than to the extremes (Bafumi and Heron 2010; Fowler et al. forthcoming). Using data from several recent high-quality national surveys, table 1.3 presents some examples of policies where a majority (typically a super-majority) of both parties agree with one another.

Table 1.3 presents findings from a wide variety of different recent surveys: the 2020 Cooperative Election Study (Schaffner, Ansolabehere, and Luks 2021),

TABLE 1.3. Shared Issue Positions as a Common Bond

Item	Source	Democrats (%)	Republicans (%)
Economic Regulations			
Support retraining programs for emerging industries	Hidden Common Ground	82	86
Create incentives for companies that onshore jobs	Hidden Common Ground	82	88
Upgrade public infrastructure, such as roads and bridges	Hidden Common Ground	82	83
Fund research in science, technology, and green energy	Hidden Common Ground	83	71
Increase the minimum wage so that jobs pay enough to keep people over the poverty line	Hidden Common Ground	87	62
Permit right to work laws	Nationscape	57	60
Require companies to provide paid maternity leave	Nationscape	90	69
Require equal pay for men and women	Cooperative Election Study Data	97	83
Trade with other countries has a positive effect on jobs for US workers	Nationscape	75	72
It is important to protect the US economy, even if it means letting China get away with unfair trade practices	Nationscape	54	64
Support "Buy American" rules	Data for Progress	75	60
Reform Social Security and Medicare			
Reduce Social Security benefits for the top 25% of wage earners	Program for Public Consultation	81	72
Raise the retirement age to 68 over the next decade	Program for Public Consultation	81	78
Raise the cap on income subject to Social Security taxes to $215,000	Program for Public Consultation	92	84
Raise the Medicare payroll tax by 0.1%	Program for Public Consultation	68	69
Health Care			
Allow the government to negotiate lower drug prices from pharmaceutical companies	Cooperative Election Study	93	87
Allow importation of prescription drugs from other countries	Cooperative Election Study	74	64
Provide health insurance subsidies for low-income workers	Nationscape	92	67
Allow those aged 55 or older to purchase a Medicare plan	Program for Public Consultation	88	70

TABLE 1.3. *(continued)*

Climate Change			
Want to take steps to reduce the effects of climate change	Hidden Common Ground	86	55
Modernize the US electrical grid to reduce waste	Hidden Common Ground	83	70
Create stronger energy efficiency standards for buildings	Hidden Common Ground	82	63
Grow new forests and protect wetlands	Hidden Common Ground	83	73
Tax credits for carbon sequestration programs	Pew Research Center	90	78
Tougher emissions standards for power plants	Pew Research Center	93	64
Tax corporations for carbon emissions	Pew Research Center	89	55
Increase fuel economy standards for automobiles	Pew Research Center	86	52

the Nationscape Project (Tausanovitch and Vavreck 2020), the Hidden Common Ground Project,[9] and the Program for Public Consultation (2021). There are other surveys that I could cite, but these different studies—conducted through different survey modes, at different times, by different vendors—provide a clear sense that there are places where the public does have some overlapping issue positions. Here, rather than organizing issues by survey, I organized them thematically, as that is an easier way of identifying areas of commonality.

The most striking example of unexpected common ground concerns workplace regulations. Americans of both parties supported things like requiring gender pay equity and providing paid maternity leave, as well as expanding infrastructure, boosting job training programs, giving tax credits for onshoring jobs (i.e., bringing jobs back to the US from overseas), funding research into new technologies, and so forth. They also thought that trade benefits American workers, and wanted politicians to stand up to China. Likewise, the public also supported a range of policies that would help to ensure the solvency of Social Security and Medicare. These are not issues that rise to the top of the policy agenda, in no small part because they are not the messaging priorities for the parties. But many of these are examples of compromise policies that would actually help to improve people's lives.

There is a parallel here to debates in Congress. When we look at congressional legislation, we tend to focus on the highly partisan fights over budget reconciliation, tax cuts, and so forth. But most policymaking remains bipartisan; it is just that these issues rarely, if ever, rise onto the media agenda and public consciousness (Curry and Lee 2020). This is not to deny congressional polarization—it is certainly very real. But it is to say that the parties still do find ways to work together: perhaps halting and grudgingly, perhaps beneath the surface, but they do come together. There's a parallel here for the public: Democrats and Republicans are divided on many issues, but not all issues, and there may be a way forward in some cases.

There is even some common ground on hot-button issues such as health care. The nation's health care system has been the subject of perennial debate since the 2010 passage of the Affordable Care Act, which might lead one to think that the parties are diametrically opposed on this issue. While there are important divisions on some parts of health care reform, when one digs beneath the surface a somewhat different picture emerges. Americans of both parties wanted to reduce costs (especially for prescription drugs) and improve affordability. There was broad support for having the federal government negotiate drug prices, for drug reimportation, for health insurance subsidies for lower-income workers, and for allowing older Americans (55+) to buy plans from Medicare. Indeed, while the parties differed sharply in their opinion of the Affordable Care Act as a whole, especially when it was called "Obamacare," there was overwhelming bipartisan consensus in favor of its actual provisions, such as allowing young adults to stay on their parent's health insurance, closing the "donut hole" in Medicare drug coverage, requiring companies to cover preexisting conditions, and so forth (Bialik and Geiger 2016). Further, even a number of heavily Republican states—such as Nebraska, Idaho, Utah, and Oklahoma—have expanded their Medicaid programs at the ballot box, suggesting that ordinary voters from both parties support this policy, even if political elites do not (Kliff 2020). The point is not that there is no disagreement in the public over health care; there is plenty. But there is also a good deal of common ground once we step beyond the flash points.

Climate change is another case in point. The link between belief in climate change and partisanship is well documented (Kahan 2010), but there is far more common ground once you ask people about actual policies, rather than the polarizing issue itself. Majorities of both parties wanted to take steps to reduce the effects of climate change, and supported modernizing the electric grid, strengthening energy efficiency standards for buildings, protecting wetlands and re-growing forests, promoting carbon sequestration (removing carbon dioxide from the atmosphere), and even toughening standards for power plants and automobiles (Tyson and Kennedy 2020). As Chris Jackson of Ipsos noted, "when you don't use partisan, tribalized language, you see that people are in the same place [on climate change]" (Weise 2020). Once we get beyond the issues where partisan symbols dominate, there is the prospect of finding some commonality between the parties. Of course, all of this is not to say that Democrats and Republicans agree on all or even most issues: very clearly, they do not. But that should not be read to imply that there is *never* agreement.

But there is an even deeper, and more important, area where there is a surprising commonality between the parties: Democrats and Republicans both systematically underestimate how similar they are to those in the other political party. This was first noted in terms of ideological beliefs and issue positions, where it was named false polarization (see, among others, Westfall et al. 2015; Levendusky and Malhotra 2016b; Yudkin, Hawkins, and Dixon 2019). But it is not simply that we mis-estimate the degree of ideological over-lap between the parties; we systematically mis-estimate how similar we are to them on many different dimensions. Partisans overestimate their dissimilarity with the other party in terms of their demographics (Ahler and Sood 2018), political interest (Druckman et al. 2022b), support for democracy (Pasek et al. 2021), support for political violence (Mernyk et al. 2022), and so forth. Indeed, we even overestimate how much the other side dislikes our party, and thereby exaggerate partisan animosity (Lees and Cikara 2020; Moore-Berg et al. 2020)! So even when disagreement exists, individuals exaggerate its extent, and they underestimate the possibility of bridging these divides.

But this poses a puzzle: how can we show Democrats and Republicans that they are not as different as they think they are from those on the other side of the aisle? There are multiple ways of doing this, but cross-party dialogue offers a particularly promising path. This is because such discussion allows both sides to see not only where they might agree with the other side (or at least disagree less than they had imagined), but also that they can, in fact, have a civil conversation with those with whom they disagree. Democrats and Republicans alike will see that they had a flawed and exaggerated view of the other side, and animus toward them will lessen.

There is one more common bond that amplifies the effect of everything I discussed above: Democrats and Republicans see political division and dissensus as problems and want to mitigate them. In a recent survey by the Hidden Common Ground Initiative, 92 percent of Republicans, and 96 percent of Democrats, thought that it was important to reduce divisiveness, and while it would be challenging to do so, they wanted to try. Roughly two-thirds of both parties said they needed to better understand those from the other side, and a majority said that they needed to learn how to engage more constructively with the other party. A super-majority of both parties—65 percent of Democrats and 76 percent of Republicans—thought that the media and political leaders exaggerated our differences (Friedman and Schleifer 2021). While there are undoubtedly some voters who want to be polarized, most do not—many Americans are receptive to finding ways to bridge the divide.

Pulling back, all these common bonds—a set of shared identities, a set of shared friendships, and a set of issues where there is common ground between the parties, highlighted through civil cross-party dialogue—offer us a way to bridge the divide between the parties. But the proof of the pudding is in the eating. To get there, this chapter concludes with a brief overview of the book to give readers a sense of what lies ahead.

Outline of the Book

Chapter 2 develops the core theoretical logic of my argument. I begin by reviewing the literature on the roots of affective polarization, and I build on that literature to explain how the psychological underpinnings of this concept also help us to reduce it. In particular, I argue that individuals think that the parties have nothing in common, but that is not true. By emphasizing our common bonds—the things that bring us together across party lines—I can lessen this animosity. I explain why each of the three strategies I discuss—priming shared identities, emphasizing cross-party friendships, and highlighting commonalities through cross-party dialogue—lessens partisan animosity.

Simply reducing partisan animosity is important in and of itself. But there is also another set of downstream consequences that flow from these efforts as well. First, when affective polarization falls, individuals also perceive the electorate to be less polarized, which in turn changes elites' incentives to engage in bipartisanship and compromise. Second, reducing affective polarization also reduces ideological polarization and heightens partisan ambivalence. The benefits of reducing partisan animosity extend quite broadly indeed.

Chapters 3 through 5 form the empirical heart of the book, and they test the three different strategies for reducing affective polarization that I outlined in chapter 2. First, in chapter 3, I test the idea that priming common identities, most notably our American national identity, can lower levels of affective polarization. Using data from a set of original experiments, as well as natural experiments surrounding the July 4 holiday and the 2008 Summer Olympics,

I show that priming American identity reduces affective polarization and lessens partisan animosity, though the effectiveness of that prime varies over time in response to how elites politicize our national identity.

While American national identity is perhaps the most salient identity shared by both Democrats and Republicans, it is not the only one. I also show that I can use sports fandom as a way to reduce affective polarization. Respondents are much less negative about individuals from the other party when they find out that they all root for the same sports team. The shared team fandom serves as a common link that makes their differing partisanship somewhat less important. But there is nothing special about sports fandom per se; it is simply a strong identity that some Democrats and Republicans have in common. There are many others as well—ties through civic organizations, community groups, colleges and universities, et cetera. Multiple types of shared identities—not just American identity—can help bridge the divide, and that in turn has important implications for other strategies to reduce partisan animus.

In chapter 4, I test the argument that cross-party friendships lower partisan animus by allowing us to remember that the other party includes individuals that we know and like. Using data from the Pew Research Center as well as two large population-based survey experiments, I show strong support for this argument. More than 80 percent of partisans have friends, family members, neighbors, or coworkers from the other party, and for most people, this cross-party friend sits closer to the center of their social network than to the periphery. When individuals reflect on these friendships, they have much lower levels of animosity toward those from the other party.

Chapter 5 tests the argument that civil cross-party dialogue can lessen partisan animus. When individuals talk across party lines, it allows them to break down stereotypes about members of the other party, and to realize what they share in common. As a result, individuals realize not only that they have friends from the other party, but that many other members of the other party are also at least somewhat reasonable, and not the belligerent media stereotypes they had imagined them to be. Using an original lab-in-the-field experiment, I show that when Democrats and Republicans come together for a cross-party discussion, levels of animus fall markedly, and the effects endure for at least one week.

In chapter 6, I examine whether there are broader attitudinal consequences to reducing affective polarization, looking at the downstream consequences on perceived polarization, cue-taking, and partisan ambivalence.

I show that all of these downstream consequences follow efforts to reduce partisan animosity. This has important implications for how we think about the links between affective and ideological polarization (and why the former has increased so much more dramatically than the latter) and how we might vitiate partisan motivated reasoning more generally. Reducing affective polarization is important, but it also has other important downstream benefits.

In chapter 7, I discuss some of the broader implications of my findings. The core logic of my argument shows how it is, in fact, possible to lessen affective polarization. In turn, this suggests that for most ordinary Americans, partisan animus is less hardened and inflexible than we might imagine: when confronted with new information, or asked to think in a slightly different fashion, most people are willing to change how they perceive the other party. In turn, this has important implications for how political scientists reason about this concept (see also Lelkes and Westwood 2017; Klar, Krupnikov, and Ryan 2018).

My findings also demonstrate that the personal is a bridge to helping improve the political. Highlighting our personal ties to the out-group—our shared identities, our friendships, our civil conversations—improves attitudes toward them as a whole. But it does more than just produce warm feelings toward the other party; it also makes us trust the other party to do what is in the country's best interest, and to be willing to interact with them in a variety of different settings. These treatments, in other words, reduce not just indicators of affective polarization, but also some of its more pernicious consequences. In the conclusion, I discuss how we can use these insights to foster cooperation and reduce the consequences of animus not just in surveys, but in the real world outside of academic studies.

But even beyond animosity itself, my findings also provide a new lens through which to see a number of other topics in political science. For example, they offer new perspectives on political participation, civic education, the role of partisanship and parties, and how we can evaluate citizen competence. The implications of reducing animosity extend quite broadly indeed.

In the end, perhaps the ultimate lesson of all of this is that focusing on what we have in common is one strategy for overcoming animus, though not the only one. In the conclusion, I also talk about ways to move beyond what I have done here and think about other mechanisms that could reduce partisan animosity. To be clear, there is no magic wand to wave that will overcome decades of anger and recrimination. While these efforts might make things somewhat better, nothing here is a cure-all for our politics; such a thing does not, and cannot, exist. But the limits of these strategies also highlight their importance. One might dismiss them as hopelessly quixotic, but that would be a mistake. Small steps are just that: small. But over time, and across many people, they can add up to something more meaningful, and to a better politics. This book is hopefully a small step toward that goal.

How Can We Mitigate Partisan Animosity?

This chapter lays out my theoretical argument explaining how our common bonds work to mitigate partisan animosity. The key word in that sentence, however, is "mitigate:" I can reduce animosity, but I cannot eliminate it altogether. This undoubtedly will disappoint some readers who had hoped for a grand unified theory of how to abolish animus. Sadly, however, no such theory can exist: many different factors cause animus, as we will see below, so there is no way to simply remove it (see also Finkel et al. 2020). A more realistic goal is to think about different strategies that allow us to reduce it, which is what I do here. To that end, this chapter lays out the logic of my argument, by first explaining why Americans have become more affectively polarized over time, and then explaining how to use our common bonds to lessen this animosity.

Why Have We Become More Affectively Polarized?

There is little doubt today that Americans are affectively polarized, and they have become more so over the past generation. While scholars have called affective polarization by a number of different names—social polarization (Mason 2015, 2018), partisan prejudice (Lelkes and Westwood 2017), negative partisanship (Abramowitz and Webster 2018; Bankert 2021), partisan animus/ partisan antipathy (Pew Research Center 2016; Pew Research Center 2019c), or partyism (Sunstein 2015)—the basic underlying idea is the same: over time, there is greater differentiation in people's sentiments between the parties, with people becoming especially negative toward the other party (see figure 1.1).

At its core, affective polarization stems from individuals' identification with a political party (Iyengar, Sood, and Lelkes 2012).[1] While we have many different identities, arguably none are as consequential in contemporary politics as our partisan identities. As a result of identifying with a political party (or any other social group), we divide the world into an in-group (our own party) and an out-group (the other party; see Tajfel and Turner 1979; Tajfel 1981). Lumping the world into in-groups and out-groups gives rise to in-group favoritism and bias, the tendency to view in-group members (one's own party) positively and out-group members (the opposing party) negatively. Identifying with a political party causes individuals to accentuate even minor differences between their own party and the opposition (Tajfel and Wilkes 1963), and to think that the other party is a distant and extreme other (Armaly and Enders 2021; Mullen and Hu 1989).[2]

But there is a puzzle that follows from this line of argumentation: if the psychological mechanism underlying affective polarization is so deeply rooted in how we see the world, why has this phenomenon only emerged in recent decades? The answer, quite simply, is politics. The political world has changed, and those changes activate the psychological forces that motivate out-group animus. Psychology alone does not explain affective polarization (West and Iyengar 2022). Instead, psychology gives us the raw ingredients (social groups that differ from one another), but it is the contemporary political environment that magnifies and weaponizes them into partisan animus. Or more succinctly, affective polarization is as much a political process as a psychological one.[3]

HOW POLITICS GENERATES OUT-PARTY ANIMUS

Three important political changes in recent decades have heightened partisan animosity. First, and most importantly, political elites genuinely are polarized, and each party will implement very different policies if elected.[4] In an earlier era, one could reasonably complain that the nation's parties "represent nothing but a choice between Tweedledee and Tweedledum," but today's parties offer much more choice than echo.[5] Comparing what President Biden would do relative to President Trump, or which bills Majority Leader Schumer would advance relative to those from Majority Leader McConnell, it becomes clear that the elite-level parties have markedly different governing philosophies. Such policy divergence fuels animus toward the other party (Rogowski and Sutherland 2016; Webster and Abramowitz 2017).[6] For many Americans, when they say they dislike the other party, what they mean is that they disapprove of the other party's elites and their policies (Druckman and Levendusky 2019).[7]

But it is not simply that today's elites are polarized. Because the mass parties

are roughly evenly divided, either party could take power in any given election (Fiorina 2017). This means that small shifts in voter behavior or elite
strategies can change the balance of power in Washington, DC, as we have
seen in election after election in recent years. If one of the parties was effectively locked out of power—as Republicans in Congress were for much
of the post–World War II period—then the stakes would be lower. But in
recent decades, the stakes are always high, as control of at least one branch
of Congress—not to mention the presidency—is typically up for grabs (Lee
2016). Given this, it is only logical that partisans would dislike and distrust
those working to implement the other party's policy agenda.[8]

Second, not only have the elite parties pulled apart ideologically; the mass
parties have changed as well. Even if voters have not polarized, they have
sorted over time, so that partisanship is now increasingly aligned with issue positions (Levendusky 2009) as well as political identities, such as race,
religion, geography, and gender (Mason 2018; Mason and Wronski 2018). Partisanship today is no longer a single social identity, but a "mega identity"
combining multiple different dimensions (Mason 2018, 14)—it represents "all
your values aligned neatly under a single label" (Gardiner 2020).

This alignment of partisanship, issue positions, and identities ramps up
animus. Partisans dislike those who hold more dissimilar issue positions—
Democrats feel much more warmly toward a moderate pro-choice Republican who believes in climate change than toward a conservative Republican
who is pro-life and a climate-change skeptic (Bougher 2017; Orr and Huber
2020). Partisan sorting magnifies affective polarization, especially among the
most politically sophisticated voters (Lelkes 2018). Indeed, as Fiorina (2017,
60) notes, "nothing . . . allows us to separate the affective from the cognitive"—
differences on the issues, driven by voter sorting and elite polarization, are a
key ingredient in why many voters dislike the opposing party.

This elite polarization and voter sorting mean that the two parties are
more distinct from one another now than they were in earlier decades. The
parties today prioritize different issues and values, and reflect different geographic bases of support. Of course, not only are the parties more distinct
than they used to be, but our underlying psychology also works to further
magnify these differences. Because our partisan identities are social identities, we naturally inflate the differences between the in-group (our own party)
and the out-group (the opposing party), and small gaps become chasms,
thereby heightening partisan animus. In short, the nature of our contemporary politics magnifies and exaggerates the divides between the parties, a
point to which I return below.

Media coverage of politics—with its focus on conflict and the loudest voices in the room—adds further fuel to this perceptual fire. Most voters' social networks are largely, though not completely, homophilous with respect to partisanship: Democrats are friends with Democrats, and Republicans are friends with Republicans (McPherson, Smith-Lovin, and Cook 2001; Mutz 2006).[9] So for most voters, when they think about those from the other party, they draw on their most accessible source of information about them—how those partisans are depicted in the mass media. But such media accounts are systematically skewed, leading to inaccurate beliefs about the other side. When the media cover political elites, they tend to focus on the most extreme voices in the room: very liberal and very conservative members of Congress get more media coverage than do their more moderate peers (Padgett, Dunaway, and Darr 2019). This same effect also occurs when the media discusses ordinary voters—it is the loudest, and most extreme, voters journalists highlight when they write about politics (Levendusky and Malhotra 2016a). The media are much more likely to interview a Trump rally attendee wearing her Make America Great Again hat, or a Sanders supporter with his Feel the Bern t-shirt, than they are to interview the far more numerous Americans who are largely politically indifferent—after all, reading about those who are disengaged is not terribly interesting (see also Fiorina, Abrams, and Pope 2005).

Mainstream outlets contribute to affective polarization, but partisan outlets are an especially potent driver of such animus. As Klein (2020, 149) notes, such outlets do not "emphasize commonalities, it [sic] weaponizes differences," by focusing on the worst and most outrage-inducing behavior from the other side (Berry and Soberaj 2014). Such content heightens animus toward the other party (Levendusky 2013), and the availability of broadband Internet—and with it the ability to seek out more partisan content online—does the same (Lelkes, Sood, and Iyengar 2017; though see Boxell, Gentzkow, and Shapiro 2017).

Social media further skew our perceptions of those from the other side. The vast majority of Americans—more than 70 percent of us—avoid political discussions on social media. But there is a small set of people, roughly 10 percent of the public, who do discuss politics online, and do so with gusto (McClain 2021). The problem is that these individuals are the most extreme and politically engaged (Cohn and Quealy 2019; Pew Research Center 2019b). As Bail (2021) aptly puts it, social media acts as a prism, magnifying extremists' voices and muting moderates', thereby skewing our perceptions of the political world and sending false polarization—our exaggeration of political polarization—"into hyperdrive" (Bail 2021, 101).[10] Unsurprisingly, then, studies consistently find that social media heighten affective polarization (Kubin and von Sikorski 2021). Even those who abstain from social media are still affected by this pattern, due to both two-step communication flows (Druckman, Levendusky, and McLain 2018) and journalists' tendency to report on social media as if they accurately reflected public opinion (McGregor 2019). So, as with the mainstream media, social media distort, rather than inform, our perceptions of those from the other party (Settle 2018). As a result, users succumb to the out-group homogeneity effect (Quattrone and Jones 1980): rather than thinking that only a small segment of the other party are rabid partisans, they think that all members of the other party are.

A COMMON THREAD: MISPERCEPTIONS

This discussion highlights that while many factors give rise to partisan animosity, a particularly important one is misperceptions. It is certainly correct that Democrats and Republicans differ on many issues, and there are genuine disagreements between them. But because of how our underlying psychology intersects with changes in the political and media environment, voters systematically exaggerate the differences between the parties. This in turn heightens the salience of our partisan identities, because it is what differentiates our own party (the in-group) from the other party (the out-group). Politics and psychology combine to skew how we perceive the other side in a vicious feedback loop.

How skewed are these misperceptions? Quite dramatically skewed, as it turns out. For example, Druckman et al. (2022b) asked a sample of Americans what percentage of the other party was simultaneously ideologically extreme and highly politically interested. While in reality only 14 percent of Americans fit this description, their respondents overestimated it by a factor of 3.5, assuming that it characterized 49 percent of the country. While the modal partisan in actuality was a moderate who was not terribly interested in politics, Americans imagined the typical member of the other party was an ideological extremist who thought about politics all the time—the type of person we see on Facebook, Twitter, or on the news at a political rally. Our perceptions look much more like political elites and activists than ordinary voters.

This finding is not limited to this one study. Americans systematically exaggerate the differences between the parties in terms of demographics (Ahler and Sood 2018), ideology (Westfall et al. 2015), specific issue positions (Levendusky and Malhotra 2016b; Yudkin, Hawkins, and Dixon 2019), values (Barasz, Kim, and Evangelidis 2019), support for democracy (Pasek et al. 2021; Braley et al. 2021; Bright Line Watch 2021), support for political/ partisan violence (Mernyk et al. 2021), motivations underlying their actions

(Schwalbe, Cohen, and Ross 2020; Freeder 2020; Goya-Tocchetto et al. 2022), and so forth. Given the logic spelled out above, it is no surprise that people assume that the disliked other party is quite different from them; the problem is that it is not true. Such misperceptions are also noteworthy because of their size: on average, people *double* the amount of distrust and animosity that exists between the parties (Beyond Conflict 2020). We *think* we are much more dissimilar to those in the other party than we are in reality.

These skewed perceptions, in turn, make the other party the enemy instead of the opposition. Because "they" are so different from "us," partisans are extremely motivated to prevent the other side from taking power (Huddy, Mason, and Aarøe 2015). This becomes even more salient when the parties are evenly matched nationally, as they are today. This is why President Trump said of the 2020 election that "at stake in this election is the survival of the nation. It's true because we're dealing with crazy people on the other side. They've gone totally, stone-cold crazy" (Tamari 2020). Not to be outdone, President Obama argued that voters' choices in 2020 would "echo through generations to come," as "our democracy" was at stake in the election—if Trump were to win, he would destroy the republic (Tamari 2020). This existential threat conveys a sense that the other side is not just wrong, but immoral—partisanship becomes not just a social identity, but a reflection of fundamental questions of right and wrong (Skitka et al. 2021; Parker and Janoff-Bulman 2013; Hetherington and Weiler 2009). Because there is a strong affective differential between the parties—and partisans especially dislike the other side—they become more likely to engage in partisan motivated reasoning and to behave in ways that will differentiate themselves from the other party (Lavine, Johnston, and Steenbergen 2012; Druckman, Peterson, and Slothuus 2013; Klar 2014).

All of this makes clear that while there are important differences between the parties, the public also systematically exaggerates how different they are from one another, which fuels partisan animus by making the other side into an existential threat, rather than simply the opposing party. Part of the problem of affective polarization, then, is a problem of misperceptions.

Is It Possible to Lessen Partisan Animosity?

The discussion above is simultaneously depressing and encouraging. It is depressing in that it highlights that animosity has deep roots in how our psychology intersects with our current political and media environment. But it is also encouraging in that it underscores that part of this animosity stems from misperceptions. To be clear, even if I removed all of these misperceptions (which is not possible), I would not cure animosity, as there are many other contributing factors. But it does suggest that if partisans realize that they have a flawed impression of the other party, their attitudes toward it should improve.

Indeed, there is good reason to think that reducing misperceptions can ameliorate partisan animosity. For example, Ahler and Sood (2018) show that individuals significantly misperceive how dissimilar the other party is to them demographically, but when they learn the correct information, hostility toward the other side decreases. Similarly, individuals *think* that the other party dislikes and distrusts them a great deal, but they significantly exaggerate the degree to which this is the case. Once this misperception gets corrected, animosity toward the other side abates (Lees and Cikara 2020; Moore-Berg et al. 2020; Ruggeri et al. 2021). Reducing misperceptions, then, can lessen animosity.

My approach here builds on this important insight from these earlier studies. I adopt the general focus of correcting misperceptions, but rather than simply giving people the corrective information directly (as these studies have done), my strategy is to emphasize the common bonds that we all share, heightening awareness of similarity between the parties that way. This is a related but distinct mechanism, and emphasizes that there is not one way to lessen animosity, but multiple ways, many of which are worth pursuing.[11] As I explain below and demonstrate in subsequent chapters, our common bonds provide a powerful technique for overcoming political adversity in America.

PRIMING SHARED IDENTITIES

Normally, individuals perceive the political world through the lens of their partisan identities. Seen from this perspective, Democrats and Republicans are members of different teams, with little in common. But this belies the fact that we have multiple identities, some of which divide us and some of which unite us. If there is a shared identity that binds Democrats and Republicans together—one that unites them rather than divides them—that should lessen their animosity toward one another (Gaertner and Dovidio 2000).

One way of doing this is to find a superordinate identity—an identity that supersedes partisanship that both Democrats and Republicans share. Given the political significance of partisanship, this task is easier said than done. Precisely because partisanship is so central to our political identities, few other identities supersede it, and that list narrows even more once you restrict it to identities shared by both Democrats and Republicans. But there is one important identity that fits the bill: American national identity, which as I showed in chapter 1, is a central identity to members of both political parties.

While there are many dimensions to American national identity (see, among many others, Smith 1997; Schildkraut 2010), in this context I mean "a subjective or internalized sense of belonging to the [American] nation" (Huddy and Khatib 2007, 65). This is not, however, tied to an endorsement of a particular ideology or political belief; rather, it reflects "being or feeling American" (Huddy and Khatib 2007, 65; see also Theiss-Morse 2009). Schildkraut (2010, 45, table 3.1) asks respondents which factors they think are important to being an American; more than 90 percent say "feeling American" and "thinking of oneself as American"; this also reinforces the findings in chapter 1. This sense of national identity transcends racial, ethnic, and partisan/ideological boundaries (Citrin, Wong, and Duff 2001; Huddy and Khatib 2007; Theiss-Morse 2009), and reflects a broadly held conception of being American. Further, American identity is also a potent identity: 50 percent of Americans strongly identify as Americans, a significantly larger percentage than those who strongly identify with their religion, race, or sex (Theiss-Morse 2009, 47, fig. 2.1; see also table 1.1).

The Common In-group Identity Model explains how identifying as an American lessens the influence of partisanship, thereby ameliorating affective polarization (Gaertner et al. 1989; Gaertner and Dovidio 2000).[12] This model argues that individuals have multiple identities, which vary in strength and relevance depending upon the situation, with the most salient identity being the one driving behavior. Normally, when Democrats think about Republicans, they see the other party through a partisan lens, and therefore dislike them. But suppose that I prime Democrats' American identity. Now they'll see those same Republicans as fellow Americans—they go from members of an out-group (the other party) to an in-group (the nation). By changing the salience of an individual's identities—partisan versus American—I can change how they evaluate those from the other party.

But superordinate identities such as American identity are not the only way to lessen partisan animus. Indeed, one limitation of a superordinate identity appeal is that there simply are not very many of them that all partisans share. But because identities are complex (Rocas and Brewer 2002), there are many identities that *some* Democrats and Republicans share. For example, as I discussed in chapter 1, members of both parties attend the same colleges, like the same actors and musicians, have the same hobbies, and, perhaps most especially, root for the same sports teams. In the contemporary context, because there is so much emphasis on what divides us, *ex ante*, partisans think they have no common identities. But if they learn that they have shared identities with those from the other party (as sports fans, college alumni, etc.), then their attitude toward them should improve—a phenomenon known as cross-cutting categorization (Crisp and Hewstone 2000; Crisp, Hewstone, and Rubin 2001). Shared identities—even if they are not shared by all members of a group—lessen partisan animosity as well.

> **Common Identity Hypothesis**: Priming common identities shared by both Democrats and Republicans will reduce affective polarization.

CROSS-PARTISAN FRIENDSHIPS

A second common bond is cross-partisan friendships. It is certainly true that most social networks are largely homophilous with respect to partisanship—Democrats are typically friends with other Democrats, and Republicans are most often friends with other Republicans, both online and offline. But largely homophilous does not mean completely homophilous. Because social networks often form for apolitical reasons—such as sharing a hobby, workplace, or neighborhood—our friendships can and do cross party lines (Sinclair 2012). For example, looking at data from the 2000 presidential election, Huckfeldt, Johnson, and Sprague (2004, 37) show that nearly 60 percent of Gore and Bush voters can name at least one person in their social network who supported the opposing party's candidate (see their table 2.1). Similarly, Mutz (2006) shows that among close friends, there is considerable exposure to diverse political views (see esp. 26–29). Even in our current political moment, most partisans report that at least some of their social network comes from the other party (Poteat et al. 2011; Pew Research Center 2017). As I showed in chapter 1, more than three-quarters of both Democrats and Republicans have at least some friendships that cross the partisan divide, and nearly all demographic groups discuss politics across party lines (Levendusky and Stecula 2021). While we might *think* that social networks are completely segregated by party, in reality they are not.

Such cross-party networks provide a mechanism for overcoming affective polarization. Normally, people's image of the other party is that of the polarized political elites or the ideologues they see discussing politics online or in the media. But this is an inaccurate perception: the other party does contain these individuals, but it also contains their friends, family members, and coworkers. When they think about these people from the other party—whom they know and like—the opposing party seems less like a distant other (Mullen and Hu 1989). As a result, empathy for the other side increases (Barlow, Louis, and Hewstone 2009) and in-group favoritism declines (Page-Gould, Mendoza-Denton, and Tropp 2008; Pettigrew and Tropp 2011).

Fascinatingly, thinking about a cross-party friend changes attitudes toward the other party overall—people use their friend to draw inferences about the other party as a whole (Pettigrew 1997; Page-Gould et al. 2010). Reflecting on a friend from the other party makes someone realize that they can, in fact, have productive encounters across the partisan divide (Barlow, Louis, and Hewstone 2009). In turn, individuals generalize from this experience, and realize that if they can do that with their friend, they can also do it more generally (Pettigrew 1997; Tropp and Pettigrew 2005).[13] In essence, the personal becomes the political—friendships are a way to improve attitudes toward those from the other side of the aisle.

The point is not necessarily that people will agree with those from the other party—they often will not. Rather, it is that they recognize that they might sometimes agree, but even if they disagree, they can do so productively. The other side is not simply the caricature presented by the media, but contains reasonable people who have legitimate rationales for their beliefs. Interviewing residents of Watertown, New York, a location characterized by low levels of polarization, Ripley (2019) finds two women who share a close friendship despite their partisan and ideological differences. In an interview, they express the core of why close ties with those from the other side can foster respect and reduce affective polarization: "It's not like my opinions are the only ones anybody can ever have . . . I have opinions, but somebody else might also. I could learn from that person, and that person could learn from me." President Obama noted a similar sentiment in a 2015 interview when he remarked that "everybody's got a family member or a really good friend from high school who is on the complete opposite side of the political spectrum. And yet, we still love them, right?" (Klein 2020, 66).

Given this, I argue that asking subjects to reflect on members of the other party that they like and respect—their cross-party friendships—will reduce affective polarization. While I use the phrase "cross-party friendships" throughout the book, this is a shorthand term that includes not just friends from the other party, but also family, coworkers, neighbors, et cetera—those that they know and like. It is the fact that one knows and respects them that changes attitudes toward the other party, not the specific nature of the relationship.

While I expect this relationship to hold generally, it should be particularly strong in two cases. First, close friendships should have stronger effects—when the cross-party friend is someone with whom the individual has spent a great deal of time, and considers to be part of their inner social circle, the effect should be larger (Tropp and Pettigrew 2005; Davies et al. 2011). Indeed, the number of cross-party friendships has little effect on one's attitudes, but the closeness of those friendships is much more important—a few deep bonds with the other party are worth more (in terms of changing attitudes) than many casual ones (Pettigrew 1997). It is our close friends—those with whom we spend significant time and interact frequently, and whom we respect a great deal—that prompt us to rethink our assessments of the other party.

Second, the effect should be larger for those who actually talk about politics with their friends from the other party. This might seem counterintuitive, as one might imagine that perhaps avoiding politics is the way forward. But this does not work: when there is no political discussion, the effect of cross-party friendship is quite weak. Without actually discussing politics—and realizing that there is disagreement, but also commonality, and the ability to learn from one another—then there is no generalization to the other party as a whole. It is the successful navigation of politics with a cross-group friend that leads people to realize that they can interact with others from the other side of the aisle. This, in turn, is crucial to transferring the warm affect from one's friend to the out-group overall (Barlow, Louis, and Hewstone 2009, see esp. 399). Discussing their cross-party marriage—a particularly striking example of cross-party friendship—Susan and Nelson Peacock noted that "we don't shy away from those conversations [about politics], but have mutual respect for each other's perspective" (Pajer 2020).[14] That highlights the key ingredient for making this sort of exchange work—engagement, but on civil terms, where individuals try to take the other person's perspective. Rather than avoiding politics, these cross-party friendships need to dive into it head-first to actually change how partisans feel about the other side.

> **The Cross-Party Friendship Hypothesis**: Reminding individuals that they have friends, family, and coworkers from the other party will reduce partisan animus. Such effects will be especially strong when the person is a close friend or is someone with whom they actually discuss politics.

CROSS-PARTY POLITICAL DISCUSSION

Finally, I argue that cross-party dialogue also provides a way to ameliorate animus by reducing misperceptions about the other side. Given the media narrative of a deeply polarized America, most Americans expect there to be little to no common ground between the parties. But as I discussed in chapter 1, there are a surprising number of issues on which there is broad agreement between them. Even more importantly, people exaggerate the extent of partisan disagreement along many different dimensions, in terms of not just issues, but also their interest in politics, their ideology, their demographics, their values, and so forth. If partisans realized the depth of this misperception, they would see what they have in common, and also recognize that they had misjudged the other party, sometimes quite markedly; their attitudes toward the other party would then likely improve.

Having a civil cross-party dialogue is a particularly effective mechanism for correcting these sorts of misperceptions. I am hardly the first to suggest that dialogue between those from different political points of view has salubrious effects, both in theory and in practice (e.g., Dryzek 2005; Delli-Carpini, Cook, and Jacobs 2004). But such discussions are an especially effective mechanism for reducing the misperceptions that give rise to affective polarization. Because it involves a give-and-take of viewpoints, political discussion prompts reflexive thinking, causing individuals to parse arguments from the opposing point of view more carefully (Levitan and Visser 2008). In turn, this increases awareness of the other side's positions (Lyons and Sokhey 2017; Mutz 2006), and recognition that the other side has a legitimate basis for its viewpoint (Lord, Lepper, and Preston 1984), thereby improving attitudes toward the other side (Caluwaerts and Reuchamps 2014). Exposure to opposing rationales also mitigates partisan motivated reasoning and moderates issue positions (Klar 2014), which fits with other arguments that discussion prompts citizens to approach politics as a cooperative dialogue rather than a battle to be won (Groenendyk and Krupnikov 2021; MacKuen et al. 2010).

Cross-party (i.e., politically heterogeneous) discussion should therefore reduce affective polarization in at least two ways. First, the discussion allows individuals to replace outdated stereotypes with more accurate information (Pettigrew and Tropp 2008; Dorison, Minson, and Rogers 2019). Second, the back-and-forth nature of political discussion allows participants to engage in perspective-taking (Pettigrew and Tropp 2008). Hearing the other side helps individuals to better understand their opponents' point of view (Lord, Lepper, and Preston 1984). Indeed, the key step of perspective-taking is really "perspective getting": hearing from the other side why they adopt the positions that they do, which allows individuals to see that their opponents have real, and legitimate, justifications for their opinions (Kalla and Broockman 2020; Kalla and Broockman, forthcoming a; Kalla and Broockman, forthcoming b).[15] This explains why exposure to compelling arguments for divergent viewpoints improves people's assessments of those on the other side of the issue (Stanley et al. 2020).

Both of these effects underscore the ways in which discussion serves to reduce misperceptions and thereby mitigate animosity. The argument is not that dialogue will erase differences and lead everyone to agree. Instead, it is that by having a reasonable exchange of views, individuals will realize that there are some issues on which they agree with the other side, and when they disagree, they are often not as far apart as they had imagined and are able to disagree without devolving into conflict (note the parallel to the argument about cross-party friendship earlier in the chapter). More generally, they will also see that the opposition is less intransigent than they'd imagined, and is willing to listen to their views. This increases their feelings of being respected and understood by the other party, which will also improve their attitudes toward the other side (Livingstone, Rodríguez, and Rothers 2020; Simon and Schaefer 2015; Voelkel, Ren, and Brandt 2021). It is both the discovery of some common ground and the realization that the other side is more reasonable than one had imagined that work to lessen animosity.

But to accrue these positive benefits, the dialogue actually has to occur; individuals cannot simply think about doing it. There is a large literature on imagined contact, or the process of how *thinking* about a constructive encounter with someone from an opposing social group reduces animosity toward them (Crisp and Turner 2009). But studies that attempted to test this argument in the partisan context generally found that it did not work (Wojcieszak and Warner 2020), or worked only in certain conditions (Rossiter 2021; more generally, on the limits of imagined contact, see Bigler and Hughes 2010). The argument above explains why: most people who imagined a dialogue with those from the other side would expect it to go poorly, with few, if any, positive exchanges, and would expect it to be unpleasant and unproductive (Dorison, Minson, and Rogers 2019). This is why most Americans do not want to engage in cross-party discussions and try to avoid them (Rainie, Keeter, and Perrin 2019; Settle and Carlson 2019). Imagining a conservation does not allow people to engage in the sort of perspective getting discussed above, so they never realize that their stereotypes were inaccurate. Especially for political topics, one needs to actually engage in dialogue to see that this works (Rossiter 2021).

It is worth emphasizing that these salubrious effects are predicated on the civil exchange engendered via face-to-face discussion. But what does a "civil" discussion entail? A civil discussion is one where there is the "free and respectful exchange of ideas" (Coe, Kenski, and Rains 2014, 658) and where there is "discourse that does not silence or derogate alternative views but instead evinces respect" (Jamieson et al. 2017, 206). This involves recognizing that differences "are philosophical not personal, that parties to a debate are entitled to the presumption that their views are legitimate even if not correct" (Jamieson and Hardy 2012, 412).

But civility should not be equated with mere politeness (Papacharissi 2004). The deeper dimension of civility is that it calls on all of us to genuinely listen to one another, and to treat each other as equals. Indeed, Keith and Danisch (2020, 18) call politeness "weak civility," to distinguish it from "strong civility," which they define as "a network of behavior and norms that can be used to engage differences in a way that will deepen a sense of community" (see also Bardon et al. forthcoming). While their conception of strong civility is somewhat broader than the type of dialogue I discuss here (in that it can contain non-discursive elements, such as protests), the underlying idea—a set of practices that entails genuinely engaging with the opposition and their ideas—is the same. Engagement need not imply acceptance, however; it simply requires that one listen to opposing viewpoints with an open mind and be willing to be persuaded (Gutmann and Thompson 2012). Civility, in short, requires that we hear the other side and listen to their arguments in good faith.

This also highlights why uncivil conversations are so harmful. Take, for example, political discussion on social media. A number of studies have shown that cross-party discussion online hurts more than it helps, exacerbating divisions and reducing understanding between the groups (Kiesler, Siegel, and McGuire 1984; Bail et al. 2018). While not the only reason, civility is a part of why these conversations go wrong: instead of trying to listen thoughtfully to better understand the other side, online discussions typically focus on simply casting aspersions on opponents and reiterating one's own talking points. In the concluding chapter, I return to this important scope condition, and discuss what this means for efforts to encourage cross-party dialogue online.

Such heterogeneous discussions are an example of inter-group contact, the argument that constructive interactions can reduce animus in a wide variety of different settings (the *locus classicus* is Allport 1954; for more recent reviews, see Pettigrew and Tropp 2011 and Paluck, Green, and Green 2019). For example, inter-group contact has been shown to reduce animus toward those of different races and ethnicities (Boisjoly et al. 2006), those of different economic or social classes (Mo and Conn 2018), and those of different sexual orientations and gender identities (Dessel 2010). That said, while contact generally ameliorates animus, its effectiveness varies considerably across contexts (Paluck, Green, and Green 2019): in some cases it does not really work (Busby 2021), and can even backfire and increase tensions (MacInnis and Page-Gould 2015). Whether cross-party dialogue reduces animosity is an important question both theoretically and for its applicability to our current political moment (see also Fishkin et al. 2021).

While there are many different types of cross-party contact in which Democrats and Republicans could engage, the civil political discussion I propose here should be a particularly effective form of it, as it satisfies a set of conditions for effective inter-group contact that were outlined in Allport's (1954) original work.[16] Contact works best when there is equal status between the groups, they share a common goal, there is between-group cooperation, and there is institutional support for cooperation. Here, all four conditions are met. Within the discussion, Democrats and Republicans have equal standing, and they are working together collaboratively toward a common goal of better understanding one another (and these effects are likely reinforced through the emphasis on civility). Finally, there is institutional support for said goal provided by the researcher—though more generally, community groups or other organizations could also provide this support (see, e.g., Graham 2018). All of this suggests that the structure of heterogeneous political discussion should be an effective vehicle for mitigating partisan bias.

While there is a great deal of value in having Democrats and Republicans come together for these conversations, most people would rather avoid them. Half of Americans say that talking about politics is stressful because there is so much disagreement, and when given the choice, many Americans would rather discuss religion than politics (Pew Research Center 2019a)! To the extent that Americans do want to talk about politics, they prefer that it occur among those from their own party, as this minimizes the possibility for conflict (Mutz 2006; though see Klar, Krupnikov, and Ryan 2018). Such partisan homogeneous political discussion heightens motivated reasoning, and increases social conformity within the group (Isenberg 1986). As a result, homogeneous political discussion will tend to *increase* both affective polarization (Parsons 2015) and ideological polarization (Druckman, Levendusky, and McClain 2018). All of this underlines the importance of cross-party discussion: it may be less common, but its consequences are particularly important.

Cross-Party Discussion Hypothesis: Bringing Democrats and Republicans together for a civil face-to-face discussion will reduce affective polarization.

Are There Downstream Consequences to Reducing Affective Polarization?

The three strategies discussed above—emphasizing a shared American identity, cross-party friendships, and civil cross-party political discussions to highlight what the parties share—all lower affective polarization. But the theoretical logic embedded therein also suggests that there are some "downstream" consequences to such efforts: by reducing affective polarization, these strategies should also change other attitudes.[17]

First, subjects should perceive less polarization and think that there is more common ground between the parties. Perceived polarization is, quite simply, the extent to which Americans *think* the mass public is divided (Westfall et al. 2015; Yudkin, Hawkins, and Dixon 2019). While humans naturally overestimate divisions between groups (Robinson et al. 1995), given the current political environment it should come as no surprise that Americans think that the mass public is deeply polarized today. Indeed, Levendusky and Malhotra (2016b, 386, table 2) find that Americans perceive twice as much polarization as exists in reality! This perceived polarization stems from the same underlying psychological dynamics as affective polarization itself: subjects harbor a desire to differentiate the opposing party from their own party, so they perceive the other party to be more ideologically distant than they are in reality. Because both affective polarization and perceived polarization are driven by this same underlying psychological phenomenon, reducing affective polarization should also decrease perceived polarization, and subjects should think there is more common ground and consensus (Armaly and Enders 2021).

Note that this implies that perceived polarization and affective polarization are likely endogenous to one another. Perceived polarization (or more exactly, misperceptions and false polarization) fuels partisan animosity, as I argued earlier in the chapter. But then as animus increases, individuals feel more of a need to psychologically distance themselves from the disliked other party, so animosity increases perceived polarization. But when animus is reduced, perceived polarization will also fall, so that should limit the growth of animus in the future.

This is not simply a matter of misperception; rather, it speaks to the broader issue of whether compromise is possible with the other side. Such common ground is important not only because it corrects misperceptions, but because it also changes the signal voters send to political elites (Gutmann and Thompson 2012). If the parties are hopelessly polarized and divided, there's little to be gained from searching for bipartisanship, and no incentive for elites to work together. But if voters perceive common ground, there is room for compromise, and hence an incentive for legislators to find bipartisan solutions.

Common Ground Hypothesis: Efforts to reduce affective polarization will also increase perceptions of common ground between the parties, and decrease perceived polarization.

Second, individuals should also become less likely to adopt their party's issue positions, a process known as party cue-taking (Zaller 1992). While much cue-taking occurs because individuals follow their party's leaders (Lenz 2012), in an era of elite polarization cue-taking may also stem from rejecting the other party's positions. For example, during the 2008 election, Nicholson (2012) found that when President Obama endorsed an immigration bill, Republicans opposed it, but an endorsement from President Bush or Senator McCain had no effect on their opinions. The exact opposite was true of Democrats—Obama's endorsement had no effect, but an endorsement by McCain or Bush led them to oppose it (see esp. 57, figure 2). In essence, cues from the other party serve as "anti-cues" of what *not* to do (Levendusky and Malhotra 2016a; Pierce and Lau 2019). So even if voters ultimately adopt their own party's position on the issue, it may be because it is the opposite of what the other party proposed (see also Merkley and Stecula 2020; Lelkes 2021; Goren, Federico, and Kittilson 2009).

This is, of course, a very similar logic to that of affective polarization—a desire to differentiate oneself from the disliked out-group—so affective polarization should drive party cue-taking (Druckman et al. 2021). Indeed, as Lelkes (2018) documents, as partisan animus rises, so too does party cue-taking, at least among those high in political sophistication (see also Bakker, Lelkes, and Malka 2020). When affective polarization falls, then, and voters view the other party less negatively, then they should be less repulsed by out-party cues, and hence less likely to unreflexively adopt their party's position on the issues. Reducing affective polarization should also reduce party cue-taking.[18]

But reducing such cue-taking has an important implication, as it is one of the primary drivers of increased levels of party sorting and ideological polarization in the electorate (Levendusky 2009; Lenz 2012). Earlier work highlights how ideological polarization helps to fuel affective polarization (e.g., Rogowski and Sutherland 2016), but this reverse possibility has been largely overlooked—affective polarization can also lead to ideological polarization. Affective polarization, ideological polarization, and party sorting are therefore very strongly linked to one another in ways not fully appreciated heretofore.

Party Cue-Taking Hypothesis: Efforts to reduce affective polarization will also reduce partisan cue-taking.

But this cue-taking shift also suggests that there is another, even broader implication: reducing affective polarization should also increase partisan ambivalence, and therefore reduce partisan motivated reasoning. Partisan ambivalence is "a disjuncture between an individual's long-term *identification* with a political party and his or her short-term *evaluations* of the parties' capacities to govern and deliver benefits to the public" (Lavine, Johnston, and

Steenbergen 2012, 3, emphasis in original). Normally, most partisans are univalent partisans: they believe that their own party is best able to govern the country and handle the most pressing issues of the day. Given this, they feel positively toward their own party, and negatively toward the other party, so their identity and evaluations align (hence the name univalent). But ambivalent partisans are those for whom this is not true: they realize that either their own party is responding poorly to a crisis (say, Republicans in the aftermath of Hurricane Katrina), or that the other party is doing an exceptionally good job at governance (say, Democrats during the peace and prosperity of the Eisenhower years). They are ambivalent because they feel either negatively toward their own party, positively toward the opposing party, or both.

Affective polarization is, not surprisingly, tied to partisan univalence—those who are more affectively polarized like their own party more and (especially) dislike the opposition more (Druckman and Levendusky 2019). But when affective polarization falls, individuals should be less likely to feel animus toward the other party, given that affective polarization is grounded in negative out-party sentiments. As affective polarization falls, partisans therefore should become less univalent, and more ambivalent.

This might seem to be a minor point, but it is not: as Lavine, Johnston, and Steenbergen (2012) demonstrate, it is univalent partisans, not ambivalent ones, who engage in partisan motivated reasoning. Partisan motivated reasoning is the tendency of individuals to interpret the political world in ways that are consistent with their partisanship (i.e., they are motivated to defend their partisan priors; see Leeper and Slothuus 2014). Empirically, this means that individuals uncritically accept arguments from their own party and reject them from the opposition (Druckman, Peterson, and Slothuus 2013), reinterpret reality in ways that portray their party in a good light (Schaffner and Luks 2018), and selectively give credit or blame to political actors for their successes and failures (Bisgaard 2019). Simply put, partisan motivated reasoning allows citizens to reinterpret the world through partisan-colored glasses. Ambivalence undercuts this tendency: it "promotes open-mindedness, doubt, and a willingness to think through alternative courses of action" (Lavine, Johnston, and Steenbergen 2012, 220), and hence helps individuals become "good" citizens. If reducing affective polarization fosters greater partisan ambivalence, then that in turn should mitigate partisan motivated reasoning more generally, with significant implications for politics more broadly.

Partisan Ambivalence Hypothesis: Efforts to reduce affective polarization will also increase partisan ambivalence, especially for attitudes about the other party.

SUMMARY OF THE HYPOTHESES

Table 2.1 provides a summary of all six key hypotheses that I will test in subsequent chapters, with an indication of the chapter in which I test each one of them, as well as the different types of data used to test them.

The next set of chapters test the three main strategies I document here, and examine how each one of them does—or does not—actually reduce affective

TABLE 2.1. Hypotheses Tested in This Book

Hypothesis Name	Argument	Chapter Tested In	Data Sources Used to Test
Common Identity Hypothesis	Priming common identities shared by both Democrats and Republicans will reduce affective polarization.	3	+ American Identity Experiment (SSI) + 2008 National Annenberg Election Study + Sports Fan Experiment (Bovitz Forthright)
Cross-Party Friendship Hypothesis	Reminding individuals that they have friends, family, and coworkers from the other party will reduce partisan animus. Such effects will be especially strong when the person is a close friend or is someone with whom they actually discuss politics.	4	+ Pew Research Center American Trends Panel + Friendship Experiment (AmeriSpeak NORC) + Friendship Experiment (Bovitz Forthright)
Cross-Party Discussion Hypothesis	Bringing Democrats and Republicans together for a civil face-to-face discussion will reduce affective polarization relative to an apolitical or same-party political discussion.	5	+ Cross-Party Discussion Experiment (Lab-in-the-Field)
Common Ground Hypothesis	Efforts to reduce affective polarization will also increase perceptions of common ground between the parties, and decrease perceived polarization.	6	+ Friendship Experiment (AmeriSpeak NORC)
Partisan Ambivalence Hypothesis	Efforts to reduce affective polarization will also increase partisan ambivalence, especially for attitudes about the other party.	6	+ Friendship Experiment (Bovitz Forthright)
Party Cue-Taking Hypothesis	Efforts to reduce affective polarization will also decrease the importance of respondent's partisanship.	6	+ Friendship Experiment (AmeriSpeak NORC) + Friendship Experiment (Bovitz Forthright)

Note: For each experiment, the vendor used to collect the data is given in parentheses.

polarization. Chapter 3 examines the effects of common identities, chapter 4 takes up the case of cross-party friendships, and chapter 5 explores the consequences of cross-party discussion and dialogue.

To be clear, if all the strategies above do is simply reduce affective polarization, that in and of itself is a valuable contribution, given the deleterious effects discussed in chapter 1. But if my argument is correct—and these other consequences also flow from it—then it becomes an even more important theoretical contribution. Chapter 6 takes up the question of the downstream effects of efforts to reduce affective polarization, and explores how they shape other behavior.

How Do I Evaluate These Claims?

But how will I actually test these hypotheses? While I have more to say about this in each chapter, it is worth having a brief discussion here of the book's overall empirical strategy.

As demonstrated in table 2.1 above, I use both observational data and experimental data to evaluate these claims. Both have their strengths and weaknesses. The strength of observational datasets—like the 2008 National Annenberg Election Study data, or the Pew American Trends data—is that they come from the "real world," so we do not have to worry about putting subjects in an artificial setting that they otherwise would never encounter (i.e., generating demand effects, though such effects are less common than many fear; see Mummolo and Peterson 2019). The downside is that, except in rare cases, we cannot be sure that we have pinned down cause and effect. For example, in the Pew American Trends data used in chapter 4, I show that those who have more friends from the other party have lower levels of animus toward it. But I cannot know which is the cause, and which is the effect: Is it that cross-party friendships reduce affective polarization, consistent with my argument above? Or instead is it that those who are low in affective polarization to begin with have more cross-party friendships? The answer is likely both (Pettigrew 1997). To be clear, such data are nevertheless extremely valuable, since they help to establish when effects can actually be detected outside of an experimental setting. But I need an additional type of data to help provide more definitive evidence to evaluate my core hypotheses.

To help show that it is the strategies that I outline above—and not some other factor—that lead to a reduction in affective polarization, I primarily rely throughout the book on a set of original experiments I designed for this project. Here, that includes both a set of survey experiments and an original lab-in-the-field experiment conducted throughout the metropolitan Philadelphia area. I use the lab-in-the-field experiment to test the Cross-Party Discussion Hypothesis in chapter 5 because it required physically bringing people together in person for face-to-face discussion, and hence could only be done with a more limited geographic scope.

The remaining experiments are all survey experiments conducted online. To carry them out, I used a variety of different vendors, including both opt-in Internet panels (from vendors such as SSI and Bovitz Forthright) and a probability sample from AmeriSpeak at the National Opinion Research Center. The latter is especially valuable, as it is a true random sample of the American public (for more on the AmeriSpeak sampling methodology, see Dennis 2018). With opt-in survey respondents, the concern is that participants are simply different from the general population somehow—for example, they likely have higher levels of political interest (Malhotra and Krosnick 2007; Yeager et al. 2011). A random sample addresses this concern, because the people who take the study are randomly selected, rather than opting into it. The limitation, however, is that such studies are many times the cost of opt-in ones, so even with the generous support I received to conduct this research, I could only field one such study. Happily, its results are very consistent with the other samples I use elsewhere in the book, which helps to allay the concern that other experimental results are an artifact of simply using such non-random samples (though to be clear, one can never completely remove this concern). Indeed, the value of blending a variety of different sources—observational datasets, a lab-in-the-field experiment, opt-in and probability survey experiments—is that I can leverage the strength of these different data sources and not rely on only one type of data.

Across these different data sources, I use a variety of different items to measure affective polarization. Because affective polarization is a complex subject, I use not one measure, but rather a series of measures, to capture it. In chapter 1, I introduced the first (and most common) measure of partisan animus: individuals' ratings of the opposing party on the 100-point feeling thermometer scale. This is an invaluable metric not only for comparability with other studies, but also for ease of interpretation. But as I noted in chapter 1, it is unclear why anyone assigns (say) the Republican Party a particular rating: is it that they like President Trump? That they like the party's emphasis on limited government? That they like the social groups they associated with the party, such as evangelical Christians? The answer is unclear. While feeling thermometers are incredibly useful, they are also limited.

Given this, I also use several other items in my experiments to try and capture other dimensions of partisan animosity (while the exact items differ slightly from study to study, this is the set of items used across experiments).

First, I use a set of trait ratings to get at how well various positive (open-minded, generous, patriotic, etc.) and negative (mean, selfish, etc.) adjectives describe each party (Garrett et al. 2014). Second, I use assessments of how much individuals trust the other party to do what is in the best interest of the nation. And finally, I use a set of social distance items, which measure how comfortable the respondent is interacting with those from the opposing party (the social distance items originally come from Bogardus 1959, and were named that long before that phrase came to mean something quite different within the context of the COVID-19 pandemic).[19] These items get at different dimensions of the underlying theoretical construct of partisan animus, and happily, they are all interrelated (Druckman and Levendusky 2019). These are also, by far, the most common set of measures in the literature (see the discussion in Iyengar et al. 2019), and by using a similar set of items across studies, I can compare across them more easily (see the discussion in chapter 5).

Given the theoretical argument above that affective polarization is, at its core, about out-party animosity, I focus throughout the text on how people assess the other party—how warmly Democrats (Republicans) rate Republicans (Democrats) on the feeling thermometer scale, how much they trust them, think that words like patriotic or trustworthy apply to them, and so forth. But some scholars prefer a slightly different measure: the gap between in-party and out-party ratings (e.g., Lelkes and Westwood 2017; Klar, Krupnikov, and Ryan 2018). The advantage of using this differenced measure is that it can help to address differences in how respondents use each item's response scale (i.e., your rating of 50 degrees on a feeling thermometer may mean something different from what my rating of 50 degrees means; see Wilcox, Sigelman, and Cook 1989). I use the out-party measures throughout my analyses for two reasons. First, in this instance, the measurement point above is less relevant since I am interested in the treatment effects, and there is no reason to think that differential scale usage is correlated with a randomly assigned treatment. Second, the treatments I examine in this book aim to reduce out-party animus (moreso than to mitigate same-party support), and therefore looking at out-party ratings is the more theoretically relevant construct.[20] That said, I have verified that I would obtain similar findings using this difference measure, so this does not influence my substantive conclusions. But now, with those preliminaries out of the way, it is time to test these hypotheses and see which, if any of them, are supported by the data.

Can Our Shared Identities Bridge the Partisan Divide?

One of the great challenges of becoming president is that you have to almost immediately overcome the fundamental divide generated by the election: while your party's supporters will have cheered when you took the oath of office, those from the other party will have grimaced. The president's first job is to bridge this divide and unite the country, bringing everyone together as one.

Especially in an age of polarization, that is not easy. But there are ways to accomplish this goal. One of the most powerful is to remind citizens of all parties that are we are in this together, and we share a common identity, and a common fate, as Americans. Recognizing this, presidential rhetoric has long echoed this notion, from Jefferson's famous remark at his first inaugural address that "we are all Federalists, we are all Republicans," to Truman's call to put country ahead of party, to Reagan's call to unite not as partisans but as Americans in common cause. President Obama's rhetoric, time and again, called on Americans to find the better angels of our nature and build bridges with the other side. For example, speaking after the 2013 government shutdown, he remarked that "we come from different parties, but we are Americans first. . . . Our regard for them [the American people] compels us all, Democrats and Republicans, to cooperate, and compromise, and act in the best interests of our nation—one nation, under God, indivisible with liberty and justice for all" (Obama 2013).

Given his background, and the unique moment in which he was elected, President Biden's rhetoric has—perhaps even more than Obama's—emphasized the power of American identity as an ideal that unites us. In his victory speech after he won the November 2020 presidential election, Biden invoked the logic of American identity when describing how he would govern: "I pledge to be a President who seeks not to divide, but to unify. Who doesn't see Red and Blue states, but a United States. . . . I ran as a proud Democrat. I will now be an American president. I will work as hard for those who didn't vote for me as those who did" (Biden 2020). His inaugural address echoed that same theme, and called on Americans to "see each other not as adversaries, but as neighbors . . . [to] stop the shouting and lower the temperature" in our rhetoric and discourse (Biden 2021), a theme his presidential rhetoric continues to invoke.

It would be easy, especially in our current moment, to say that such flowery oratory ignores our harsh political reality. But to do so would be a mistake, as these calls for unity reflect a deep psychological insight: by highlighting a shared identity, they help to reduce the animosity between Democrats and Republicans (Gaertner and Dovidio 2000; Gaertner et al. 1989). Normally, Democrats and Republicans see each other as rivals competing for control of the government and the ability to set policy. But when the president, or anyone else, primes their identity as Americans, and reminds them of their common bonds, they see the other side in a different light. They are no longer a rival partisan out-group, but members of a national in-group. As such, thinking of those from the other party as fellow Americans, rather than as partisan competitors, should reduce partisan animus; this is the logic of the Common Identity Hypothesis from chapter 2. In this chapter, I first test it using American identity, as it is among our strongest and most powerful identities; later in the chapter, I explore how other types of shared identities can also help to bridge the partisan divide.

Does American Identity Bridge the Partisan Divide?

To test the Common Identity Hypothesis, I designed an original survey experiment. To prime American identity, those assigned to the treatment condition read an article celebrating America, modeled on Novarro (2014). Originally published on the Fourth of July, it outlines a set of reasons why Americans should be proud of their national identity—our system of government, our freedoms, our natural beauty, and so forth. After reading the article, subjects then write a brief paragraph reflecting on why they themselves are proud to identify as an American. Control group subjects read an apolitical article about a New Mexico cat library that allows office workers to borrow a cat to play with in their office (Mackie 2015), and then write an unrelated paragraph about the types of restaurants they like to visit and why (to mimic the length and format of the treatment condition). I recruited 1,729 respondents to take this experiment through Survey Sampling International (SSI; now known as

Dynata) between July 15 and July 18, 2015. These data are not a true random (probability) sample of the US population; rather, they come from an opt-in Internet panel (i.e., a set of respondents who sign up online to take surveys in exchange for small rewards). That said, using a non-probability sample here should not be a terribly important impediment to drawing valid conclusions, because American identity does not vary much by demographics, and because I also use other, more representative data (described below) to examine this hypothesis in other contexts.

As I discussed in chapter 2, I use a common set of items across experiments to measure partisan animosity. In this analysis, I ask subjects to assess the other party using a feeling thermometer, as well as a trait battery, asking them to rate how well various adjectives (i.e., American, honest, trustworthy, etc.) describe those from the other party. Here and throughout the book, independents who lean toward one of the political parties are treated as partisans (Keith et al. 1992), and pure independents are excluded from these analyses (Levendusky 2010). I focus primarily on graphical analyses of my data, and as much as possible, relegate regression results to the appendix of each chapter. Readers interested in more detailed analyses of these particular data are referred to Levendusky (2018a), where they are experiment 1.

Before turning to an analysis of the treatment effects, it is worth considering *why* participants felt proud to be Americans—when given the opportunity to write about this, what did they say in their open-ended responses? To do this, I had a research assistant code their answers and classify them into a set of categories; figure 3.1 displays this data. While respondents could list as many responses as they wanted to, most focused on one or two reasons they are proud to be an American.[1]

Not surprisingly, the modal answer is that Americans are proud of our freedoms—the fact that we have freedom of speech, freedom of the press, freedom of religion, and so forth. Indeed, more than half of respondents mention freedom as a core rationale for their pride in their national identity. Second, but far less popular (selected by 25 percent of respondents), was the idea that America is a land of opportunity: anyone who works hard enough can succeed here, they are not constrained by where they started in life, and they too can achieve the "American dream."[2] Those are—by far—the most common answers, which in and of itself is telling about the American creed and American identity.

The next set of answers—each of which was provided by approximately 5–10 percent of respondents—spoke of America's diversity (i.e., America is a melting pot, we are a land of immigrants, etc.) or our system of government and founding documents (especially the Constitution and the Bill of

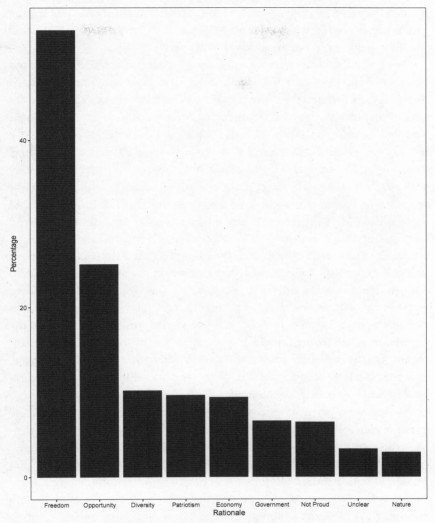

FIGURE 3.1. Sources of Pride in American Identity, 2015

Note: Bars show the percentage of respondents who listed a given category as a reason they were proud of their American identity. Because respondents could pick more than one category, the bars do not sum to 100 percent.

Source: American Identity Experiment

Rights), or expressed patriotism. This last category is particularly interesting, as it typically did not say anything in particular, but rather simply stated that America is the best nation on earth, noted how proud the flag made them, and so forth—it is more a general sentiment than a specific argument. The other substantive rationales were pride in our economy (6 percent of subjects;

this was largely focused on American innovation and our standard of living), pride in our natural beauty (3 percent of subjects), or an answer that could not be coded into one of these categories (3 percent).

Fascinatingly, approximately 6 percent of subjects rejected the prime, and they noted that they were *not* proud of their American identity. These came from both the left and the right, invoking their shame in America's legacy of slavery and racism, as well as claiming that America had lost its way, become a socialist nation, and so forth. I include these individuals in the analysis below, so the effects I estimate are really intent-to-treat (ITT) effects. If anything, these ITT estimates are a lower bound on the effects, as the treatment likely had no effect (or perhaps even increased affective polarization) for these individuals who rejected the treatment (though additional data would be needed to establish this point). As I note below, while American identity is a powerful identity, it is clearly not embraced with equal gusto by all Americans.

Looking across all these categories, however, the pattern is clear: Americans have a variety of reasons why they are proud to be an American, focused largely on our national story: American is a nation born in freedom, and one where anyone can work hard and achieve success. The notion of America as a melting pot and a land of immigrants clearly also remains a core part of the American ethos. While the study was conducted prior to the Trump presidency, by 2015 (when the study took place) immigration had already become a hot-button issue, suggesting that while it is divisive, it is also an important part of how Americans see themselves.

Regardless of what subjects wrote about, the key question is whether the treatment changed their levels of partisan animus. To begin, consider respondents' assessment of the other party on the feeling thermometer scale. If the Common Identity Hypothesis is correct, then I would expect to find that those in the treatment condition—who had their American identity primed and should have seen those from the other party as fellow Americans more than as rival partisans—should have rated the other party more positively than those in the control condition (who, given the political climate of 2015, likely will have rated the other party quite negatively). Figure 3.2 plots the distribution of feeling thermometer scores in both treatment and control groups to test this logic.[3]

Figure 3.2 follows a number of graphical conventions that I will use throughout the book. Here, the control group is shown in dark gray with a solid outline, while the treatment group is shown in light gray with a dotted outline. The x-axis shows the feeling thermometer scores from 0 (coldest rating) to 100 (warmest rating), and the y-axis shows the relative number (density) of respondents who provided a given response, with higher values

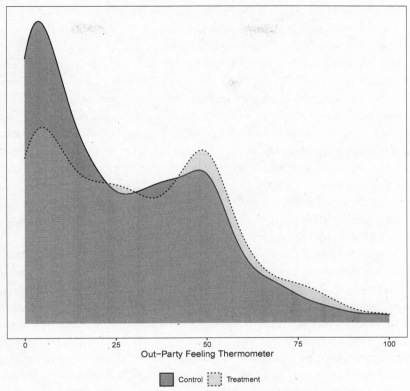

FIGURE 3.2. American Identity Improves Out-Party Feeling Thermometer Ratings

Note: The distribution of out-party feeling thermometer ratings for control group respondents is given in dark gray; the corresponding data for treated subjects is in light gray.

Source: American Identity Experiment

indicating that more people gave that response. Here we can see that in the control condition, most respondents rated the other party quite negatively: the modal response was a rating at 0 degrees, the coldest rating, which 13 percent of respondents in the control condition gave. Further, 50 percent of subjects in the control condition rated the other party at 20 degrees or lower, reinforcing my expectations: absent any intervention, partisans have considerable animus for those from the other party.

But what happened to those in the treatment condition? Here, responses were quite different. While many respondents still rated the other party at the low end of the feeling thermometer scale, the distribution shifted markedly to the right, and many respondents gave warmer evaluations of the other party. On average, subjects in the treatment condition rated those from the other party six degrees warmer than those in the control condition (p < 0.01), a one-quarter of a standard deviation difference.

This treatment effect is immediately visible in figure 3.2. Note that there are far fewer responses at the coldest end of the scale, and far more responses at 50 degrees or higher. For example, the number of ratings of the other party at 0 degrees—the coldest rating—fell by 25 percent, from 13 percent in the control condition to only 9 percent in the treatment condition (p < 0.05). Not only did the number of cold ratings fall; the number of warm ratings rose. Ratings of 50 degrees (neutral) or warmer grew from only 19 percent of respondents in the control condition to 28 percent in the treatment condition, an increase of nearly 50 percent. This provides us with strong initial evidence in favor of the Common Identity Hypothesis: priming American identity—and thinking of the other party as fellow Americans rather than rival partisans—decreased animus and improved attitudes toward them.

Looking at figure 3.2, readers might wonder if there is any partisan heterogeneity: were Democrats or Republicans especially moved by the treatment? What about by strong versus weak partisans? The answer, perhaps surprisingly, is no, not only for the feeling thermometer item, but also for the other items used in this study—for many different subgroups, the story is the same. This finding was replicated throughout the analyses in the book, and except in a few instances clearly noted in the text, the story was one of homogeneous effects, not heterogeneous ones. I therefore pooled Democrats and Republicans, as well as strong, weak, and leaning partisans, together in my analyses throughout the book.[4] Overall, the story is one where all respondents—Democrats and Republicans, weak partisans and strong—respond similarly to the treatments.

Figure 3.2 tells a clear story about the reduction of animus from this treatment, but it is worth commenting more generally on the effect size from this treatment, as the same point arises in later experiments as well. Here, the modal response in both the treatment and control groups is to rate the other party at 0 degrees, and the average rating in the treatment condition is still a relatively chilly 31 degrees—warmer certainly than in the control condition, but still not especially warm. While the effects of the treatment are real, they are modest rather than massive. This makes good sense, as this is brief and relatively simple treatment, and it would be unrealistic to expect a wholesale change in attitudes as a result. As I noted in earlier chapters, these treatments are about reducing animus, not eliminating it.

That said, these reductions in animus are important and substantively meaningful. To help grasp their magnitude, consider the data on the over-time feeling thermometer ratings presented in figure 1.1. Between 2016 and

2020, out-party feeling thermometer ratings fell by 6 degrees (from 25 to 19 degrees, using only the online respondents for consistency). Here, I found that the American identity prime increased feeling thermometer ratings by 6 degrees, so the treatment effect is equivalent to turning back the clock from 2020 to 2016, before Trump's election. To be clear, such a move would not eradicate animus, but it represents an important change in it. My treatments do not cure partisan animosity, but they do ameliorate it.

The evidence above demonstrates that priming American identity improves out-party feeling thermometer ratings, but does it also improve trait ratings of the other party? Subjects were asked how well eight adjectives described the other party: American, intelligent, honest, generous, open-minded, hypocritical, selfish, and mean. For each item, respondents could select one of five responses: "not at all well," "not too well," "somewhat well," "very well," or "extremely well." If the Common Identity Hypothesis is correct, then when a respondent has their American identity primed, they should think that the positive traits (American, intelligent, honest, generous, open-minded) better describe those from the other party, and the negative traits (hypocritical, selfish, and mean) are less applicable. In an earlier publication, I showed that the treatment improved these trait ratings on average by one-fifth of a standard deviation (Levendusky 2018a, 64, table 1). But to better unpack what that means substantively, consider the responses to one particular item: how well "intelligent" describes to the other party. Figure 3.3 shows the distribution of responses to this item in both the treatment and control conditions.

Figure 3.3 shows clear graphical evidence of the treatment effects noted above. In both conditions, the modal response is that intelligent described the other party "somewhat well"—35 percent of subjects in both conditions felt this way. But in the treatment condition, far more subjects thought that the term intelligent described the other party "very well" or "extremely well." In the control condition, only 16 percent and 8 percent of subjects gave these ratings, but that jumped to 22 percent and 11 percent in the treatment condition, an increase of 38 percent. Likewise, those who say that intelligent described the other party "not at all well" or "not too well" fell by 18 percent (from 39 percent to 32 percent). Clearly, treated subjects rated the other party more positively.[5]

So far, the evidence above is consistent with the Common Identity Hypothesis, but nothing there can directly speak to the particular mechanism underlying it. If this hypothesis is correct, then the treatment should also make respondents more likely to say "American" is an apt description of those from the other party (after all, it is their shared American identity that is

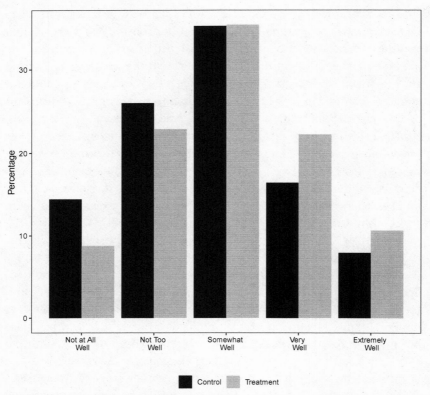

FIGURE 3.3. American Identity Increases Perceptions of Out-Party Intelligence

Note: Control subjects' ratings of how well the term "intelligent" describes the other party are given in black; the ratings for treated subjects are given in light gray.

Source: American Identity Experiment

driving these effects). Figure 3.4 shows the distribution of responses to this item in both conditions.

Here, we see that even in the control condition, most respondents thought that American does a good job of describing those from the other party. But note that, relative to those in the control condition, treated subjects were more likely to say that American described the other party "very well" or "extremely well" (an increase of 16 percent), and less likely to say it described the other party "not at all well" or "not too well" (a decrease of 30 percent). By priming American identity, Americans saw the other party as more American, exactly as the Common Identity Hypothesis predicted. Of course, one cannot really prove a particular mechanism (Bullock, Green, and Ha 2010), but this evidence is certainly consistent with my underlying argument. When

American identity is primed, subjects come to view those from the other party as more American, and indeed, view them more positively along a number of different dimensions.

The evidence from this experiment is clear: American identity can serve as a bridge between the parties, uniting them rather than dividing them. But of course, this is just one experiment, with a single manipulation used to prime American identity. In particular, this is a strong treatment (containing both a newspaper article and a brief writing task) that also conflates American identity with pride in that identity (by asking subjects what makes them proud to be American). Would other primes, especially weaker ones, produce similar results? The results in Levendusky (2018a) speak directly to this point. In that study, I conducted two additional experiments with different,

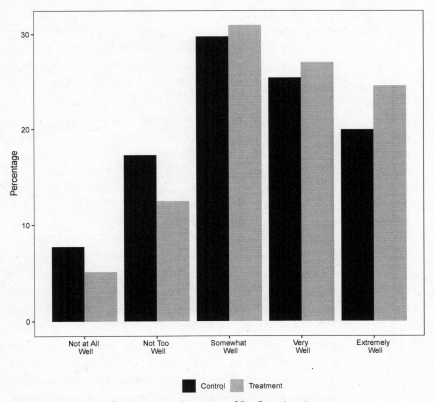

FIGURE 3.4. American Identity Increases Perceptions of Out-Party Americanness

Note: Control subjects' ratings of how well the term "American" describes the other party are given in black; the ratings for treated subjects are given in light gray.

Source: American Identity Experiment

and weaker, treatments to explore the robustness of these findings. In one experiment, I simply had respondents complete the free writing task on why they were proud to be American (without first reading the newspaper article), and in the other, I had them answer a few close-ended items about whether they saw themselves as Americans (without reading any articles or completing any writing task). The results from both of these experiments confirmed the results above: even a weaker prime of American identity had similar effects on reducing affective polarization. American identity helps to bridge the partisan divide.

Evidence from Outside the Experimental Context

The analysis above provides strong experimental evidence in support of the Common Identity Hypothesis. But do these effects extend beyond the experimental context—can I find evidence of them in the "real world"? To do so, I need to find some event that exogenously increases American identity. Happily, there is a real-world event that does so: America's Independence Day, July 4. The day is a celebration of America, and many Americans commemorate the day by displaying national symbols such as the American flag, attending parades, and singing patriotic songs. As a result, Americans feel more American on that day (Madestam and Yanagizawa-Drott 2012). July 4 therefore serves as a natural experiment to test this hypothesis, and allows me to gather valuable non-experimental evidence of these effects.

To examine the effects of the July 4 holiday, I turn to the 2008 National Annenberg Election Study (NAES) Online Panel, which interviewed over 30,000 respondents during the course of the 2008 campaign. Not only is this dataset extremely large, allowing me to search for small effects; the interview date is also randomly assigned within wave, so that there should be no systematic differences between the subjects who respond to the survey near July 4 and those who answer it at other times (see Johnston 2008 for more on the NAES design). Here, I use the responses from wave 3 of the NAES panel, which interviewed subjects between April and August 2008. Because the Democratic Party primaries in 2008 ran until early June, responses before June could be different from those that come afterward (due to learning about the candidates in the Democratic primary). To avoid this potential confound, I focus my analyses on those interviewed between June and August. Unfortunately, the NAES does not include party feeling thermometers, but they did ask respondents to rate Barack Obama and John McCain, the major-party nominees, on the feeling thermometer scale. As Lelkes, Sood, and Iyengar

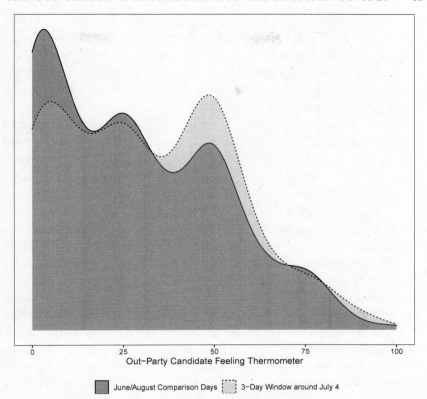

Out-Party Candidate Feeling Thermometer

▨ June/August Comparison Days   ┊┄┊ 3-Day Window around July 4

FIGURE 3.5. July 4 Reduces Out-Party Animus

Note: Out-party candidate feeling thermometer ratings for those interviewed in the three-day window around July 4 are given in light gray; the data for those in the comparison windows in June/August are given in dark gray.

Source: 2008 National Annenberg Election Study Online Panel

(2017) demonstrate, these candidate feeling thermometer ratings closely track party feeling thermometers, so this should not be a significant limitation to my analysis (see the supplemental appendix of Levendusky 2018a for more on this point). So here, I examine how Democrats (Republicans) rate McCain (Obama) on the feeling thermometer scale, and whether those responses are more positive for those interviewed near July 4.

My expectation is that those interviewed "close" to July 4 will evaluate the other party's nominee more positively. But what does "close" mean? The answer is unclear, so in Levendusky (2018a), I operationalized this difference in a wide variety of different ways. Here, for the sake of simplicity, I say that those who were interviewed in a three-day window around July 4 were interviewed close to the holiday, and I compare them to those interviewed in similar three-day windows earlier and later in the summer. Figure 3.5 shows the results.

Here, we see results similar to those in figure 3.2 above—on average, for those interviewed close to July 4, feeling thermometer ratings increased by roughly 3.6 degrees (p < 0.05), and that shift was driven by fewer ratings at the coldest end of the scale, and more ratings at 50 degrees and higher. Of course, this is just one potential operationalization of closeness to July 4; there are many others. In the earlier publication (Levendusky 2018a), I showed that a variety of different operationalizations of this concept—windows of various sizes, as well as measuring the number of days or weeks from the holiday—give substantively similar results. Measured many different ways, those interviewed around Independence Day feel warmer toward the other party.[6]

But is this the only time when national sentiments rise? Fortuitously, there is another time when I can examine the effects of priming national identity: the 2008 Beijing Summer Olympics.[7] The Olympics are structured around competition between nations, where individuals march with their country's flag, compete under their country's banner, and wear uniforms bearing their country's national colors. As a result, the Olympics increase a sense of national identity among viewers (Elling, Van Hilvoorde, and Van Den Dool 2014), especially during salient events, such as when their nation does particularly well in the medal count (Van Hilvoorde, Elling, and Stovkis 2010).[8] The 2008 Beijing Summer Olympics featured a particularly noteworthy event for Americans: the weekend of August 15–17, when Michael Phelps won his sixth, seventh, and eighth Olympic gold medals in the Beijing games, which approached, tied, and then broke Mark Spitz's 1972 record for most gold medals won by an individual athlete in a single Olympics. This historic event, widely covered in the US press, should bring all Americans together around this achievement, thereby priming American identity and reducing partisan animus. To assess this effect, I compare the effect among those interviewed over that weekend (August 15–17) to the effect among those interviewed on the weekend that preceded the start of the Olympic games. Figure 3.6 presents these results.

The results here directly parallel those in figures 3.2 and 3.5 above: subjects interviewed during Phelps's gold medal weekend—which should prime American identity—view the other party's nominee more positively. Here, the average feeling thermometer rating for the other party's candidate increased by 4.8 degrees (p < 0.05), ratings at 0 degrees fell considerably (by 20 percent), and those at 50 degrees or warmer rose notably (by 25 percent). Much like July 4, a record-breaking Olympic result can bring us together as a nation and bind us as one, reducing hostility toward those from the other party.

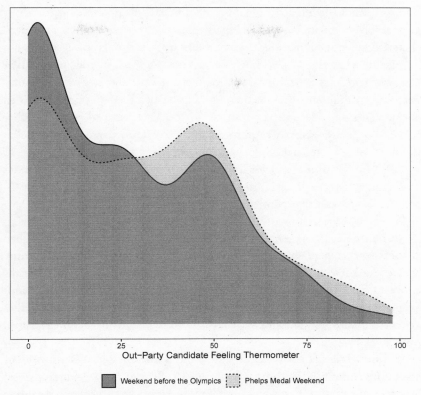

Out−Party Candidate Feeling Thermometer

▮ Weekend before the Olympics   ⬚ Phelps Medal Weekend

FIGURE 3.6. Olympic Victories Reduce Out-Party Animus

Note: Out-party candidate feeling thermometer ratings for those interviewed on Michael Phelps's record-breaking weekend are given in light gray; the data for those interviewed just before the Olympic games are given in dark gray.

Source: 2008 National Annenberg Election Study Online Panel

Overall, then, in both instances—July 4 and the Olympic games—I find strong non-experimental evidence buttressing my experimental findings. When we come to see those from the other party as fellow Americans, rather than as rival partisans, we view them more positively. American identity can serve as a powerful bridge to those from the other side of the aisle.

Does American Identity Still Bind Us Together?

The data so far in this chapter suggest that priming American identity reduces partisan animosity. But all of those data—both the experimental data and the NAES data—were collected before Donald Trump's term in office. President

Trump's tenure in office might have eliminated the power of this sort of prime, for two related sets of reasons. First, past political leaders have used American identity as a bridge beyond politics, as the discussion at the start of the chapter suggests. Trump, however, did not. He was a divider, not a uniter (to use Jacobson's 2006 phrasing); his instinct was to cast blame and emphasize our differences rather than our similarities (Leibovich 2020). When former President George W. Bush called for Americans to come together and avoid partisanship in response to the COVID-19 pandemic, President Trump mocked him (Baker 2020a). When evaluating the nation's response to COVID-19, racial justice, or really any other topic, "Trump regularly divides the country into the parts that support him and the parts that do not, rewarding the former and reproving the latter" (Baker 2020b).

Trump's politicization of the July 4 holiday—holding a military parade in 2019 and a de facto campaign rally in 2020 at Mount Rushmore—exemplified this tendency. Normally, July 4 is a day to celebrate all Americans, but Trump instead took it as an opportunity to attack his opponents. In his Mount Rushmore address, Trump argued that "our nation is witnessing a merciless campaign to wipe out our history, defame our heroes, erase our values and indoctrinate our children," linking these efforts to his 2020 rival, Joe Biden (Karni 2020).

Second, Trump's rhetoric has—time and again—linked American identity with Whiteness. His campaign narrative calling to "Make America Great Again" seeks a return to a world where White Americans—particularly White men—held unquestioned political power in this country. Trump's arguments are about activating the fear of "the erosion of the ability to define mainstream America as white," as Ashley Jardina succinctly put it (Chotiner 2019). For example, he emphasized his desire for immigrants from Norway and other European countries rather than "sh**hole" countries like Haiti (Dawsey 2018), told several prominent non-White Congresswomen to "go back" to their home countries, despite the fact that all but one of them were born in the United States (Sonmez and Bade 2019), and gave what many heard as tacit support for a widely disparaged white supremacist group (the Proud Boys) during the first presidential debate in 2020 (Timberg and Dwoskin 2020). Trump's rhetoric linked and activated racialized understandings of American identity (Smith and King 2021), drawing on long-standing tropes that Whites are the quintessential Americans (Devos and Banaji 2005).

Given the ways in which Trump has manipulated American identity, this raises the possibility that it may no longer serve to bridge the partisan divide. Instead, the appeal may only work for Republicans and White respondents, because Trump effectively defines them as Americans (and removes others from that in-group). It is therefore worth considering the effectiveness of the prime overall, as well as its effects by race and party, in a more recent sample. In the experiments analyzed earlier in the chapter, the prime worked for all Americans, and there were no differential effects by race or party, but that homogeneity may no longer hold.

Beyond simply replicating the American Identity prime used in the earlier experiments, I propose an additional treatment to further probe the limits of using our shared bonds to overcome animus.[9] This is not an identity per se, but a collective memory of a time when Americans came together as one. Over time, societies form a collective memory of an event, and how we remember an event is, in many ways, more important for our politics than what actually happened (Edy 2006). Events that we remember as moment of national unity could be another effective mechanism for overcoming dissensus by triggering a recollection of a time when divisions were subsumed by appeals to national unity. This is, effectively, an indirect route to priming national identity (by triggering the memory of a specific event, rather than the general concept of national identity).

There are a number of examples of such events in the American past. The Olympic games are a perennial source of these events, from the famous "Miracle on Ice" in 1980, to Mary Lou Retton's gold medal in 1984, to Michael Phelps's record-breaking eight gold medals in 2008, as I discussed above. Military victories—such as World War II and the Cold War—also serve as powerful reminders of national unity.

Here, I investigate whether evoking the memory of the aftermath of 9/11 can trigger this sense of national unity. In the wake of that tragedy, members of Congress locked arms across party lines and sang "God Bless America" on the steps of the Capitol, and ordinary Americans rushed in record numbers to volunteer, donate blood and money, and help those who were affected by the attacks. The increased salience of such national unity pushed President Bush (temporarily) to the highest approval rating on record (Kam and Ramos 2008) at 90 percent, according to Gallup,[10] and pride in American identity to reach an all-time high (Brenan 2019).

Americans collectively remember the time after those attacks in a similar way. Every year around September 11, there are renewed calls to rediscover this sense of unity and to come together to solve our common problems. Such articles have appeared in major papers, such as the *Washington Post* (Dvorak 2020) and the *Wall Street Journal* (Henninger 2011), as well as scores of smaller, more regional outlets (see, e.g., Falce 2020, *Gainesville Times* 2020). Priming this post-9/11 unity, therefore, may also heighten national identity and reduce animus toward the other party. Here, to parallel the article used to prime American national identity, I adapted an article about how the nation's post-9/11 unity should inspire us to come together once again (Cobern 2020).

To measure out-party animus, I replicated the items from my earlier study—the feeling thermometer ratings and trait ratings of the other party—and also ask an additional item, how much respondents trust in the other party to act in the country's best interest. I tested these hypotheses in a study using respondents from the Bovitz Forthright Panel collected between October 5 and October 13, 2020. This is a particularly strong test of my argument, as it occurs not only during the Trump era, but also in the final month of a highly competitive presidential election. If the prime works even here, it is a testament to its power to bridge the partisan divide.

As before, prior to examining the treatment effects I had a research assistant go through and code the open-ended responses about why respondents were proud of their American identity, using the same coding scheme I used for the original experiment. These responses are presented in figure 3.7. There is a great deal of continuity, but also some change, in these responses relative to the patterns seen in figure 3.1 using the data from the original 2015 experiment. As before, the modal answer was that Americans are proud to be American because of our freedoms (50 percent), with the idea of opportunity (the American dream) coming in second (30 percent). But the third answer was markedly different—now it was those who were *not* proud of their American identity (12 percent). In 2015, only about 6 percent of respondents rejected the prompt, but here that figure doubled. This suggests that American identity may be more contested in 2020 than it was in earlier eras.

Why were respondents not proud of their American identity? Their reasons fell into three roughly equally sized groups. The first group pointed to the structural racism in America, especially in light of the disproportionate impact of the coronavirus pandemic on racial and ethnic minorities, as well as the deaths of many Black Americans, such as Breonna Taylor and George Floyd, at the hands of the police; these themes were acutely highlighted during that summer's Black Lives Matter protests. A second group pointed to the corrosive effects of the Trump presidency and the ways in which he damaged American democracy (Carey et al. 2019), especially with his claims that he would only lose the upcoming 2020 election if there was voter fraud (a false claim Trump repeated again and again after the election, even after the tragic events of January 6 and his second impeachment). Finally, the last group pointed to a litany of other problems, most notably the rising cost of a college education, health care, and the explosion in income inequality in recent decades.

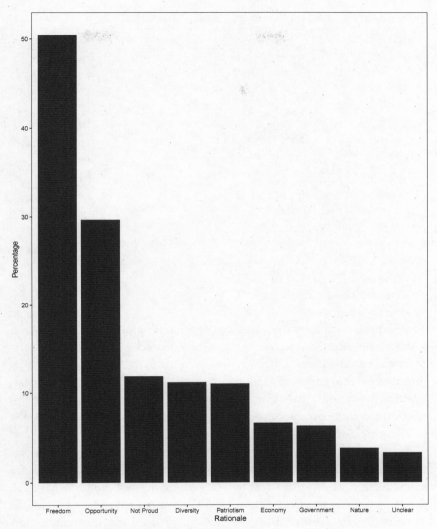

FIGURE 3.7. Sources of Pride in American Identity, 2020

Note: Bars show the percentage of respondents who listed a given category as a reason they were proud of their American identity. Because respondents could pick more than one category, the bars do not sum to 100 percent.

Source: 2020 American Identity Experiment

TABLE 3.1. Treatment Effects of Trump-Era Common Identity Primes

	AP Index	Out-Party FT	Out-Party Traits	Out-Party Trust
Constant	0.313***	16.123***	2.222***	1.654***
	(0.006)	(0.794)	(0.032)	(0.033)
American Identity				
Prime	0.019**	2.392**	0.101**	0.079*
	(0.009)	(1.153)	(0.046)	(0.047)
9/11 Prime	0.015*	2.591**	0.061	0.029
	(0.009)	(1.143)	(0.046)	(0.047)
American Identity				
Prime	N	N	N	N
More Effective?				
p-value	0.62	0.87	0.39	0.3
N	1988	1958	1988	1984
R-Squared	0.003	0.003	0.002	0.001

Note: Cell entries are OLS regression coefficients with associated standard errors in parentheses.
*p<0.1; **p<0.05; ***p<0.01.

Source: 2020 American Identity Experiment

But it was not simply that more people were not proud of their American identity: in 2020, these responses took on a distinct partisan cast. In 2015, there were no significant differences between the parties in the rate at which they rejected the prompt and said that they were not proud of their American identity. But in 2020, there was a marked difference: 85 percent of those who rejected the prompt were Democrats. This is the first hint that the prime may be a less effective bridge in 2020 than it was in 2015.

Table 3.1 presents the results of my experiment to test whether American identity still reduces affective polarization. The table presents a seemingly happy picture, as it appears that both the original American identity prime and the 9/11 prime both lessened animus. The results in the first column show the effects of the treatments on an index of all three affective polarization measures included in this study ($\alpha=0.82$), with higher values indicating lower levels of partisan animus. The remaining three columns show the effects on each of the individual measures: out-party feeling thermometers, out-party trait ratings, and out-party trust (again, scaled so that higher values indicate lower levels of animus). Both the index and the individual measures indicate that both treatments mitigated partisan animus. Even in the Trump era, American identity helped to bridge the partisan divide.[11]

Fascinatingly, there was also no significant difference in the effectiveness of the two treatments. While the effect of the 9/11 treatment on trait ratings and trust fell just shy of conventional levels of statistical significance,

TABLE 3.2. Racial & Partisan Heterogeneous Effects, Trump-Era Identity Primes

	Type of Heterogeneity:	
	Race	Partisanship
Constant	0.343***	0.315***
	(0.012)	(0.008)
American Identity Prime	-0.010	0.030**
	(0.018)	(0.012)
9/11 Prime	-0.013	0.024**
	(0.017)	(0.012)
White Respondent	-0.039***	
	(0.014)	
American Identity*White	0.039*	
	(0.021)	
9/11 Prime*White	0.037*	
	(0.020)	
Democrat		-0.004
		(0.012)
American Identity*Democrat		-0.022
		(0.017)
9/11 Prime*Democrat		-0.018
		(0.017)
Non-White/Dem Treat Effect? (Amer. Iden.)	N	N
p-value	0.62	0.87
Non-White/Dem Treat Effect? (9/11)	N	N
p-value	0.39	0.3
N	1986	1988
R-Squared	0.007	0.007

Note: Cell entries are OLS regression coefficients with associated standard errors in parentheses.
*p<0.1; **p<0.05; ***p<0.01.

Source: 2020 American Identity Experiment

the effect could not be differentiated from the effect of the American identity prime (Gelman and Stern 2006). In the rows labeled "American Identity Prime More Effective?" and "p-value," I give the p-value from the test of the null hypothesis that the two treatments were equally efficacious.[12] In every case, I fail to reject the null hypothesis. Priming American identity and priming the unity in the aftermath of 9/11 both worked to lessen the partisan divide, and did so to a similar extent. Table 3.1 presents a salubrious finding for our democratic politics: even when the president works to divide us, our national identity still serves as a powerful balm to help reduce inflamed partisan passions.

But before celebrating too much, I need to examine whether there were heterogeneous effects by race or party—perhaps American identity was a more powerful tonic for some groups than for others, and hence this aggregate effect may have masked important heterogeneity. Table 3.2 presents the results testing for heterogeneous treatment effects by race and by party. Consistent with the concern I expressed above, we see here that the treatment was more efficacious for Republicans and White respondents. For simplicity, I only present results here for the combined index of affective polarization, but the results look very similar for the individual items. Indeed, if I examine whether the treatment effect for non-White or Democratic respondents could be differentiated from 0,[13] I find that it could not (see the middle portion of the table). That paints the results in table 3.1 in a different light: I found an overall effect of both primes, but that was due to effects among White respondents and among Republicans. In the Trump era—unlike earlier eras— there is clear evidence of differential treatment effects in response to appeals to American identity.

This is consistent with the findings in figure 3.7 above about why individuals were not proud of their American identity in 2020: systemic racism, Trump's actions as president, and other problems in America such as the rising cost of college education and health care. These are all factors disproportionately cited by Democrats, rather than Republicans, so it is perhaps no surprise that the prime is less effective for Democrats and non-White voters. For Whites and Republicans (identities that are obviously linked in an era of socially sorted parties; see Mason 2018), their American identity was still seen in overwhelmingly positive terms, and it reminded them of unity and coming together for a common purpose. But for people of color, and for Democrats, the experience was quite different: they saw American identity as politicized, with more negative overtones, and hence the prime divided rather than unified them. To be clear, animus still fell overall, and that is a valuable finding. But that decrease was due to shifts in a particular subgroup.

This highlights how American identity works to unify the country only if the president—and other political leaders—work to use that identity as a bridge. If American identity becomes politicized and/or racialized, it becomes just another political symbol, and it loses its power to unite us all as one. This highlights the fragility of these appeals: while they worked in the past, it was because past presidents sought to reach across the aisle and bring us together as one. If leaders no longer do that, then their effectiveness wanes. The obvious solution is to have leaders speak to what unites us and brings us together across party lines. But even if they do—as President Biden has done—it may not be enough. Once an identity like this has become politicized, the damage is long-lasting. That does not mean that American identity cannot bring us together—I discuss this point more in the conclusion to this chapter, as well as the final chapter of the book—but it certainly complicates its cross-party appeal.

Are There Other Identities That Can Bridge the Partisan Divide?

So far, I have tested the Common Identity Hypothesis by evaluating the power of American identity to bridge the partisan divide. But the underlying theoretical argument was focused on common identities more generally, not just superordinate identities such as American identity. If the hypothesis is correct, then shared identities beyond our national identity should also lessen partisan animosity.

But what identities do Democrats and Republicans share? As I illustrated in chapter 1, sports fandom is a salient—and widely shared—identity across party lines. If (say) a Democratic Green Bay Packers fan meets a Republican Packers fan, then their shared passion for the Packers should mitigate some of the partisan animus they would otherwise feel for one another. Indeed, as George Dorfman, the author of *Superfans*, an account of die-hard sports fans, notes, sports team identity is "one of the few things left in our society that bridges our divides" (*New Yorker* 2018).

More generally, sports team fandom is crucial to many Americans' lives. Americans spend over $56 billion per year attending live sporting events (O'Brien 2017), and that does not count the billions more spent on branded apparel, cable packages to receive sports channels, and so forth. Sports fans don their team's colors, tattoo their bodies with their team's logo, and see their team identifications as an important part of their self-conception (Heere and James 2007). They work references to their teams not only into their everyday lives, but even into life's most significant rituals, like weddings and funerals (Cottingham 2012). Indeed, identifying with a sports team is a quintessential example of social group identification, and much like other types of social identity, team fandom serves as an in-group/out-group boundary (Wan and Branscombe 1993).

Prior work suggests that such fandom can be politically consequential as well. Harrison and Michelson (2017) show that messages from athletes and sports league officials supporting same-sex marriage persuade their fans to become more supportive of marriage equality, and Healy, Malhotra, and Mo (2010) show that local sports team wins can affect election outcomes. While sports fandom is ostensibly apolitical, it can provide a bridge to political persuasion. Indeed, a recent paper by Engelhardt and Utych (2020) tests a question distinct from but related to the one I examine here. They ask whether shared partisanship can help bridge the divide between rival teams. If a (say) Michigan fan finds out that an Ohio State fan is from the same party, do they trust each other more? They find, consistent with my expectations, that they do. Here, however, I want to see if shared fandom reduces affective polarization between parties, which calls for the converse of their design.[14]

To test whether sports team fandom can reduce the partisan divide, I recruited a sample of 2,121 fans of professional football from the Bovitz Forthright Panel between November 24 and December 2, 2019.[15] After recording baseline demographics, the study asked respondents for their favorite football team, and then primed their identification with that team using the social identity measures proposed by Huddy, Mason, and Aarøe (2015), as well as by asking them to write a brief paragraph explaining why being a fan of their team is important to them.

To measure attitudes toward the other party, I showed respondents a vignette of an individual they were asked to evaluate. The experimental treatment was the information they were told about that person (for a similar setup, see Orr and Huber 2020). Respondents were told either four or five different pieces of information about the person: their age, race, gender, favorite sports team, and partisanship. All subjects were shown someone matched to their gender, race, and age range to avoid confounds on these variables; the variation comes from whether the person's favorite sports team and/or partisanship were provided. There were five experimental conditions:

1. The target individual shared the respondent's favorite sports team and partisanship
2. The target individual shared the respondent's favorite sports team, but their partisanship was not stated
3. The target individual shared the respondent's favorite sports team, but belonged to the opposite political party
4. The target individual shared the respondent's partisanship, but their favorite sports team was not stated
5. The target individual came from the opposite political party and their favorite sports team was not stated

Respondents were shown their randomly assigned vignette, and then asked to rate the person represented therein using the three measures of affective polarization included in the 2020 American Identity Experiment: out-party feeling thermometer ratings, out-party trait ratings, and how much they trust the other person to do what is in the best interest of the nation as a whole.

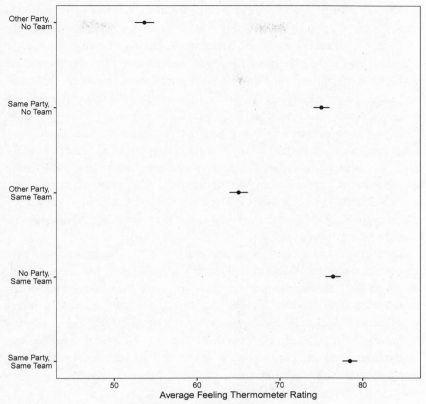

FIGURE 3.8. Shared Sports Fandom Reduces Partisan Animus

Note: Data show the mean in each condition, with bars indicating the 95 percent confidence interval.

Source: Sports Fandom Experiment

Here, the question is whether shared team fandom can overcome the partisan divide. To answer that, I estimated two different quantities of interest using this data. First, does shared fandom reduce animus toward the outparty? This is simply comparing the responses of those in condition 3 to those in condition 5; I would expect lower levels of animus in condition 3 (shares respondent's team identity but from a different party) than in condition 5 (no team affiliation, and different partisanship from the respondent).

Second, and very relatedly, does shared fandom reduce the gap between the parties? This is a difference-in-difference estimator: (condition 1 – condition 3) – (condition 4 – condition 5); put into words, the partisan gap in the same-team condition minus the partisan gap in the no team condition. This is, in many ways, a refinement of the estimate above, but it adjusts for same-party ratings, much like the estimator used in Lelkes and Westwood (2017).

In the analysis below, I focus on the feeling thermometer item given that it is easy to interpret. The regressions needed to formally test these effects are given in the appendix, where I also show that if I use all three measures of affective polarization, I get the same answers. To begin, it is useful to look at the estimated mean (with its standard error), by condition; figure 3.8 presents this data.

Figure 3.8 shows strong support for my argument that sports fandom reduces partisan animus. Take the first quantity of interest: did shared fandom improve assessments of the other party? In the different party / no sports team condition, the average feeling thermometer rating was 53.7 degrees, but that increased by 11.4 degrees—or 21 percent—when that person rooted for the same sports team (p < 0.01). Shared team identity reduced animus toward those from the other party.

Similarly, shared fandom also reduces the affective gap between the parties. When no team affiliation was provided, individuals rated those from their own party 21.4 degrees warmer than those from the other party (75.1 degrees versus 53.7 degrees). But when those hypothetical individuals rooted for the same NFL team, that gap was only 13.4 degrees (78.5 degrees versus 65.1 degrees). In the same-team condition, the gap between the parties was almost 40 percent smaller (p < 0.01)! Sports fandom—much like American identity—helps to bridge the partisan divide.[16]

Conclusions

Can shared identities bridge the partisan divide? The Common Identity Hypothesis from chapter 2 argued that they could, focusing in particular on the role of American national identity. When we see those from the other party as fellow Americans, rather than rival partisans, we perceive them differently. As members of the other party they are part of a disliked out-group, but as fellow Americans they are members of a liked in-group—our fellow citizens. Testing this hypothesis with both an original survey experiment and survey data exploiting the natural experiments of the July 4 holiday and the 2008 Summer Olympics, I find strong and persuasive evidence in support of the Common Identity Hypothesis. When individuals are primed to think about members of the other party as Americans rather than partisans, their feelings toward those others improve quite markedly (Levendusky 2018a). While this held in the pre-Trump era, it becomes more complicated in the post-Trump world, with implications to which I return below.

But American identity is not the only identity shared by Democrats and Republicans—far from it. I ask further whether sports fandom can also bridge the partisan divide. If individuals root for the same team, but come from different parties, their shared team loyalty should blunt the animus they would normally feel for one another. Using another original experiment, I find strong support for my argument: rooting for the same team makes individuals like those from the other party more than they otherwise would. So not only does American identity help to bridge the partisan divide; other identities can do so too.

But these results raise several important questions. First, if rhetorical appeals to American identity, or other shared identities, lessen animus, why don't politicians employ them more frequently? The short answer is that most politicians do employ them, as the examples earlier in the chapter demonstrate. Anyone who doubts this need only listen to nearly any speech by President Biden, who constantly invokes American identity and appeals to American ideals when speaking to the public. And these appeals do work, at least in the short run. But such effects fade as the warm glow of the speech recedes and those from the other party rebut and reframe these appeals. In the end, it is challenging for these sorts of appeals to overcome the typical partisan rhetoric that characterizes our contemporary politics.

There is a further limitation to using American identity. American identity is a powerful identity that brings us together, but it can mean different things to different people.[17] Perhaps this is nowhere more apparent than with respect to race: because Whiteness is typically symbolically linked to Americanness (Devos and Banaji 2005), White and Black Americans often have different understandings of what it means to be American, especially in the wake of public controversies surrounding race (Dach-Gruschow and Hong 2006). For example, while there was no evidence of this heterogeneity in the original American identity experiment from 2015, I found evidence of this heterogeneity by race and party in 2020, in the wake of the Trump presidency and that summer's Black Lives Matter protests. This type of heterogeneity problematizes the use of these primes to reduce partisan animosity.

This also suggests the potential limitation to using another important identity to bridge the partisan divide: our identity as parents. The data I presented in chapter 1 showed that Democrats and Republicans alike attach a great deal of importance to their identity as parents, so this could, in theory, be a bridge to overcoming partisan divisions. And in some cases, this can work. For example, Zeng (2021) shows that priming parental identity shrinks the partisan polarization on how to respond to COVID-19 by making

Republicans more likely to think that COVID-19 is a serious threat. This sort of prime—reminding parents that they have children who depend on them, and who are vulnerable to the disease—uses a powerful identity to mitigate the influence of partisanship. But such identities only work to bridge the gap when the parties want the same thing, and that is not always the case. Pitched battles over critical race theory in schools (really, debates about the central role played by racism and slavery in American history and even our contemporary society) are an example of where parental primes might well fail: if Democratic and Republican parents want different things, then appealing to their parental identity would likely deepen, rather than bridge, the gap between them (see Klar 2018 for an example in the context of gender). Shared identities only work when the two sides understand them in the same way.

Where does this leave us in terms of appeals to American identity? Can it still work to lessen animus? The answer is complicated, but there is, I believe, a path forward; I discuss this point in the book's concluding chapter. But for now, I would make two points. First, the role of American identity reminds us of how much overcoming our divides depends on the actions of political elites. If the president and other politicians use our national symbols to unite us, rather than to divide us, then they can potentially bring us together, but if not, then they shatter our consensus rather than reifying it. When the president calls on our worst impulses rather than our best—when making America great again requires a return to a world where one race and one gender held unquestioned political power—a tool of unity becomes a tool of division. As we see again and again when analyzing political behavior, where elites lead us—good or bad—is where we often end up.

Second, this underlines the importance of apolitical factors like sports teams serving as a bridge between the parties. Here, I chose sports as a meaningful and compelling identity, one where people spend tremendous sums of money and invest considerable emotional energy in the success of their teams. But this is not the only identity that can bridge these divides; so could many groups, such as college and university alumni organizations, churches, civic and community groups, organizations like Rotary or Kiwanis Club, and so forth. Indeed, this provides another argument in favor of these organizations that foster social capital (e.g., Putnam 2000; Mutz 2006). Of course, while such cross-cutting organizations are vital to our political life, they are also becoming less common, as people self-sort into more reinforcing groups (Mason 2016). Finding ways to connect with others from across the political aisle independent of politics would help our politics, even if it is difficult to do.

Appendix: Regression Analysis of the Sports Fandom Experiment

In the body of this chapter, I argued that shared sports fandom can reduce affective polarization, relying primarily on presenting graphical results, and I referred readers interested in the statistical results to this appendix.

Consider the two models I discussed in the body of the chapter. First, consider whether shared fandom reduces animus toward the other party. Using the numbering of conditions from the body of the chapter, this is simply $y_i = \beta_0 + \beta_1 C_3 + \epsilon_i$ if $(C_3 = 1 \mid C_5 = 1)$, where C_3 and C_5 are indicators for conditions 3 and 5. Second, we can ask whether shared fandom reduces the partisan gap. To estimate this quantity, I run the regression: $y_i = \beta_0 + \beta_1 C_1 + \beta_2 C_3 + \beta_3 C_4 + \epsilon_i$ if $! C_2$ (i.e., exclude subjects assigned to condition 2). So here, C_5 (different party, no team) is the baseline (β_0), and the others are offsets relative to that condition. So this hypothesis test becomes: $Ho: (\beta_1 - \beta_2) = \beta_3$, with the expectation that $\beta_3 > \beta_1 - \beta_2$. First, I run these models on just the feeling thermometer data, since that is what I focused on in the chapter; table A3.1 presents these results.

TABLE A3.1. Effects of Shared Fandom on Feeling Thermometer Ratings

	Model 1 (1)	Model 2 (2)
Same Party, Same Team		24.80***
		(1.46)
Other Party, Same Team	11.39***	11.39***
	(1.60)	(1.45)
Same Party, No Team		21.39***
		(1.45)
Constant	53.66***	53.66***
	(1.13)	(1.02)
Observations	849	1,677
R^2	0.06	0.17

Note: Cell entries are OLS regression coefficients with associated standard errors in parentheses.

*p<0.1; **p<0.05; ***p<0.01.

Source: Sports Fandom Experiment

TABLE A3.2. Effects of Sports Fandom on Affective
Polarization Index

	Model 1 (1)	Model 2 (2)
Same Party, Same Team		0.19***
		(0.01)
Other Party, Same Team	0.07***	0.07***
	(0.01)	(0.01)
Same Party, No Team		0.18***
		(0.01)
Constant	0.57***	0.57***
	(0.01)	(0.01)
Observations	849	1,677
R^2	0.04	0.22

Note: Cell entries are OLS regression coefficients with associated
standard errors in parentheses.
*p<0.1; **p<0.05; ***p<0.01.

Source: Sports Fandom Experiment

Note that the results follow from the discussion in the body of the text. Using the data from Model 2 I can test H_0: $(\beta_1 - \beta_2) = \beta_3$ to see if the partisan gap shrinks in the same-party condition. Here, $F = 14.979$, $p < 0.01$, which suggests that we can easily reject the null of no difference between the same-party and no-party conditions.

To ensure that these effects are not simply due to using only the feeling thermometer scale, I can re-scale all three measures to lie in the [0,1] range (where higher scores imply lower levels of animus toward the other party) and then take the average between them ($\alpha = 0.81$); table A3.2 presents these results. Note that these results replicate the feeling thermometer results presented in the body of the text. Again using the data from Model 2, I can test H_0: $(\beta_1 - \beta_2) = \beta_3$ to see if the partisan gap shrinks in the same-party condition. Here, $F = 18.17$, $p < 0.01$, so once again we can reject the null of no difference between the same-party and no-party conditions.

Why Can't We Be Friends: Can Cross-Party Friendships Mitigate Affective Polarization?

I never considered a difference of opinion in politics, in religion, in philosophy, as cause for withdrawing from a friend.

THOMAS JEFFERSON, in a letter to William Hamilton, April 1800

Take a moment and think about your social network—your friends, family members, coworkers, neighbors, and other acquaintances. Do any of them come from the other political party? You might initially be tempted to say no, as you probably see the other party as somewhat distant from yourself. But upon closer reflection, the answer is likely yes, at least if you are similar to most Americans—more than 8 in 10 Americans have at least some partisan heterogeneity in their social networks, as I showed in chapter 1. While we might think that we don't know anyone from the other party, on reflection almost all of us do.

And these cross-party social ties can help to reduce partisan animus. Normally, when we think about the other party, we bring to mind the party leaders in Congress or the White House, or the extreme exemplars we see depicted on the nightly news or Facebook. But if we remember that the other party includes people we know and like as a part of it, then our attitudes toward it improve, as the Cross-Party Friendship Hypothesis predicts.

This chapter tests this hypothesis, and in so doing examines whether our existing social networks might be able to help us mitigate and reduce affective polarization. The findings in this chapter show that they can. Even in our contemporary political moment, the vast majority of Americans can name someone they know and respect from the other party, and briefly reflecting on this friendship sharply lowers their animosity toward it. While Americans might *think* that they have nothing in common with those from the other side of the political aisle, that is not true, as nearly all of us have friends, family, coworkers, and neighbors from the other party. Reflecting on this fact, and what it tells us about who is actually in the other party, provides a first step toward overcoming these partisan divides.

Do Cross-Party Friendships Mitigate Partisan Animus?

As a first test of whether cross-party friendships can reduce partisan animus, I turn to data collected by the Pew Research Center. In spring 2016, the Pew Research Center asked respondents in its American Trends Panel how many friends they had from the other party, as part of a larger survey on political polarization.[1] I use these data to examine whether having more cross-party friendships actually helps to reduce partisan animus, as the Cross-Party Friendship Hypothesis predicts that it would.

The advantage of using this Pew data is that it is a large, nationally representative sample, as Pew uses both random-digit dialing and address-based sampling to recruit subjects into its American Trends Panel (for more on the methodology behind the American Trends Panel, see Keeter 2019). Further, because this is an observational study rather than an experiment, there is less concern about the artifice of the situation. The downside, however, is that cross-party friendships are not randomly assigned, and those whose social networks are bipartisan are likely different from those who have only same-party friends. Given this, I use these results to verify that a link exists between cross-party friendships and lower levels of partisan animus before I turn to experimental tests later in the chapter.

First, just at a descriptive level, how many Americans had friends from the other party? Pew asked respondents how many of their close friends came from the other party: a lot, some, just a few, or none. Note that by asking respondents about "close friends," this item implicitly gives us a conservative estimate of cross-party friendship, as (all else equal) close friends will tend to be more similar to us in partisanship than those with whom we have weaker ties. Figure 4.1 plots the percentage of respondents who had a lot, some, just a few, and no friends from the other party.

This figure shows us unequivocally that friendships did cross party lines, even in 2016.[2] While few people had a lot of cross-party friendships, the modal partisan had some cross-party friendships, and only roughly 10 percent had no friends from the other party. At the outset, it is worth noting that in a large, nationally representative survey, the vast majority of partisans did have friends from the other side of the aisle.

But did those with such cross-party friendships actually report lower levels of partisan animus? To assess this, I used two items from the Pew study: a feeling thermometer rating of the other party, and an item asking whether the other party has any good ideas. To begin, consider the effect on feeling thermometer ratings of the other party. If the Cross-Party Friendship Hypothesis is correct, then I would expect those who report higher levels of cross-party

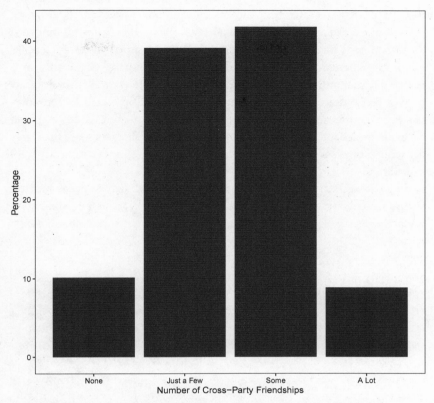

FIGURE 4.1. Frequency of Cross-Party Friendships

Note: Bars show the percentage of respondents who have each level of close friends from the other party.

Source: Pew American Trends Panel

friendships to also give higher feeling thermometer ratings of the other party. Figure 4.2 plots this relationship. Consistent with the Cross-Party Friendship Hypothesis, those with more friends from the other party rated them more positively on the feeling thermometer scale. Those with no friends from the other party rated the other party at a chilly 19 degrees. But those who had at least some friends from the other party rated them 37 percent more warmly (almost half of a standard deviation higher), and those with a lot of friends from the other party rated them a full 10 degrees warmer, a 60 percent increase from those with no cross-party friendships. Those with more bipartisan social networks felt more warmly toward those from the other party.[3]

Did this effect also extend to thinking that the other party had good ideas? Figure 4.3 plots this relationship. Once again, we see a strong correlation between cross-party friendship and lessened animus toward the other party. Only about 11 percent of those with no cross-party friendships thought that the other party had some good ideas, but that jumped to 26 percent—a 136 percent increase—for those who had some cross-party friendships. It is not simply that individuals rated the other party more warmly; they also saw them as having more good ideas, suggestive of greater possibilities for bipartisanship, compromise, and consensus. This suggests—foreshadowing what we will see in chapter 6—that these cross-party friendships do more than simply reduce animus; they also shape other important attitudes toward politics more broadly.

Together, these results show that those whose social networks are more bipartisan also report lower levels of partisan animus. But of course, the limitation is that the degree of partisan homophily in one's social network is not randomly

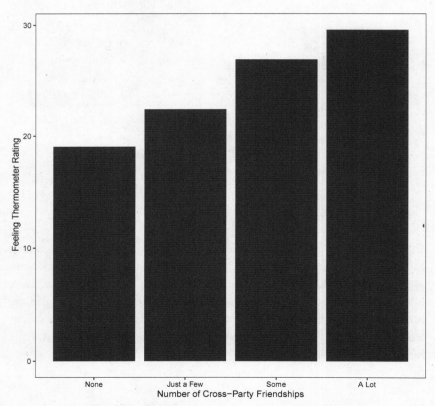

FIGURE 4.2. Cross-Party Friendships Improve Out-Party Feeling Thermometer Ratings

Note: Bars show the average out-party feeling thermometer rating by the frequency of cross-party friendships.

Source: Pew American Trends Panel

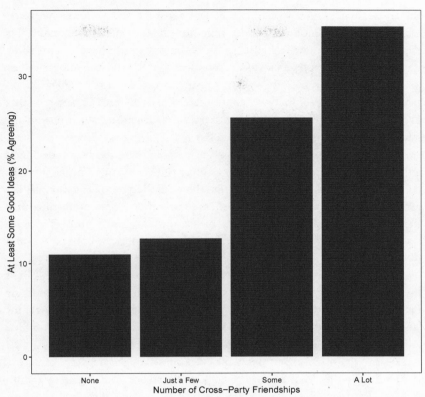

FIGURE 4.3. Cross-Party Friendships Increase the Belief That the Other Party Has Good Ideas

Note: Bars show the percentage of respondents who think that the out-party has at least some good ideas by the frequency of cross-party friendships.

Source: Pew American Trends Panel

assigned, but rather is the result of deliberate choices individuals make. Indeed, in the appendix, I show that stronger partisans and stronger ideologues are less likely than others to report cross-party friendships, perhaps not surprisingly. Given that partisan strength, as well as ideological strength, predict affective polarization, this suggests that part of the effect above is due to these differences.[4] To see if there is a treatment effect—that is, if bipartisan social networks reduce partisan animus—I need to turn to experimental techniques.

An Experimental Test of the Effects of Cross-Party Friendships

In an ideal world, I would randomly assign people to have either partisan homogeneous or partisan heterogeneous friendship networks and then examine the consequences. For a variety of ethical and practical reasons, that obviously cannot happen. But I can do something similar that approximates this experiment. As we saw in figure 4.1, most Americans do have at least some cross-party friendships. I can ask respondents to think about someone they know and like from the other party, and then to write a brief paragraph explaining why they feel that way about them. Previous research suggests that even the act of thinking about such cross-party friendships can powerfully affect attitudes (Crisp and Turner 2009).

To deliver this treatment, I fielded a population-based survey experiment with the National Opinion Research Center's (NORC) AmeriSpeak Panel. To construct the panel, NORC uses its national sampling frame to randomly select households, and then contacts them via a variety of methods to recruit them to join the panel and complete surveys online (Dennis 2018). These respondents are therefore a true random sample of American households, and not simply an opt-in sample, which are biased toward those with higher levels of political interest and engagement (Malhotra and Krosnick 2007). Given the extraordinary cost of a random sample, this is the only experimental one included in the book; elsewhere I rely on opt-in samples to test my claims (though note that the NAES data from chapter 3, and the Pew data from this chapter, are also random samples). But the fact that these results parallel those from my other experiments provides some reassurance that other experimental findings in the book are not simply artifacts of using non-random samples. Between December 6 and December 18, 2018, 1,805 individuals completed this survey, with a cumulative response rate of 8.32 percent.

If the Cross-Party Friendship Hypothesis is correct, treated subjects should rate the other party more warmly on the feeling thermometer scale, evaluate them more positively on various traits, and say that they are more trusting of the other party to do what is right for the country.

DID SUBJECTS COMPLY WITH THE TREATMENT?

Before examining whether the treatment prime actually reduced affective polarization, it is worth digging into the open-ended responses to consider whether treated subjects were actually willing to comply with the prompt. That is, did they actually write about someone from the other party that they like and respect? In an era of elite polarization, merely complying with this sort of treatment is an indicator of affective polarization. In a previous publication (Levendusky 2018b), I attempted to mitigate affective polarization by having subjects say two things they dislike about their own party and two things they like about the opposing party (i.e., priming partisan ambivalence;

see Lavine et al. 2012). Unfortunately, subjects in that study did not comply: only 38 percent were willing to actually say something they liked about the other party. Many respondents simply responded that they liked nothing about the other party or replied (often quite creatively) with vitriol and profanity. While that treatment was designed to mitigate affective polarization, it ironically ended up augmenting it.

Did the same thing happen here—did subjects reject this treatment as well? To determine this, I had a research assistant go through and code each response to see if the respondent actually wrote about someone from the other party that they like and respect. Overall, 81 percent of treated subjects did so. Three percent of subjects wrote gibberish (i.e., just a nonsense string of characters) or skipped the item, and 16 percent responded that they did not like or respect anyone from the other party. This has several important implications. First, subjects complied with the treatment, so it makes sense to examine treatment effects below. Second, because any failure to comply with the treatment is highly non-random, I present the intent-to-treat (ITT) effects (i.e., the effects of being assigned to the treatment condition, whether or not subjects actually complied with it) for all analyses here, consistent with what I did in chapter 3.

But it's also worth considering why subjects might have been willing to write positive things about a friend from the other party, when they were unwilling to do so about the other party more generally. This contrast highlights an important theoretical point I made in chapter 2: when people think about the Democratic and Republican *Parties* without any further prompting, they imagine stereotypes and polarized political elites (Druckman and Levendusky 2019). But when they think about someone they know and like from the other party, their mental image of the party shifts. In part because we cannot know "the Democratic Party" as a collective, we fall back on the cognitively accessible stereotypes that are in our heads (Druckman et al. 2022b). But when asked to think about those we know in the other party, we do not bring those stereotypes to mind. This is not simply a manifestation of person-positivity bias (Sears 1983), but rather suggests the importance of how individuals conceptualize the other party, as that powerfully shapes their reaction to it.

In addition to having my research assistant determine if subjects actually complied with the treatment, I also had them note any other features of how the respondents talked about those from the other party. Two important features of these open-ended responses stick out. Sixteen percent said that, for them, politics and political views are simply irrelevant to whether you like someone, and they would not let politics stand in the way of a personal relationship. This suggests that while we hear stories of people ending friendships over politics in the age of Trump (Wehner 2016), that is a particular segment of the population—the most partisan and politically engaged segment. Most Americans are like President Jefferson—they think of friendship as something too important to end over a political disagreement. Another 10 percent noted that they had some common ground with this person, and agreed with them on some issues, again reinforcing the point made in other work that most voters are not strict ideologues (Fiorina 2017). This is a hint that, for many voters, politics does not sit at the center of their identities, even in an age of affective polarization, and it may well be possible to build bridges to the other side.

WHO ARE THESE CROSS-PARTY FRIENDS?

But who are these cross-party friends? I had my research assistants attempt to code the nature of these relationships in this data, but it proved impossible to do so systematically. Subjects wrote about why they liked and respected the person, but not who that person was. To address this limitation, I ran a second study with the Bovitz Forthright Panel between October 28 and November 5, 2019. In this follow-up study, I repeated this prime and then asked respondents to classify the person they had just written about: was this person a friend, a family member, a coworker, a neighbor, or someone else? All "someone else" responses were asked to clarify. I then had my research assistants code these clarifications; nearly all of them could be classified into one of the existing categories. Figure 4.4 presents this data.[5]

The data show a clear pattern: nearly 8 in 10 respondents wrote about a friend or family member! My *ex ante* expectation was that more people would name a family member than a friend, but that turned out not to be the case: 45 percent named a friend, while only 30 percent named a family member. Eleven percent named a coworker, consistent with the arguments from Mutz and Mondak (2006) that the workplace fosters cross-party interaction, and another 6 percent named a neighbor, consistent with arguments that most neighborhoods are politically mixed (Mummolo and Nall 2017; Martin and Webster 2020). Finally, roughly 6 percent of subjects named a celebrity, mostly politicians like the late Senator John McCain or former President Jimmy Carter; in less than 1 percent of cases, my research assistants and I could not classify the response.[6] These findings underline that far from existing in partisan bubbles, Americans do, in fact, interact with those from the other side of the political aisle. Friendships—as well as families, neighborhoods, and workplaces—straddle the partisan divide.

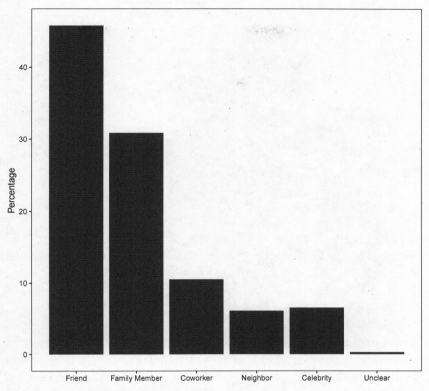

FIGURE 4.4. Who Are People's Cross-Party Friends?

Note: Bars indicate the type of relationship respondents have with the person they know and respect from the other party.

Source: Bovitz Forthright Friendship Experiment

I also asked respondents how close they were to the individuals they named in the prompt. One concern might be that individuals can name someone from the other party, but this isn't someone that they know well, and all of their close friendships are with those from their own party. The Pew data presented above suggested that this is not the case, as there we saw cross-party friendships even among respondent's "close friends" (as you may recall, that is how Pew asks the question). Figure 4.5 shows us whether this is true in these data as well. Here, I removed the 6 percent of subjects who named a celebrity or public figure; the subjects who named such figures do not know these individuals well, so including them would skew the results. Of the remaining sample—those who named an actual *personal* acquaintance—the data

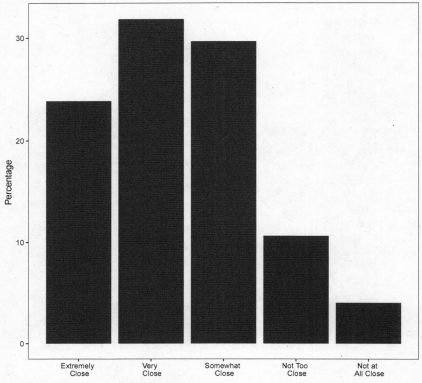

FIGURE 4.5. How Close Are People to Their Cross-Party Friends?
Note: Bars indicate degree of closeness with the person respondents know and respect from the other party.
Source: Bovitz Forthright Friendship Experiment

overwhelmingly show that these were close friends and family. Eighty-five percent of subjects were at least "somewhat close" to the person they named, with roughly one-quarter being "extremely close" and nearly a third being "very close," which was the modal answer. People reported being closest to their family members, then their friends, then coworkers, and finally neighbors, but in all of those cases the average respondent was at least "somewhat close" to the person they named. It is simply not the case that people are naming those from the periphery of their social networks; rather, cross-party friendships occur even among those at the center of our social milieu. For many people, such cross-party interaction occurs quite regularly.

Together, these findings provide important evidence that our social networks are not as politically homogeneous as they might appear at first glance, and that many Americans have very close friends and family members from the other party. It is simply incorrect to conclude that most Americans do not interact across party lines.

DO THESE FRIENDSHIPS LESSEN ANIMUS?

But did priming these cross-party ties actually reduce affective polarization? The results above showed that subjects were willing to comply with the treatment, but did not show whether it had any effects. Consider first whether the treatment changed feeling thermometer ratings for the other party. Figure 4.6 follows the exact same conventions as in chapter 3: the responses for those in the control condition are plotted in the darker gray with a solid line,

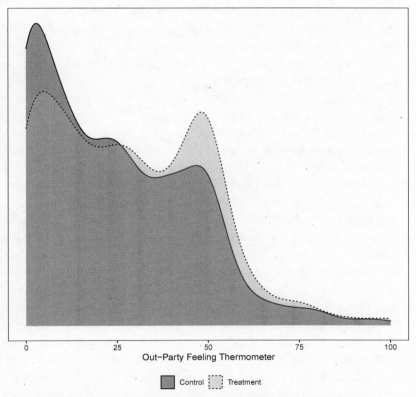

FIGURE 4.6. Cross-Party Friendships Improve Out-Party Feeling Thermometer Ratings

Note: The distribution of out-party feeling thermometer ratings for control group respondents is given in dark gray; the corresponding data for treated subjects is in light gray.

Source: AmeriSpeak Friendship Experiment

responses from those in the treatment condition are in the lighter gray with a dashed line. With even a quick glance at the figure, it is immediately obvious that treated subjects rated the other party more positively. Here, the treatment effect was 4.5 degrees, or approximately 20 percent of a standard deviation ($p < 0.01$). This was not simply due to the treatment increasing positivity more generally: in the appendix, I show that the treatment had no effect on feeling thermometer ratings for one's own party. Consistent with the Cross-Party Friendship Hypothesis, the treatment only changed respondents' assessment of the other party. When individuals reflect on those they know and respect from the other party, their mental image of the other party changes, and as a result, they feel less animus toward it. Cross-party friendships help to bridge the partisan divide.

To further clarify the effect on other-party feeling thermometer ratings, I also considered the effects on three different types of ratings: (1) the percentage of subjects who rated the other party at 0 degrees, the coldest rating; (2) the percentage of subjects who rated the other party at 5 degrees or lower, which is the bottom quartile of feeling thermometer ratings in the control condition; and (3) the percentage of subjects who rated the other party at 50 degrees or warmer (neutral or positive ratings). All of these analyses reinforce the message of figure 4.6: the treatment reduced out-party animus. In particular, treated subjects were one-third as likely to rate the other party at 0 degrees: 15 percent of control group subjects, but only 10 percent of treated subjects, assigned the other party the coldest rating of 0 degrees. Similarly, the treatment reduced ratings of 5 degrees or colder by 25 percent, and it increased neutral or warm ratings (50 degrees or warmer) by 40 percent. Cross-party friendships reduce animus toward the other party.

But there is a deeper and more fundamental insight to glean from these effects as well. In chapter 3, in the sports fandom experiment, I asked if common identities—there, sports fandom—improved assessments of a *particular* individual, and found that they did. In this chapter, I show that this prime has effects on the other party as a whole. Individuals primed to think about cross-party friendships rate "the Democratic Party" or "the Republican Party" more positively, not just their one friend. The effects generalize from the specific friendship to the group at large, just as the Cross-Party Friendship Hypothesis predicted they would. Knowing someone that you like and respect from the other party is a bridge to improving aggregate assessments of that party as a whole.

I also asked subjects to rate the other party on an eight-item trait battery, the same one used in chapter 3.[7] If the Cross-Party Friendship Hypothesis is correct, then I expect to find that those in the treatment condition rate those in the other party more positively along all of these trait measures. Figure 4.7 shows

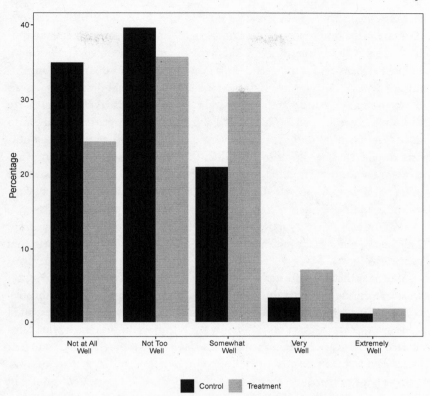

FIGURE 4.7. Cross-Party Friendships Increase Perceptions of Out-Party Honesty

Note: Control subjects' ratings of how well the term "honest" describes the other party are given in black; the ratings for treated subjects are given in light gray.

Source: AmeriSpeak Friendship Experiment

how the treatment affects ratings of the other party as "honest." The graph shows a sharp improvement in assessments of the other party, with the average rating improving by 0.15 scale points on the 1–5 scale (p < 0.01). In the control condition, more than one-third of subjects (34 percent) said that the word "honest" described the other party "not at all well," but in the treatment condition, that figure dropped to 25 percent, a nearly 30 percent decline. Further, those who said that honest described the other party at least "somewhat well" increased by over 50 percent: only 25 percent of control condition subjects assigned ratings in this range, but 40 percent of treated respondents did. This one trait is not an aberration. In the appendix, I show that when I analyze the traits pooled into various indices, I find the same pattern: treatment subjects gave more positive assessments of those from the other party than did control subjects.

As a final indicator of affective polarization, consider whether respondents trust the other party to do what is right for the country. Figure 4.8 presents these results, underlining what many other studies of trust have found: in our current political moment, most Americans have little trust in our political parties and other institutions (Hetherington and Rudolph 2015). Even in the treatment condition, most respondents only trusted the other party to do what is right "once in a while," and virtually no one trusted them to do what is right "almost always." Nevertheless, those in the treatment condition did have higher levels of trust than those in the control condition (p < 0.01). In the control condition, 31 percent of subjects "almost never" trusted the other party to do what is right, but that fell to 28 percent in the treatment condition, a decline of roughly 10 percent. Likewise, the proportion of those who trusted the other party "about half the time" increased by roughly one-quarter. Trust in the other party increases when we think about those we know in that party.

The fact that trust in the other party increases is also particularly noteworthy, as it suggests that this treatment helps to overcome the *political* consequences of affective polarization. It is not simply that individuals rated their cross-party friends more warmly on a feeling thermometer; they also trusted the other party to do what is right for the nation. This suggests that by building on the personal ties between individuals, we can help to improve politics—the personal can be a bridge to the political. I return to this point in chapters 6 and 7 later in the book.

But the consistency of results here also suggests something important about *why* these effects occur. Much of the psychological literature on this topic suggests that cross-party friendships, like other types of cross-party contact, reduce prejudice through an affective, not a cognitive, pathway: individuals like those from the other side more, even if the contact does little to change underlying attitudes about them (Tropp and Pettigrew 2005). Yet that's not quite what happens here. While there is certainly an affective shift— feeling thermometer ratings improve—so do more cognitive assessments: trait ratings get better, and individuals trust the other party more as well. What explains why this scenario does not fit the typical pattern? The answer, I suspect, is that the cross-party friendships here are working to provide disconfirming information to respondents. Normally, they think of the other party as quite remote and distant, but remembering that they have friends or family in it—and they actually agree about politics sometimes, and can disagree without being disagreeable—disrupts this image of the other side. As they shift how they think about the other party, individuals not only like

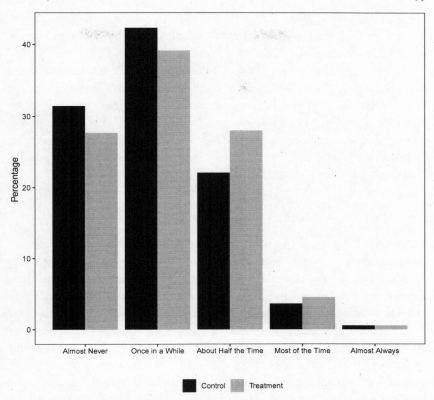

FIGURE 4.8. Cross-Party Friendships Increase Out-Party Trust

Note: Control subjects' ratings of how often they trust the other party are given in black; the ratings for treated subjects are given in light gray.

Source: AmeriSpeak Friendship Experiment

the other side more—their stereotypes about it break down as well (Rothbart and John 1985). This type of cross-party exchange—where one builds a lasting friendship across party lines—is a particularly powerful type of interaction.[8]

Looking across these various measures of affective polarization, a clear pattern emerges: irrespective of the metric used, treated subjects felt less animus toward those from the other party. They liked the other party more, rated them more positively on the feeling thermometer, gave them more positive trait ratings, and trusted them more to do what is the country's best interest. To be clear, it is not that affective polarization completely dissipated in the treatment condition—these are modest, not massive, effects. But they should also give pause to those who claim that the divides between the parties are irreconcilable and insurmountable. Affective polarization is real, but it is more malleable than we would have thought given what we hear about in both the media and the scholarly literature.

So far, I have focused the results on the data from the AmeriSpeak study, but readers might also be curious about the effects in the Bovitz Forthright data as well—did I find that cross-party discussion reduced partisan animus in that study as well? I did, and I present the results in the appendix in to this chapter (and discuss them in table 4.2 below). I also present similar results on the effects of cross-party friendship elsewhere (Levendusky 2022), suggesting that this is a quite robust treatment for overcoming partisan animus.

WHAT EXPLAINS THESE EFFECTS?

In chapter 2, I argued that while cross-party friendships should generally reduce partisan animus, there were two subgroups for whom these effects should be especially strong: those who have political discussions with their cross-party friends, and those who are especially close to their cross-party friends. It is having political discussions and seeing how to bridge the partisan divide that make these friendships so efficacious. Further, these types of conversations—and the trust they require—are more likely to occur with our close friends and family, those with whom we have a reservoir of trust and mutual respect from which to build. In the AmeriSpeak data, I asked about the frequency of political discussion; in the Bovitz Forthright data, I asked about the closeness of the relationship (see figure 4.5). In table 4.1 I test whether those who discuss politics with their friends have stronger effects, and in table 4.2 I test whether those who are closer to their friend have stronger effects. Here, we see that political discussion with a cross-party friend improves attitudes toward the out-party. The results in the first column show the effects on an index of the three affective polarization measures ($\alpha = 0.76$), and the remaining columns report the effects for each measure individually. Happily, they all tell the same story. Those who talked about politics more with their cross-party friend rated the other party more warmly on the feeling thermometer, evaluated them more positively on positive traits (though there was no significant effect on negative traits), and trusted the other party more. Cross-party political discussions attenuated animus.

Because these regression coefficients can be difficult to understand, consider the feeling thermometer ratings of subjects who reported different levels of political dialogue with the other party. As a baseline, in the control condition the average feeling thermometer rating for the other party was

TABLE 4.1. Effects of Frequency of Political Discussion on Partisan Animus

	Affective Polarization Index (1)	Out-Party Feeling Therm. (2)	Positive Trait Ratings (3)	Negative Trait Ratings (4)	Out-Party Trust (5)
Frequency of Political Discussion	0.02***	3.36***	0.06**	-0.002	0.10***
	(0.01)	(0.89)	(0.03)	(0.04)	(0.03)
Constant	0.37***	21.83***	2.34***	2.58***	1.91***
	(0.01)	(1.90)	(0.06)	(0.08)	(0.07)
Observations	878	780	876	873	875
R^2	0.01	0.02	0.005	0.0000	0.01

Note: Cell entries are OLS regression coefficients with associated standard errors in parentheses.
*$p<0.1$; **$p<0.05$; ***$p<0.01$.

Source: AmeriSpeak Friendship Experiment

23.9 degrees. In the treatment condition, that average rating increased to 28.4 degrees, but as we can see in table 4.1, this varied based on the frequency of political discussion. Among respondents who talked about politics "not at all frequently" with the person they named, feeling thermometer ratings were actually very slightly lower than in the control condition: 23.5 degrees. But among those who talked about politics with them more than this, we saw larger effects. For those who talked about politics "not too frequently," the average rating was 30.9 degrees; for those who talked about it "somewhat frequently," the average rating was 30.7 degrees; and for those who talked about it "very frequently," the average rating was 31.6 degrees. The fact that there was any discussion was the crucial factor, and the extent of political discussion mattered less. It is those who are willing to dialogue with the other party—and see where they might either agree or at least recognize that the opposition has a reasonable point—who feel more warmly toward the other party. Of course, knowing and liking someone may reflect that you've positively discussed politics with them, so I want to avoid pushing this argument too far. But it is not simply that cross-party friendships work because they are apolitical. Rather, discussion across party lines is a mechanism to mitigate affective polarization and discord, a point upon which I expand in chapter 5.

This also speaks to why these effects occur in another subtle but important way. Part of why the political nature of the conversation is key is that it reinforces that their friend is, in fact, an exemplar of their larger political party.

If a respondent never discusses politics with their cross-party friend, respondents see them as atypical of the members of that party: they are the proverbial exception that proves the rule, and even if they like their friend, that need not have implications for their feelings about the other party (Hewstone and Brown 1986). But if they actually engage in a political discussion—and see that they can converse about politics without it ending their friendship—then they realize that they might be able to do that with other members of that party, and attitudes toward the group improve (van Oudenhoven, Groenewoud, and Hewstone 1996). Constructive discussions allow individuals to generalize from this one friend to the other party as a whole.[9]

Do we similarly see larger effects when individuals are closer to the person they named? Table 4.2 presents these results. Here, because the main goal of the Bovitz Forthright friendship study was to study downstream effects of reducing partisan animus (see chapter 6), I only included two measures of affective polarization in this study: the opposite-party feeling thermometer rating, and trust in the other party to do what is right for the nation. And just as in table 4.1, the results confirm the logic from chapter 2: it is those who are closer to their cross-party friends that drive these effects. Indeed, just looking at the effects for the feeling thermometer rating, those who were "not at all close" or "not too close" to their cross-party friend had ratings at or below the mean in the control condition. The positive treatment effects seen in figure 4.6 above were driven by those who were at least "somewhat close" to the person they named, with feeling thermometer ratings (and trust) increasing as closeness increases.

Taken together, these analyses flesh out *why* cross-party friendships reduce partisan animus. Cross-party friendships lessen animus (1) when they are close relationships, and (2) when those involved actually discuss politics with one another. Both factors matter: it is not as effective to have these conversations on the periphery of our social networks; we need to have them at the very core (and luckily, most people do). And these friendships need to confront politics, rather than sidestepping it. Political discussion seems to be especially key, because it is how we recognize where there is common ground, and equally importantly, how to disagree without letting it harm the bonds of friendship. Our personal relationships can help us to see how to bridge the partisan divide more generally.

Conclusions

Can friendships that cross the political aisle help mitigate affective polarization? The Cross-Party Friendship Hypothesis argues that they can. Normally,

TABLE 4.2. Effects of Closeness to the Cross-Party Friend on Partisan Animus

	Out-Party Feeling Thermometer (1)	Out-Party Trust (2)
Closeness to Cross-Party Friend	2.48***	0.07***
	(0.47)	(0.02)
Constant	18.28***	1.69***
	(1.79)	(0.07)
Observations	1,856	1,871
R²	0.01	0.01

Note: Cell entries are OLS regression coefficients with associated standard errors in parentheses.

*p<0.1; **p<0.05; ***p<0.01.

Source: Bovitz Forthright Friendship Experiment

when someone brings to mind the other political party, they think about partisan stereotypes, extreme media exemplars, and polarized political elites. But when they think about the fact that they know and like many people from the other party—their friends, family, coworkers, and neighbors—their image of it changes. Rather than simply thinking that the other party is full of people quite different from them, they remember that it contains people they know and like, and their assessment of it improves.

I found strong support for this argument. First, more than 80 percent of Americans know and like someone from the other party, and indeed, a nontrivial fraction of Americans explicitly say—without prompting—that they would not let partisanship get in the way of friendship. We might think that many of these cross-party friendships occur on the edges of our social networks, but that too is incorrect—the people named are typically close friends, and the plurality of them are friends, rather than family members, coworkers, or neighbors. As political identities have become important social identities, there are no doubt some friendships that have broken apart over politics, especially in the aftermath of the Trump presidency. But these data suggest that this is a relatively atypical pattern. For most Americans, friendships—as well as family ties, workplaces, and neighborhoods—can and do cross the political divide.

Not only do people have friends from the other party—those friendships matter. When Americans are asked to reflect on their friendships with those from the other party, their assessments of the other party improve. They rate them more warmly on the feeling thermometer, give them more positive trait ratings, and trust them more to do what is in the best interest of the nation. Further, and importantly, these results are not simply driven by respondents who avoid talking about politics with those from the other party. Rather, they come from those who are willing to talk politics at least some of the time: it is political discussion, and the recognition that there can be some common ground and mutual understanding, that improves sentiments toward the opposition. The effects are also larger when those cross-party friendships are with our closest friends, rather than our more distant ones. Our close friendships—where we have a reservoir of goodwill and trust built up over time—allow us to probe these political differences most effectively with one another.

These results suggest the importance of partisan diversity in social networks, but if anything, they are an underestimate of these effects. One of the classic findings from network studies is that most Americans overstate the partisan homogeneity of their social networks: we project our own views onto our friends and family members (Huckfeldt and Sprague 1987). Further, because of social conformity, people often do not disclose their own political views, especially if they think it will lead to strife (Cowan and Baldassarri 2018; Noelle-Neumann 1974). For most Americans, there are people within their social network who are from the other party, and they just don't realize it. In reality, people likely know and respect even more people from the other party than they think they do, which in turn has important implications for how we think about not only these effects, but more generally the role of our social networks in the broader political environment—a point to which I return in the concluding chapter.

Appendix: Regression Results from This Chapter

Here, I provide results for those interested in the regressions rather than the graphs presented in the body of the chapter. Below, in table A4.1, I analyze the data from the Pew Research Center.

Column 1 shows that those with more cross-party friendships report lower levels of partisan animus, consistent with figure 4.2. As I noted in note 3, the feeling thermometer item used in this analysis was asked in wave 15 of Pew's American Trends Panel, while the friendship item was asked in wave 16, approximately one month later. Because it is unlikely that one's friendship network would change dramatically in a one-month span, and the Pew Research Center (2016) presented a similar analysis, I include the item here. To

TABLE A4.1. Effects of Cross-Party Friendship

	Other Party Feeling Thermometer (1)	Other Party Candidate Feeling Thermometer (2)	Belief the Other Party Has Good Ideas (3)
Number of Cross-Party Friendships	3.83***	2.26***	0.25***
	(0.48)	(0.36)	(0.02)
Constant	15.02***	10.94***	1.21***
	(1.25)	(0.95)	(0.05)
Observations	2,106	2,256	2,244
R^2	0.03	0.02	0.07

Note: Cell entries are OLS regression coefficients with associated standard errors in parentheses.
*p<0.1; **p<0.05; ***p<0.01.

Source: Pew American Trends Panel

ensure that there is not some odd reverse causality here (i.e., those who are less polarized toward the other party in wave 15 then construct more bipartisan social networks in the month before wave 16), I analyzed the candidate feeling thermometer items included in wave 16 of the study. In that wave, Pew asked respondents to rate all of the leading candidates still seeking their respective party's presidential nomination: Hillary Clinton, Ted Cruz, John Kasich, Bernie Sanders, and Donald Trump. I average these ratings by party and then ask whether more bipartisan friendship networks also raise feeling thermometer ratings of these candidates; column 2 shows that they do. Column 3 gives the results for the item asking respondents whether the other party has good ideas.

In table A4.2, I use respondents' political and demographic characteristics to predict which individuals are most likely to have more cross-party friendships. Because the dependent variable is ordinal (respondents can have no, a few, some, or a lot of cross-party friendships), I analyze this item using ordinal logistic regression. Column 1 uses only political variables, and finds that partisan and ideological strength are both negatively associated with the number of cross-party friendships. Fascinatingly, so too is being a Democrat—on balance, Democrats have fewer cross-party friendships. Technically, in the limit, this cannot really be true, but it likely reflects that Republicans may simply be more *aware* of cross-party friendships. Note that in column 2, these relationships survive controlling for a whole set of demographic variables. While there is a modest effect of political participation (such as attending a rally or donating money) in column 1, once we control for these other factors, the effect is no longer statistically significant. The main demographic factor—not surprisingly—is race, with Black Americans being less likely to have cross-party friendships. This, however, is almost certainly due to patterns of racial, and hence partisan, segregation (White and Laird 2020). That said, as I noted in the body of the chapter, there are no heterogeneous effects based on race or party, so while there are differences in the frequency of cross-party friendships, their effects are quite similar.

But what about the regression results from the experimental data? Table A4.3 presents the results for the AmeriSpeak data used in figures 4.6 through 4.8. Here, column 1 shows the effects on other-party feeling thermometer ratings, and column 2 shows that the treatment had no effect on same-party feeling

TABLE A4.2. Predicting Frequency of Cross-Party Friendship

	Political Variables Only (1)	Including Demographic Controls (2)
Democrat	-0.82***	-0.68***
	(0.11)	(0.12)
Partisan Strength	-0.15***	-0.14***
	(0.05)	(0.05)
Ideological Strength	-0.52***	-0.56***
	(0.06)	(0.06)
Political Participation	0.22***	0.11
	(0.08)	(0.08)
Female		-0.02
		(0.08)
College Graduate		0.16*
		(0.09)
Caucasian		0.12
		(0.16)
African-American		-0.86***
		(0.21)
Hispanic		-0.24
		(0.22)
Income		0.11***
		(0.02)
Observations	2,253	2,219

Note: Cell entries are ordinal logistic regression coefficients with associated standard errors in parentheses.

*p<0.1; **p<0.05; ***p<0.01.

Source: Pew American Trends Panel

TABLE A4.3. Treatment Effects of Cross-Party Friendship

	Out-Party Feeling Therm. (1)	Same-Party Feeling Therm. (2)	FT Rating of 0 (3)	FT Rating of 50+ (4)	Positive Trait Ratings (5)	Negative Trait Ratings (6)	Trait Rating Index (7)	Out-Party Trust (8)	AP Index (9)
Treatment	4.54***	1.23	−0.05***	0.06***	0.22***	0.14***	0.19***	0.12***	0.03***
	(1.07)	(1.11)	(0.02)	(0.02)	(0.03)	(0.04)	(0.03)	(0.04)	(0.01)
Constant	23.87***	65.66***	0.15***	0.15***	2.23***	2.44***	2.31***	2.00***	0.37***
	(0.76)	(0.78)	(0.01)	(0.01)	(0.02)	(0.03)	(0.02)	(0.03)	(0.005)
Observations	1,571	1,800	1,571	1,571	1,796	1,785	1,797	1,798	1,804
R^2	0.01	0.001	0.005	0.01	0.02	0.01	0.02	0.004	0.01

Note: Cell entries are OLS regression coefficients with associated standard errors in parentheses.

*p<0.1; **p<0.05; ***p<0.01.

Source: AmeriSpeak Friendship Experiment

thermometer ratings; columns 3 and 4 show that the treatment reduced the number of ratings of 0 degrees and increased the number of ratings of 50 degrees of higher. Columns 5–7 show the effects on trait ratings: the treatment improved positive and negative traits (both scaled so that higher values indicate more positive trait assessments, i.e., higher values on positive traits and lower values on negative ones), as well as an aggregate index of all trait ratings. Column 8 provides the results for the "trust in the other party" item, and column 9 shows the results on an omnibus measure where I rescaled all three measures (out-party feeling thermometer ratings, average trait ratings, and out-party trust) to the [0,1] scale and averaged them. These findings confirm the discussion from the body of the chapter.

While the analysis in the chapter relied primarily on the AmeriSpeak data, I also ran a second study using this prompt with Bovitz Forthright in 2019. Given space constraints, I could only include a few items to measure out-party animus. Here, I included just the out-party feeling thermometer ratings, as well as the out-party trust measure to capture partisan animosity. Table A4.4 presents the results. Here, we see that the treatment once again successfully reduced partisan animus—treated subjects had higher out-party feeling thermometer ratings, as well as higher trust in the other party. Note, however, that these effects were somewhat smaller than those in the Ameri-Speak study. There, the treatment effect on feeling thermometer ratings was 4.5 degrees, here it was only 1.85 degrees. It is difficult to compare the effect size magnitudes, however, because of the order of the survey instrument. In the AmeriSpeak study, as in most of the other studies in this book, the key

TABLE A4.4. Treatment Effects of Cross-Party Friendship

	Out-Party Feeling Therm (1)	Out-Party Trust (2)
Treatment	1.85***	0.05*
	(0.64)	(0.03)
Constant	24.42***	1.88***
	(0.45)	(0.02)
Observations	4,723	4,771
R^2	0.002	0.001

Note: Cell entries are OLS regression coefficients with associated standard errors in parentheses.

*p<0.1; **p<0.05; ***p<0.01.

Source: Bovitz Forthright Cross-Party Friendship Experiment

dependent variable items are asked immediately after the treatment. In the Bovitz Forthright study, however, subjects answered another block of items first, so the smaller effects might either indicate a less effective treatment, or some dissipation of the treatment effect (or both). The key result, however, is the substantive effect replication.

Does Cross-Party Dialogue Reduce Partisan Animus?

Growing up, every student learns the classic aphorism that politics and religion should not be discussed in polite company, lest one create an uncomfortable atmosphere. While experts on manners might endorse this advice, political scientists, psychologists, and communication scholars would not. The academic literature is full of studies that document the benefits of "hearing the other side" and being exposed to different points of view (Mutz 2006). Heterogeneous political discussions help participants to better understand the perspectives of those from across the political aisle (Mutz 2002), and also lower attitudinal polarization (Isenberg 1986; Druckman, Levendusky, and McClain 2018). Indeed, the vast literature on deliberative democracy argues that political discussion is crucial to legitimately resolving political controversies (Gutmann and Thompson 1996). While there are, of course, critics of this approach (e.g., Gardner 1995; Sanders 1997), most scholars see political discussion among people of different perspectives as something of an unalloyed good.[1]

Given the value of such discussions, then, one might assume that Americans engage in them frequently and with gusto, but such an assumption would be incorrect. A litany of work shows that most political discussion, like most discussion overall, occurs among like-minded individuals (McPherson, Smith-Lovin, and Cook 2001; Mutz 2006). This sets up a paradox: if discussion with those holding different viewpoints is so valuable, why do most Americans avoid it? Mutz (2006, 9) nicely summarizes this puzzle:

> But if everyone is so deliriously enthusiastic about the potential benefits of exposing people to oppositional political perspectives, then what exactly is the problem? Given the unusually strong consensus surrounding its assumed value, one would assume this activity to be widespread. Why don't people go

home, to church, or to work and discuss politics with their non-like-minded friends or acquaintances?

The answer is that most Americans find such discussions to be deeply uncomfortable, as they assume it will expose conflicts that will damage their relationships. Fifty percent of Americans think that discussing politics with those with whom they disagree is stressful and frustrating (Pew Research Center 2019a), and nearly 60 percent think their fellow Americans cannot have such discussions across lines of difference in a civil manner (Rainie, Keeter, and Perrin 2019). Many Americans do not even want to discuss apolitical topics like sports and pop culture with those from the other party (Settle and Carlson 2019)!

This desire to avoid cross-cutting dialogue, however, carries a hefty price. As I noted in chapter 2, because of both the power of partisanship and the contemporary political and media environment, individuals' perceptions about the other party are skewed and inaccurate. While there is some common ground and consensus between the parties—at least on some issues, as I discussed in chapter 1—because people rely on inaccurate stereotypes of the other party, they typically fail to recognize it, and higher levels of animus are the result.

But discussion across lines of difference offers a way to address this. As I argued in chapter 2, when individuals talk to those from the other party, they realize both that they have shared values and agree on some issues, and that the other party is not simply the stereotypical caricatures presented in the media. In short, they learn not only that they share some common ground with the other party, but also that the other party is less unreasonable than they had imagined. This logic explains the rationale for the Cross-Party Discussion Hypothesis— engaging in civil discussion across party lines will reduce partisan animus.

So even if individuals are not enthusiastic about cross-party discussion, it has some particularly valuable consequences. Cross-party discussion provides individuals with an important mechanism to learn about the other party and to substitute accurate information for inaccurate stereotypes. Much as cross-party friendship offers a route to improved attitudes toward the other party (see chapter 4), so too does cross-party discussion. Cross-party discussion is the political equivalent of eating kale: it might be mildly unpleasant, but it has tremendous benefits.

The Cross-Party Discussion Experiment

To test this argument, I designed an original lab-in-the-field experiment, the Cross-Party Discussion Experiment, which I then fielded working jointly with Dominik Stecula (for more details, see Levendusky and Stecula 2021).

The crux of this experiment involves comparing subjects who participated in an apolitical discussion (which serves as the baseline control condition) to those who participated in a cross-party (politically heterogeneous) discussion.[2] If the Cross-Party Discussion Hypothesis is correct, then I would expect those who took part in the heterogeneous discussion, with members of both parties, to have lower levels of affective polarization than those who took part in the apolitical discussion.

To recruit participants for this experiment, we worked with a team of research assistants to run Facebook advertisements about our study in the metropolitan Philadelphia area. We conducted studies throughout the broader metropolitan area, focusing in particular on politically heterogeneous suburban and exurban areas (where we were more likely to attract both Democratic and Republican participants), between November 2018 and July 2019. To appeal to the broadest set of respondents, we organized our group discussions at easily accessible locations throughout the region, mostly public libraries and community centers. While our subjects in no way approximate a random sample, even of the Philadelphia area, they constitute a diverse sample.[3] Participants who took part in our one-hour study were compensated with $20 for their time. We recruited 553 subjects, spread across 28 different sessions over that nine-month period, to take part in our study.

When subjects showed up at one of the sites we had chosen for our study, the actual experiment proceeded in several steps. They first filled out a brief pre-test questionnaire to record their partisanship and baseline demographics. Next, they completed a brief distractor task (a set of logic puzzles), during which we randomly assigned subjects to experimental conditions, subject to two related constraints. First, when forming heterogeneous discussion groups, we ensured that there were an even number of Democrats and Republicans in each group so that the groups would be balanced with respect to party. Second, subjects were assigned to discussion groups of approximately four individuals, consistent both with prior studies (Druckman, Levendusky, and McClain 2018) and with work suggesting that political discussion networks are often this size (Klofstad, McClurg, and Rolfe 2009).[4]

Once subjects had been assigned to discussion groups, each group was seated together at a table, and we distributed an article to them that provided the basis for their discussion. Here, subjects in the apolitical control condition read an article about the best beach towns on the New Jersey shore, and subjects in the heterogeneous discussion condition read an article suggesting that there is a surprising amount of consensus and common ground between the parties. Once everyone in the group had finished reading the article, they proceeded to the discussion. We began the discussion by asking each person in the group to state briefly whether or not they agreed with the article. Once everyone had an opportunity to offer their initial opinion, subjects spent the remaining time in open discussion about the article and the topic more generally. In total, the discussion lasted fifteen minutes. After the discussion was finished, subjects completed a brief post-test battery to measure their attitudes, received their payment, and left.

To be clear, this is a strong treatment, as it combines the newspaper article with the political discussion. In this experiment, I cannot separate out these effects, and simply present the results of this treatment *in toto*; an important task for future work is to unpack these different dimensions of the treatment and estimate the effects of discussion without reading anything beforehand (for a discussion of potential strategies for doing so, see Levendusky and Stecula 2021).

To measure affective polarization, I use the same items as in the previous chapters: the feeling thermometer rating of the other party, the trait rating battery, and whether or not the respondent trusts the other party to do what is in the best interest of the nation. In this experiment, however, I also asked a set of social distance items that measure how comfortable the respondent would be interacting with those from the other party. Here, I asked how comfortable individuals would be having a political discussion with someone from the other party, having them as a neighbor on their street, having them as a friend, and finally, how upset they would be if their son or daughter wanted to marry someone from the other party. As Druckman and Levendusky (2019) note, these social distance items are only modestly correlated with other measures of affective polarization, such as the feeling thermometer and trust items. But I include them here to measure a different dimension of affective polarization, and to see whether it too changes in response to cross-party discussion. Indeed, the social distance items are a particularly valuable addition here, because they simulate exactly the sort of contact and interaction with the other party that is alleged to be so valuable.

Does Cross-Party Discussion Reduce Partisan Animus?

To begin, consider the effects of heterogeneous (cross-party) discussion on feeling thermometer ratings of the other side. If hearing the other side does allow people to substitute accurate lived experiences for inaccurate stereotypes, and to realize what they have in common with the other side, then I would expect to find that cross-party discussion improves feeling thermometer ratings of the other party. Figure 5.1 presents the results. As in earlier chapters, we see a large effect on ratings of the other party. In the treatment condition, subjects rated the other party at a very cold 17 degrees, with roughly one-quarter of them rating the other party at the coldest possible rating. Those ratings

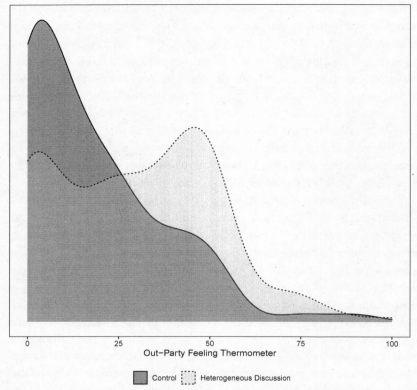

Out–Party Feeling Thermometer

■ Control ┊ ┊ Heterogeneous Discussion

FIGURE 5.1. Cross-Party Discussion Improves Out-Party Feeling Thermometer Ratings
Note: The distribution of out-party feeling thermometer ratings for control group respondents is given in dark gray; the corresponding data for heterogeneous discussion group respondents are in light gray.
Source: Group Discussion Experiment

improved by 70 percent in the cross-party discussion treatment: the average feeling thermometer rating jumped to 29 degrees, 12 degrees warmer than in the control (obviously, such large differences are statistically significant; for the regression analyses of these data, see Levendusky and Stecula 2021).

Just as in the experiments in earlier chapters, this average increase came because respondents replaced especially cold ratings—particularly ratings at 0 degrees—with much warmer ones, often over 50 degrees. Ratings of 0 degrees fell by 35 percent, from 28 percent of subjects in the control condition to 18 percent in the cross-party discussion condition, and ratings of 50 degrees or higher increased by an astounding 150 percent, from 11 percent in the control condition to 26 percent in the cross-party discussion treatment. Cross-party discussion markedly shifted feeling thermometer ratings.

These effects are not only statistically significant; they are substantively significant as well. Here, the heterogeneous discussion treatment improves feeling thermometer ratings by 12 degrees. To put that in perspective, out-party feeling thermometer ratings declined by approximately 12 degrees between 1992 (when they stood at 42 degrees) and 2016 (31 degrees; using only face-to-face respondents for consistency). This experimental effect is equivalent to taking the country from the end of the Obama era back to the start of the Clinton era. Simply put, this is a noteworthy, and important, shift in partisan animosity, erasing more than two decades' worth of heightened ill will between the parties.

Similarly, much as it improves average feeling thermometer ratings, the cross-party discussion condition should also improve trait ratings of the other party. Here, as in other chapters, I show the effects for one particular trait, but other traits show similar effects. Figure 5.2 shows how the treatment changes perceptions of out-party generosity. Once again, participating in cross-party discussion changed how respondents perceived the other party. In the control condition, 31 percent of subjects said that "generous" described the other party "not at all well"; that negative rating fell to only 18 percent of subjects in the treatment condition, a 40 percent decline. Likewise, the percentage that said "generous" described them "somewhat well," "very well," or "extremely well" increased by 85 percent, from 28 percent in the control condition to 52 percent in the treatment condition. As with the feeling thermometer ratings above, cross-party discussion engendered sizable shifts in how individuals viewed those from the other party.

Does the discussion also increase trust in the other party? Figure 5.3 shows that it did. As in chapter 4, the modal respondent in both conditions said that they trusted the other party only "some of the time," consistent with the relatively low trust levels in nearly all institutions and organizations in contemporary America (Rainie, Keeter, and Perrin 2019). But the shift in the second most popular option is particularly striking. In the control condition, the second most popular option was to trust the other party "almost never," but that changed to trusting them "about half the time" in the treatment condition. Indeed, relative to the control condition, the lowest trust rating ("almost never") fell by 40 percent, and the more trusting responses ("about half the time" or greater) more than doubled. Cross-party discussion markedly increased political trust.

DOES CROSS-PARTY DISCUSSION REDUCE SOCIAL DISTANCE?

But what about the social distance measures? Bogardus (1959) developed these indicators to measure comfort interacting across lines of difference, so

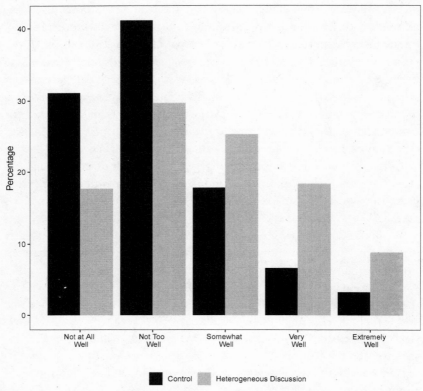

FIGURE 5.2. Cross-Party Discussion Increases Perceptions of Out-Party Generosity

Note: Control group respondents' ratings of how well the term "generous" describes the other party are given in black; the ratings for heterogeneous discussion group respondents are given in light gray.

Source: Group Discussion Experiment

here, if out-party animus declines, subjects should feel less socially distant from the other party—they should be more comfortable having a political discussion with them or having them as friends or neighbors, and less upset if their child were to marry someone from the other party. To begin, I first analyze the cross-party marriage item. Did a heterogeneous political discussion reduce how upset a cross-party marriage would make respondents?

Figure 5.4 shows that it did. In the treatment condition, nearly half of subjects (49 percent) were "not at all upset" by their child's cross-party marriage, an increase of 53 percent relative to the control condition, where only 32 percent felt that way. Further, those who were "somewhat upset" or "extremely upset" declined by 46 percent (from 41 percent of subjects in the control to 22 percent of subjects in the heterogeneous discussion condition). So even on this canonical item—one of the key pieces of evidence that Iyengar, Sood, and Lelkes (2012) used to argue that affective polarization had increased—I find strong evidence that the treatment reduced partisan animus.

But there is another social distance item that speaks quite powerfully to the efficacy of this treatment: are individuals willing to have a political conversation with someone from the other party? This is a crucial question, because this item speaks to the power of the treatment to become self-reinforcing: if individuals participate in one cross-party exchange, are they willing to participate in others? Figure 5.5 presents the data.

The data show, once again, the remarkable power of cross-party discussion—treated subjects were much more likely to be willing to discuss politics across party lines in the future. In particular, the shifts in the "not too

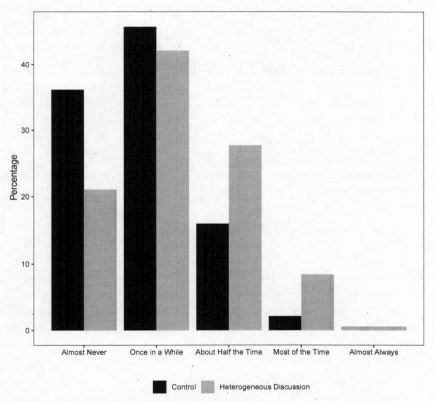

FIGURE 5.3. Cross-Party Discussion Increases Out-Party Trust

Note: Control group respondents' ratings of how often they trust the other party are given in black; the ratings for heterogeneous discussion group respondents are given in light gray.

Source: Group Discussion Experiment

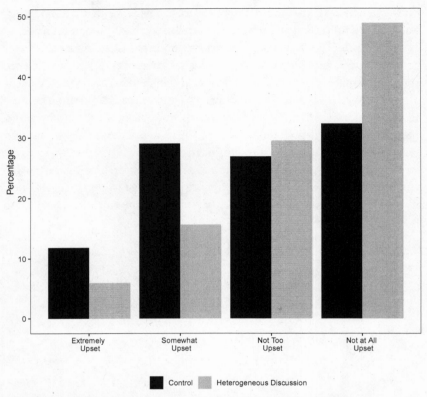

FIGURE 5.4. Cross-Party Discussion Decreases Discomfort with Cross-Party Marriage

Note: Control group respondents' ratings of how upset they would be if one of their children married someone from the other party are given in black; the ratings for heterogeneous discussion group respondents are given in light gray.

Source: Group Discussion Experiment

comfortable" and the "extremely comfortable" categories are noteworthy. In the control condition, 31 percent of subjects were "not too comfortable" with a cross-party discussion, but that fell by 39 percent in the control condition (to 19 percent of subjects). Likewise, the percentage of subjects who were "extremely comfortable" with such conversations increased by 55 percent (from 18 percent to 28 percent). This highlights that cross-party discussion can, indeed, become self-reinforcing.

While cross-party discussion did reduce social distance, another aspect of figures 5.4 and 5.5 is equally important: even in the control condition, most respondents were quite comfortable interacting with those from the other party. For example, for the cross-party marriage item (figure 5.4), nearly 60 percent of respondents (59 percent) were either "not at all upset" or "not too up-set" by their child marrying someone from the other party, and with respect to cross-party discussion (figure 5.5), 62 percent were "somewhat comfortable" or "extremely comfortable" having a political conversation with those from the other party. The other two measures show very similar results: 85 percent of control condition subjects were either "somewhat comfortable" or "extremely comfortable" being neighbors with those from the other party, and 73 percent felt the same way about being friends with them. So even though there is a treatment effect, and comfort interacting with the other party increases after cross-party discussion, the baseline level of comfort interacting with the other party is reasonably high as well.

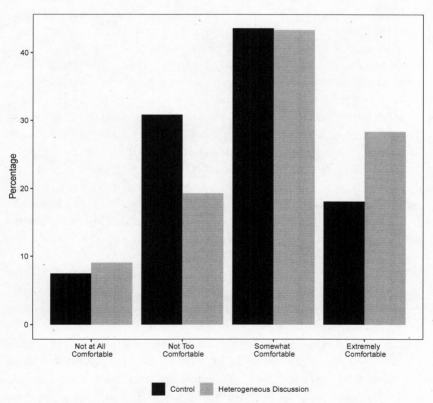

FIGURE 5.5. Cross-Party Discussion Is Self-Reinforcing

Note: Control group respondents' ratings of how comfortable they would be having a conversation with someone from the other party are given in black; the ratings for heterogeneous discussion group respondents are given in light gray.

Source: Group Discussion Experiment

One might wonder if this is just a fluke of one study—perhaps I just drew an odd group of individuals who were especially willing to interact with those from the other. This is not the case. In another publication (Levendusky 2022) I show the exact same pattern of results using a very different sample (a set of respondents from the Qualtrics panel) and a different treatment (priming cross-party friendship). In that study, I find the same substantive conclusion: even in the control condition, respondents are quite willing to interact with those from the other party. Even if individuals say that they do not like the other party, they are willing to interact with partisans from across the aisle.

This has both methodological and substantive implications. First, from a methodological perspective, this highlights a finding from Druckman and Levendusky (2019): social distance measures are only modestly correlated with other measures of affective polarization. In theory, they tap similar underlying constructs, and it makes sense that those who feel more animus toward the opposition would be less willing to interact with them. But in actuality this relationship is not an especially strong one. There is an even deeper point, though, that reinforces a finding seen in earlier chapters. Individuals draw a distinction between "the party" as an entity and individual members of it. The treatments change attitudes toward "the Democratic Party," but in all cases, individuals feel even more positively toward individual Democrats. This highlights the argument from chapter 4—personal relationships and conversations are a bridge to changing attitudes about the other party.

This is also a win from the perspective of normative theory. These data show that social distance is actually quite low. Individuals are, by their own account, quite willing to interact with those from the other party, even if they dislike "the Democratic Party" or "the Republican Party." While affective polarization is a real—and significant—component of American life, it is also important not to exaggerate its extent (see also Klar, Krupnikov, and Ryan 2018).

DOES DISCUSSION CHANGE BELIEFS ABOUT THE OTHER PARTY?

The data above show strong support for my argument that cross-party discussion reduces partisan animosity. In chapter 2, I argued that it would do so both by highlighting where the parties might agree, and by showing individuals that the other side was more reasonable than they had thought. To assess whether discussion shifted these sorts of beliefs, I asked respondents whether they agreed with three items: "I have a good understanding of the experiences, feelings, and beliefs of [the other party]"; "Even when I disagree with them, [the other party] adopt reasonable policy positions"; and "[The other

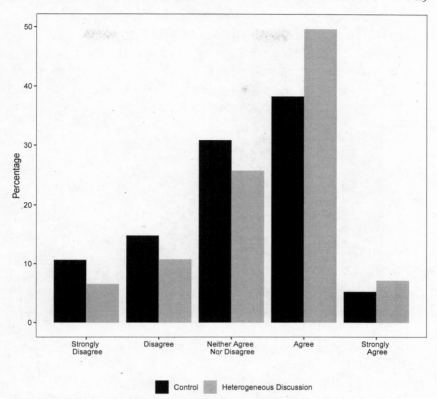

FIGURE 5.6. Cross-Party Discussion Increases Understanding of the Other Party

Note: Bars give the percentage of respondents who think they have a good idea of the feelings, beliefs, and ideas of the other party. Control group respondents are given in black; heterogeneous discussion group respondents are given in light gray.

Source: Group Discussion Experiment

party] respect my political beliefs and opinions," where [the other party] is replaced with Democrats or Republicans, as appropriate. These items tap whether individuals think the other party is, in effect, more reasonable than they'd imagined, and whether they have legitimate rationales for their beliefs, consistent with the perspective-taking argument outlined in chapter 2.

Begin with whether individuals feel that they understand the other side. Did heterogeneous discussion affect this belief? Figure 5.6 shows that it did. While the modal category stayed the same (respondents in both conditions agreed that they understood the other party), 35 percent fewer respondents disagreed with the statement, and 30 percent more agreed with it, in the treatment condition. Understanding of the other side's point of view increases.

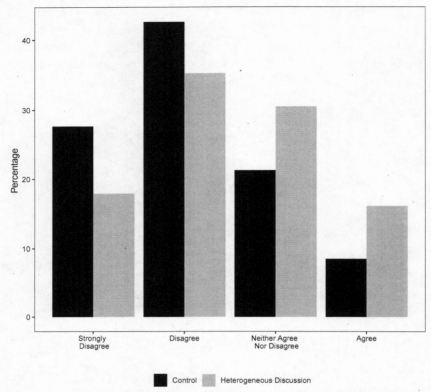

FIGURE 5.7. Cross-Party Discussion Increases Belief That the Other Party Takes Reasonable Positions
Note: Bars give the percentage of respondents who think the other party takes reasonable positions, even when they disagree with them. Control group respondents are given in black; heterogeneous discussion group respondents are given in light gray.
Source: Group Discussion Experiment

Similarly, did cross-party discussion increase the prevalence of the belief that the other side has a legitimate rationale for their beliefs? This is perhaps the core dimension of perspective-taking: realizing that the other can justify their opinions with facts, rather than just prejudice. In figure 5.7, we see evidence of this effect, but with notable limitations. Disagreement with the statement fell by 25 percent, and agreement doubled (from 8 percent to 16 percent), so there were treatment effects. But there were also real, and important, limits on how much respondents changed their attitudes. Note that no one in this study strongly agreed with the statement, and even among those assigned to the discussion condition, a majority disagreed with it. This highlights that discussion is not a magic salve that heals all political wounds.

Yes, it can improve attitudes, but there are limits: years of angry politics and recrimination do not simply disappear as the result of one conversation.

We see a similar pattern in respect for the other party in figure 5.8. Again, attitudes clearly improved, and respect for the other party increased, though the aggregate effect was largely driven by the decrease in those strongly disagreeing with the item in the discussion condition. But again, while more people felt respected by the other side post-discussion, many did not, which again highlights both the power and the limits of discussion to change attitudes.

But pulling back and looking across all three measures, the more important point is that discussion did perform the vital perspective-taking functions discussed in chapter 2. Part of why discussion improves attitudes is that it allows individuals to see both where common ground exists, and

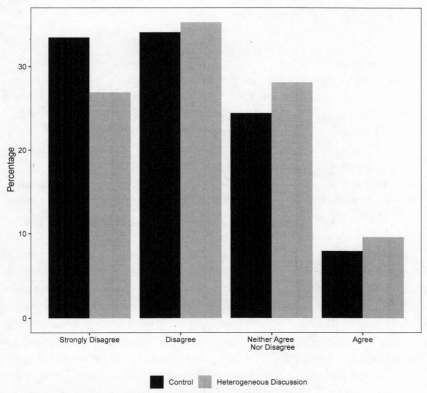

FIGURE 5.8. Cross-Party Discussion Increases Respect from the Other Party

Note: Bars give the percentage of respondents who think the other party respects them. Control group respondents are given in black; heterogeneous discussion group respondents are given in light gray.

Source: Group Discussion Experiment

TABLE 5.1. The Effects of Cross-Party Discussion Persist for at Least One Week

	Out-Party FT (1)	Out-Party Trust (2)	Social Distance (3)
Heterogeneous Discussion	11.86**	0.45**	0.47***
	(4.63)	(0.22)	(0.15)
Constant	24.76**	2.03***	3.13***
	(11.79)	(0.15)	(0.64)
Observations	98	110	110
R^2	0.38	0.27	0.21

Note: Cell entries are OLS regression coefficients with fixed effects for experimental session; standard errors (clustered by discussion group) are in parentheses.
*p<0.1; **p<0.05; ***p<0.01.

that the other side is more reasonable than they might have suspected. Post-discussion, respondents can use that lived experience to replace inaccurate stereotypes about the other party, and hence attitudes toward them improve.

DO THESE EFFECTS ENDURE?

One concern with any experiment is that the study simply creates a transitory shift in attitudes that quickly fades once subjects leave the study. To help address these concerns, as part of the Cross-Party Discussion Experiment I conducted a follow-up study with respondents one week later. In the follow-up study, subjects were asked to complete a brief online survey, which simply asked them the key dependent variables from the post-test instrument; 35 percent of the sample completed this follow-up survey. In any panel study like this, non-random attrition is a significant concern. I tried to combat this by incentivizing respondents to participate (all of those who completed the follow-up study were entered into a lottery to win a $50 Amazon gift card), but this only reduces this concern—it does not eliminate it entirely. Here, neither treatment assignment nor political characteristics (partisanship, strength of party, liberal-conservative self-identification, political activity, political interest, or frequency of political discussion) predict taking the follow-up survey (see the appendix to Levendusky and Stecula 2021 for more details). While there are some expected demographic differences (i.e., younger and better-educated participants are more likely to take the follow-up study), they are relatively minor, and controlling for these factors does not change the substantive results.

The key question here is whether the effects found above can still be detected one week later; table 5.1 presents those results.[5] The results demonstrate that the effects lasted for at least a week. One week later, those assigned to the heterogeneous discussion condition still rated the other party more warmly on the feeling thermometer scale, trusted the other party to do what is in the nation's best interest, and felt less socially distant from them (i.e., they are more comfortable interacting with them in a variety of different settings).[6] Overall, this suggests that these effects were not simply transitory shifts, but endured for at least several days after the study. Cross-party discussion meaningfully changes attitudes toward the other party.

Comparing Across Experiments: Which Treatment Is Most Effective?

Over the past three chapters, I have presented results from several different experiments examining the effectiveness of using different strategies to reduce affective polarization: the American Identity Experiment, the Cross-Party Friendship Experiment, and the Cross-Party Discussion Experiment. All of these experiments asked respondents about the same target—the other party—and did so using a common measure—the feeling thermometer scale.[7] So I can use this item to compare across the three treatments to say something about their comparative effectiveness.

Looking back at the evidence in the past three chapters, we can see that the American identity prime in chapter 3 increased out-party feeling thermometer ratings by 6 degrees, the cross-party friendship prime in chapter 4 improved out-party feeling thermometer ratings by 4.5 degrees, and the cross-party discussion prime in this chapter improved ratings by 12 degrees. Clearly, the cross-party discussion prime is the most effective, but that is not really surprising—the first two treatments are simple primes that are delivered within the context of a brief survey, whereas the third involves a more elaborate treatment.

But this also makes an important theoretical point: survey experimental results are really akin to existence proofs. They demonstrate that it is possible to change people's beliefs, but because they are not terribly realistic, we do not know what sort of longer-term change they engender (likely not much). To get larger and longer-lasting results, we need more comprehensive interventions like the one here, where subjects get a more sustained dose of cross-party contact. And indeed, to be truly effective, such discussions need to take place over an extended period of time. The sort of intervention I conduct here is a beginning, rather than an end.

Conclusions

Can cross-party discussion lessen partisan animus? The Cross-Party Discussion Hypothesis argues that it does so by allowing respondents to substitute accurate information—from their interaction with the other party—for inaccurate stereotypes. In the discussion, respondents will see that the parties sometimes agree on the issues, and that even when they do not, the other side is more reasonable than they had imagined. Using an original experiment, I show that affective polarization falls sharply as a result of heterogeneous political discussion, with subjects rating those from the other party much more positively after these encounters. Further, these effects persist for a week after the study, indicating that they are not simply momentary aberrations forgotten soon after the treatment is administered.

These results might be a bit surprising, as some readers might suspect that attempting to bridge the partisan divide in the present moment would lead to angry shouting matches and fisticuffs rather than greater understanding and unity. There are two important reasons why I find the more positive effects here. First, as I have argued elsewhere in the book, respondents are not as affectively polarized as they think they are (Druckman et al. 2022b). When they actually meet someone from the other party and talk to them, and realize what they share in common, animus falls. The argument is not that someone from the resistance can meet a Trump devotee and start singing kumbaya. Rather, it is that ordinary people from both parties—who are less political and less ideological than is commonly assumed (Druckman et al. 2022b)—can do so. The partisan rancor we see depicted in the media occurs primarily in a narrow swath of the electorate.

Second, the setup of the experiment itself facilitated this productive encounter. Because respondents discussed politics in a face-to-face setting, this engendered a strong set of social norms about how they should interact with one another. Social norms of interpersonal dialogue emphasize politeness and respect, and those who violate these norms are sanctioned (van Kleef et al. 2015). But if these norms are absent, heterogeneous discussion can be deleterious. For example, online discussions, which lack these norms, often exacerbate divisions and reduce understanding between groups (Kiesler, Siegel, and McGuire 1984; Bail et al. 2018). Indeed, one need only glance at Facebook or Twitter to see this pattern confirmed time and time again. This suggests that a genuine conversation centered on mutual respect—and not just a shouting match—will be needed to overcome political differences. Whether the discussions are face-to-face or online, maintaining these norms underlying discussion will be important to having productive cross-party dialogue; I return to this point in the conclusion to this book.[8]

This also helps to explain the scope conditions for this sort of study. To reduce animus, discussion needs to involve members of both parties—individuals actually have to hear from the other party, and listen to their point of view, to change their opinion. Simply interacting with those from their own party is unlikely to improve anything, as that conversation likely just reflects on inaccurate stereotypes of the other party. But these discussions actually need to be centered on politics. There's a parallel here to chapter 4, where I found that cross-party friendships that avoid politics do little to ameliorate partisan animus. Individuals actually need the disconfirming evidence from dialogue and discussion to change levels of partisan animosity (Rothbart and John 1985). One can use something apolitical to open up the conversation and build bridges with the other side. But if the conversation never moves beyond that, and participants do not learn that they have more in common with the other side than they had realized, its effects will be more limited. The value here is not just in learning that there are decent people on the other side; it is in learning that they are not so different from us.

There is a wrinkle here, though: as I noted at the start of the chapter, Americans do not like to engage in these sorts of cross-party dialogues. But there is an important implication to this research. Americans *think* they will not like cross-party encounters, because they expect them to devolve into shouting matches. But this typically does not happen, and most people end up enjoying such interactions much more than they thought they would (Dorison, Minson, and Rogers 2019). This also helps us to reinterpret past findings about Americans' hesitancy to engage in these conversations—people do not want to have them because they imagine the worst-case scenario, and see themselves shouting at a stereotype from the other side of the aisle. But in a more normal, and reasonable, exchange, they can find some common ground, and they realize that it need not be so uncomfortable. If people have conversations across political lines, things are likely to go better than they expect, and perhaps they will be less hesitant to do so again.

This also highlights the importance of everyday political discussion. Yes, people want to avoid cross-party political dialogue. But most political conversations are incidental, not purposive (Minozzi et al. 2020): people do not seek out political conversations, they just happen in the course of everyday life. People might want to avoid cross-cutting discussion, and they might try to use social cues to avoid it (Carlson and Settle 2021), but it occurs nevertheless. This is exactly the sort of "everyday talk" that Mansbridge (1999) emphasizes: the small encounters between different people that help us to better understand and tolerate one another. Conversation is not a cure-all, but it does help us learn what we share in common across the aisle. This sort of everyday dialogue really is crucial, and I return to this point in the concluding chapter.

Are There Downstream Consequences
to Reducing Affective Polarization?

So far, the analysis in the book has focused on testing whether various strategies actually reduce affective polarization. But as I argued in chapter 2, if those strategies succeed, then there should be a set of downstream consequences that also follow from those efforts. This chapter focuses on three such effects. First, perceived polarization should also fall—when affective polarization declines, individuals should think that the parties are less divided and polarized, and they should perceive that there is more common ground between them (the Common Ground Hypothesis). Second, individuals should be less likely to adopt the positions espoused by their party leaders—they should be less likely to follow party cues (the Party Cue-Taking Hypothesis). Third and finally, individuals should also have higher levels of partisan ambivalence (the Partisan Ambivalence Hypothesis)—which in turn should reduce partisan motivated reasoning more generally. As I explain below, these latter two effects—on party cue-taking and partisan ambivalence—are especially important, as they have broader implications for theories of ideological polarization, partisan sorting, and partisan motivated reasoning. If I find support for these hypotheses, then, it suggests that reducing affective polarization has quite wide-ranging implications for citizens' attitudes, and is even more important than it seems at first glance.

This chapter tests whether such downstream effects exist. I find strong support for all three of them—reducing affective polarization has further attitudinal consequences, with important normative implications for our understanding of American political behavior more broadly.

Does Reducing Affective Polarization Decrease
Perceived Polarization?

As I argued in chapter 2, part of why Democrats and Republicans dislike and distrust one another is that they think they have less in common than they actually do, following on the logic of social identity theory and how it intersects with our contemporary media and political environment. As a result, ordinary voters greatly exaggerate the degree of polarization in the mass public: they think Democrats and Republicans are more divided than they actually are (Levendusky and Malhotra 2016b). But if affective polarization falls, and the other party is seen less as a dissimilar other, then perceived polarization should also fall—individuals should think that the parties are less polarized and there is more common ground between them. This is the logic of the Common Ground Hypothesis.

To test this argument, at the end of the AmeriSpeak Cross-Party Friendship Experiment used in chapter 4 I asked respondents two different items. They were asked to assess how much common ground exists between the parties on a scale ranging from "a great deal" to "none at all," and how often Democrats and Republicans agree on the issues of the day, on a scale ranging from "all the time" to "never." I expect that treated subjects (those primed to think about their cross-party friendships) will perceive more common ground, and think that the parties agree on more issues, relative to subjects in the control condition. Figures 6.1 and 6.2 show the distribution of responses to these items for subjects in both the treatment and the control conditions.[1]

Both results strongly support the Common Ground Hypothesis. In figure 6.1, note that treated subjects were more likely to perceive there to be more common ground: in the control condition 37 percent of respondents perceived at least some common ground between the parties, but that rose to 46 percent in the treatment condition—a 25 percent increase. Likewise, the fraction of those who said that there was no common ground at all fell by 27 percent, from 11 percent in the control to 8 percent in the treatment.

In figure 6.2, we see a similar increase in assessments of the frequency of agreement between the parties. Not surprisingly, in both the treatment and the control condition, most respondents felt that there was not too much agreement between the parties, reflecting the reality of high levels of perceived polarization seen elsewhere (Levendusky and Malhotra 2016b). Nonetheless, the treatment led respondents to perceive more cross-party agreement. Thirty percent more subjects agreed that the parties agree "sometimes," and 25 percent fewer subjects say that they "never" do so in the treatment

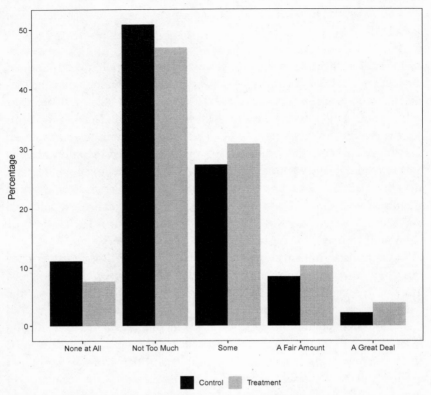

FIGURE 6.1. Cross-Party Friendships Increase Perceptions of Common Ground
Note: Control group respondents' assessment of how much common ground exists between the parties is given in black; the assessment for heterogeneous discussion group respondents is given in light gray.
Source: AmeriSpeak Friendship Experiment

relative to the control. Reminding subjects of what they share across parties (here, cross-party friendships) increases their perception of shared common ground (readers interested in the regression analyses of the data underlying figures 6.1 and 6.2 are referred to the appendix to this chapter).

This tells us something powerful about the link between partisan animus and perceptions of polarization. Part of the reason why perceptions of polarization are so high is that animosity toward the other side leads us to expect that the other party is very distant from our own—it's similar to the contrast effect in candidate placements (Judd, Kenny, and Krosnick 1983). But if we lessen that animosity, then there is less psychological need to distance ourselves from them, and hence perceived polarization falls (see also Armaly and Enders 2021).

This is not simply a matter of reducing misperceptions, a valuable goal in and of itself; it has two broader implications as well. First, it strengthens legislators' incentives to find compromise and consensus. If citizens are truly divided by party, and there is no common ground, what incentive do legislators or other elected officials have to compromise with one another? But if there is actually overlap in the public's attitudes, then there is more reason to find the "spirit of compromise" and look to reach across the aisle (Gutmann and Thompson 2012). Indeed, support for compromise and bipartisanship in the mass public drives elite support for bipartisan legislation (Harbridge and Malhotra 2011). A divided America would support little such consensus building. But if, instead, Americans of both parties have at least some shared commonalities, and can agree on some issues, then compromise is a more fruitful activity.

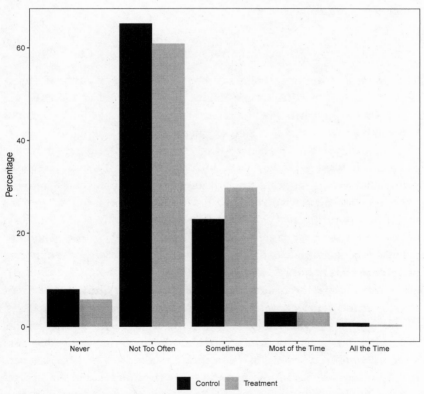

FIGURE 6.2. Cross-Party Friendships Increase Perceptions of Cross-Party Agreement

Note: Control group respondents' assessment of how much the parties agree with one another is given in black; the assessment for heterogeneous discussion group respondents is given in light gray.

Source: AmeriSpeak Friendship Experiment

Second, as citizens perceive more common ground between the parties, then it becomes possible for them to consider voting for the other party. Affective polarization nationalizes elections, so that voters are unwilling to vote for even down-ballot candidates from the other party (Abramowitz and Webster 2016)—how could you support a candidate from the other side when they disagree with your core values and issue positions? But if there is some common ground between the parties, then voters can see that there are some areas of consensus, even if many differences remain. This strengthens accountability, because it allows voters to support someone from the other party in a case, say, where their own party has performed poorly or has been involved in scandal. The point is not that voters will suddenly begin frequently splitting their tickets—that's not realistic. The argument is that it makes them more open to voting for a candidate from the other party under some circumstances, and to using their ballot to help discipline elected officials to better promote accountability.

Does Reducing Affective Polarization Reduce Partisan Cue-Taking?

The evidence above supports the first hypothesis about the downstream effects of lessening partisan animus: reducing affective polarization also reduces perceived polarization and increases perceptions of common ground between the parties. But does it also reduce partisan cue-taking, as the Party Cue-Taking Hypothesis predicts? Affective polarization heightens individuals' desire to differentiate their own liked party from the disliked other party, which implies that as affective polarization increases, individuals are more likely to follow their own party's cues and less likely to follow those from the other party (Druckman et al. 2021). When affective polarization falls, so too does the psychological desire to differentiate between the parties, and individuals are both less tied to their own party and less repulsed by the opposing party. Given this, partisan cue-taking should fall.

To test this hypothesis, at the end of the AmeriSpeak Cross-Party Friendship Experiment subjects were asked to provide their opinion of two policies: how much the government should expand urban growth (modeled on the item from Chong and Druckman 2007) and whether the government should place additional restrictions on class-action lawsuits. Both of these issues are the sort of low-salience issues where this type of treatment could plausibly affect respondents' attitudes (Bartels 1993), and they are issues where the parties have a position, but one that is not especially widely known in the mass public (to avoid pre-treatment effects). Subjects are told the parties' positions on the issues (Democrats support limits on urban growth but oppose restrictions on

TABLE 6.1. Cross-Party Friendships Reduce Party Cue-Taking

	AmeriSpeak Data (1)	Bovitz Forthright Data (2)
Treatment Prime	-0.03*	-0.03*
	(0.02)	(0.02)
Constant	0.55**	0.50**
	(0.01)	(0.15)
R^2	0.018	0.013
N (Total)	3540	3706
N (Respondents)	1780	1595

Note: Cell entries are OLS regression coefficients, with standard errors are clustered by respondent given in parentheses. Both models include fixed effects for issues.

*p<0.1; **p<0.05; ***p<0.01.

class-action lawsuits, Republicans the reverse), and then asked where they themselves stand. If my hypothesis is correct, treated subjects should be less likely to follow the party cue and therefore will be less likely to adopt their party's position on these issues.

To test this claim, I pool across issues and estimate the following model: $PartyPosition_{ij} = \beta_0 + \beta_1 Treated_i + \varphi_j + \varepsilon_{ij}$, where $PartyPosition_{ij}$ indicates whether subject i adopted their party's position on issue j, $treated_i$ is an indicator for whether subject i was assigned to the treatment condition, φ_j is an issue fixed-effect, and ε_{ij} is a stochastic disturbance term. Column 1 in table 6.1 below presents the results, with standard errors clustered by respondent.

As I hypothesized, treated subjects were less likely to adopt their party's position on the issues. In the control condition, approximately 55 percent of subjects adopted their party's position on the issues, but that decreased to 52 percent in the treatment condition—a 5 percent relative decrease. This is undoubtedly a very modest shift. But this is what we should expect: it would hardly be realistic for this sort of simple affective polarization treatment to cause major shifts in cue-taking, but it does have some effect.

In the Bovitz Forthright Cross-Party Friendship Experiment, I included a replication of this party cue study, with the same setup as before. Here, all respondents received the class-action lawsuit item from the original study and were then randomly assigned to answer one of two additional items: whether we should allow more citizens to vote by mail, and whether we should expand the use of nuclear power.[2] While vote by mail became a higher-salience partisan issue in 2020 given Trump's argument that it would be used to perpetuate voter fraud, it was a much lower-salience, less partisan issue when the study took place: for example, Pennsylvania adopted Act 77 (which greatly expanded mail balloting in the state) on a bipartisan basis in 2019. Column 2 of table 6.1 shows that I found an almost identical effect here: once again, treated subjects were less likely to adopt their party's position on the issues, all else being equal.

The analysis above looks at whether respondents adopt their party's position on the issue, which makes sense given the theoretical logic of the Party Cue-Taking Hypothesis. But subjects answered the items on five-point Likert scales (strongly agree to strongly disagree). Digging into the raw data, I found that treated subjects moved away from their own party's position, but they did not adopt the other party's position. Instead, they became more likely to select the scale midpoint. For example, in the AmeriSpeak Cross-Party Friendship Experiment, in the control condition 19 percent of subjects adopted the other party's position (i.e., a Democrat who wants to restrict the use of class-action lawsuits), 33 percent adopted the scale midpoint (neither supporting nor opposing the policy), and 48 percent adopted their party's position. In the treatment condition, those figures were 18 percent, 37 percent, and 45 percent, respectively; the same pattern appears in the Bovitz Forthright data as well.[3] The treatment here does not shift people to adopt the other party's position; rather, it moves them away from their party's position and onto the scale midpoint. With lower levels of animus, they move away from their party, even if they do not embrace the other side's positions.

What drives these cue-taking effects? There are two non-exclusive possibilities. First, subjects might become less likely to follow their party's cues because they feel a weaker identification with their own party (i.e., they become less univalent partisans, see Lavine, Johnston, and Steenbergen 2012). Second, they might feel less negativity toward the opposing party's cue, and it would therefore be less of an "anti-cue" (Nicholson 2012; Goren, Federico and Kittilson 2009; Merkley and Stecula 2020). Undoubtedly, both factors matter, but which one is dominant? Here, given the design, I cannot say definitively. I followed the standard format of party cue studies, and presented subjects with the positions of both parties, so these results cannot directly address this debate. Even if I presented subjects with just one party's position, they would most likely be able to infer the other party's position (i.e., if I tell you that the Democrats support position X, then you will most likely infer that the Republicans support not-X), so providing dispositive evidence here would be extremely difficult and would require a more complicated research design (and as I discussed in chapter 2, additional theorizing as well).

Regardless of the particular mechanism, though, the fact that these primes decrease cue-taking has broad and important implications. Party cue-taking is one of the main mechanisms driving both ideological polarization and partisan sorting (Lenz 2012; Levendusky 2009; Levendusky 2010). What my findings here show is that affective polarization causes ideological polarization and sorting via cue-taking. While earlier work highlighted how ideological polarization could fuel affective discord (Bougher 2017; Orr and Huber 2020), this reverse possibility has been largely overlooked. This suggests that we cannot really untangle affective and ideological polarization, that the two are inextricably linked (see also Druckman et al. 2021). Part of the reason why affective polarization has risen is that the parties have pulled apart on the issues, but part of the separation on the issues is the result of increasing animus between the parties. The two are intertwined at a deep level (see also Fiorina 2017).

These results also help to explain Lelkes's (2018) findings about the linkage between affective polarization and partisan sorting. In that study, he examines the effects of affective polarization on partisan sorting, and finds that the relationship is rather modest. Such a finding is entirely consistent with my results here. Partisan sorting and affective polarization are linked, but that linkage is via cue-taking, which occurs predominantly among those with more cognitive resources (Bakker, Lelkes, and Malka 2020; Bang-Peterson et al. 2013). So affective polarization does increase partisan sorting, but only among a subset of the mass public, and hence the relationship is modest rather than massive.

This also explains why sharp increases in affective polarization have not generated large increases in ideological polarization: the cue-taking mechanism works best for a subset of respondents who were likely already quite ideologically polarized *ex ante*. While ideological polarization has a large effect on affective polarization, the reverse causal process—from affective polarization to ideological divisions—is considerably weaker. There are deep, but subtle, connections between affective polarization, ideological polarization, and party sorting.

But there is another implication of these cue-taking effects for how we think about citizens' behavior. Numerous studies argue that party cues serve as a type of heuristic shortcut for voters (e.g., Sniderman, Brody and Tetlock 1993), a way for them to make some sense of the political world (Sniderman and Stiglitz 2011) and even hold elected officials to account (Achen and Bartels 2016). If I reduce party cue-taking, am I also undercutting these more desirable effects of cues? This is a reasonable concern, but the results above suggest that it is not a serious limitation. The effect on cue-taking is quite modest, and is very unlikely to shift factors like vote choice (see, e.g., Broockman, Kalla, and Westwood forthcoming). If anything, this is about reducing reflexive party cue-taking, and as the results below suggest, getting citizens to be slightly more even-handed in how they view the political world. But that will not remove all effects of partisanship—it will just dampen down some of its excesses.

Does Reducing Affective Polarization Heighten Partisan Ambivalence?

The results above suggest that reducing affective polarization works to lessen partisan cue-taking. But, as I argued in chapter 2, there may be a related, but even more fundamental, shift engendered by falling levels of partisan animus— partisan ambivalence may also fall, as I predicted in the Partisan Ambivalence Hypothesis. As animus toward the other party falls, individuals have less incentive to differentiate their liked party from the disliked other party. As a result, they should become more ambivalent toward the other party, seeing both its good and its bad sides. This is obviously closed tied to animus itself, but as I explain below, it has a broader, and important, implication in how it connects to partisan motivated reasoning more generally.

To measure partisan ambivalence, in the Bovitz Forthright Friendship Experiment I included the items suggested by Lavine, Johnston, and Steenbergen (2012). These questions first ask respondents whether they have any favorable thoughts or feelings toward a given party, and if they do, how positive those feelings are. It then repeats the process for the unfavorable thoughts and feelings about that party. Then subjects repeat the battery for the other party. This procedure ultimately generates four measures: same-party positive thoughts, same-party negative thoughts, other-party positive thoughts, and other-party negative thoughts. The resulting metrics parallel the classic party likes and dislikes format of the ANES (which I used in Levendusky 2018a), but in a way that is less cognitively demanding, as well as more accurate (see the discussion in Lavine, Johnston, and Steenbergen 2012, 57–60).

Here, I expect that treated subjects (those primed to think about cross-party friendships) display more positivity, and less negativity, toward the other party—rather than simply disliking it (as we would normally expect), they now see some positive aspects as well.

The data in table 6.2 show that there were modest, but real, effects: treated subjects were more ambivalent about the other party, with more positive, and fewer negative, thoughts about it. For example, column 1 contains a summary measure of out-party ambivalence, which is simply the difference between positive and negative out-party feelings, with higher values indicating more positive thoughts about the other party. Here, the treated subjects were 0.036 units more positive (on a [-1,1] scale). In the control condition, only 28 percent of subjects were neutral or positive toward the other party (note that that constant term is negative, suggesting that in the control condition,

TABLE 6.2. Cross-Party Friendship Increases Partisan Ambivalence

	Net Out-Party Effect (1)	Out-Party Positive Feelings (2)	Out-Party Negative Feelings (3)	Net Same-Party Effect (4)	Same-Party Positive Feelings (5)	Same-Party Negative Feelings (6)
Treatment	0.036***	0.018***	-0.017	-0.013	-0.0005	0.011
	(0.014)	(0.007)	(0.011)	(0.013)	(0.009)	(0.008)
Constant	-0.505***	0.131***	0.634***	0.291***	0.538***	0.228***
	(0.009)	(0.005)	(0.008)	(0.009)	(0.007)	(0.006)
Observations	4,680	4,767	4,684	4,154	4,158	4,767
R^2	0.002	0.001	0.001	0.0002	0.00000	0.0004

Note: Cell entries are OLS regression coefficients with associated standard errors in parentheses.
*p<0.1; **p<0.05; ***p<0.01.

Source: Bovitz Forthright Friendship Study

subjects have more negative than positive thoughts toward the other party). In the treatment condition, this increased to 32 percent, a 14 percent increase. Likewise, treated subjects had more positive thoughts toward the other party, as well as fewer negative thoughts ($p = 0.12$, two-tailed, so this just misses standard cutoffs for statistical significance).

Note that these effects were not simply due to the fact that respondents liked both parties more. I asked these same items for the respondent's own party as well, as a placebo check; the treatment had no effect on these ratings (columns 4–6 of table 6.2).[4] Rather than just being about positivity overall, the effect was about changing attitudes toward the other party (due, as I argued in chapter 4, to changing one's conception of it). So when animus falls, partisan ambivalence increases.[5]

These downstream consequences speak more broadly to the *political* consequences of affective polarization. As Iyengar et al. (2019) note, we have learned a tremendous amount about the apolitical consequences of affective polarization—everything from its effect on dating and relationships (Huber and Malhotra 2017), to the length of time people spend at Thanksgiving dinner (Chen and Rohla 2018), to roommate preferences (Shafranek 2021), to economic and consumer behavior (Gift and Gift 2015; McConnell et al. 2018; Panagopoulos et al. 2020), to medical decisions and health care (Hersh and Goldenberg 2016; Lerman, Sadin, and Trachtman 2017). But despite this impressive array of effects, much less is known about how animosity has changed politics (though see Hetherington and Rudolph 2015; Druckman et al. 2021; Druckman et al. 2022a). These findings highlight how animosity also shapes perceived polarization, partisan cue-taking, and partisan ambivalence, helping to further document the political relevance of animosity.

All of the downstream consequences have important implications for how we understand American politics more broadly, but the implications of increasing partisan ambivalence are arguably the most important of all, as partisan ambivalence vitiates partisan motivated reasoning (Lavine, Johnston, and Steenbergen 2012). Such partisan motivated reasoning weakens democratic accountability, because it makes subjects more responsive to partisan cues than to factual information (Lavine, Johnston, and Steenbergen 2012; Druckman et al. 2013; Little, Schnakenberg, and Turner 2022) and skews how citizens assign credit and blame to government figures (Bisgaard 2015; Bisgaard 2019). It prompts a "partisan" type of citizenship (MacKuen et al. 2010), one where citizens see politics through a lens of debate and argumentation rather than deliberation and reasoned consideration (Groenendyk and Krupnikov 2021). As such, scholars have invested considerable effort in thinking about how to minimize this type of thinking (e.g., Druckman 2012), but it turns out to be quite difficult (Lavine et al. 2012). The results here offer a potential path to doing so.

But there is another point here as well. Because partisan motivated reasoning also drives party cue-taking (Lavine, Johnston, and Steenbergen 2012; Druckman et al. 2013), in many ways the Party Cue-Taking Hypothesis is really a corollary of the Partisan Ambivalence Hypothesis: if partisan ambivalence increases, and partisan motivated reasoning falls, then cue-taking will also abate. And because cue-taking is so intimately tied to partisan sorting and ideological polarization, this implies that to study any one of these concepts—partisan motivated reasoning, affective polarization, party sorting, ideological polarization, and partisan ambivalence—is to study all of them. While they have some unique causes and consequences, they are also inextricably bound together.

This, in turn, has a further implication. Because they are so closely linked, if you can reduce one, you should be able to reduce others of them as well. Typically, moderating these sorts of tendencies—especially motivated reasoning—is very difficult (Redlawsk, Civettini, and Emmerson 2010). But by working to reduce affective polarization, the strategies outlined in this book also reduce these other pernicious effects. This has considerable importance for our contemporary politics, as I discuss in the concluding chapter.

Conclusion

Are there downstream consequences to reducing affective polarization? Even simply lessening partisan animus is an important goal in and of itself, but the consequences become even more important and significant if there are other downstream effects. This chapter tests the three downstream effects hypotheses from chapter 2: reducing affective polarization should reduce perceived polarization and increase perceptions of common ground between the parties (the Common Ground Hypothesis); reducing affective polarization should reduce partisan cue-taking (the Party Cue-Taking Hypothesis); and finally, reducing affective polarization should increase partisan ambivalence (the Partisan Ambivalence Hypothesis). Using the data from my original experiments, I find strong support for all three of these hypotheses.

These results have several broader consequences. First, as the discussion earlier in the chapter highlights, affective and ideological polarization are deeply intertwined, and cannot really be disentangled. The results here show that when affective polarization falls, so too does party cue-taking. But the converse is also true: as affective polarization has increased, so too has cue-taking, and because cue-taking is one of the primary mechanisms driving partisan sorting and ideological polarization (Levendusky 2009; Levendusky 2010), rising affective polarization helped to fuel ideological polarization as well. So sorting and ideological polarization are both causes and consequences of affective polarization, and they should be understood to be endogenous to one another. Ideological polarization helps to fuel affective discord, but affective discord contributes to ideological polarization as well.

Further, and even more broadly, these results also show that there are significant political consequences to reducing affective polarization. While much of the extant work in this area focuses on the counterintuitive effects of affective polarization on apolitical outcomes, my work here also shows how this matters politically. This is true not just for party cue-taking, but also for partisan ambivalence: reducing affective polarization reduces partisan motivated reasoning more generally. This implies that when affective polarization falls, subjects should be less likely to engage in a host of related behaviors—less likely to engage in expressive survey responding (Schaffner and Luks 2018), less likely to show confirmation and disconfirmation bias (Taber and Lodge 2006), and so forth. Just as rising affective polarization has shaped American politics in recent decades, if it were to fall, there could be equally broad consequences.

Appendix: Regression Results from This Chapter

TABLE A6.1. Effects in Perceptions of Common Ground & Party Agreement, Ameri-Speak Friendship Data

	Perceptions of Common Ground (1)	Extent of Party Agreement (2)
Treatment	0.16***	0.08**
	(0.04)	(0.03)
Constant	2.40***	2.24***
	(0.03)	(0.02)
Observations	1,801	1,794
R^2	0.01	0.003

Note: Cell entries are OLS regression coefficients, with associated standard errors in parentheses.

*p<0.1; **p<0.05; ***p<0.01.

What Does This All Mean?

A Recap of the Argument: Where Have We Been?

Our Common Bonds lays out an argument for how we can reduce the affective polarization that plagues American society. Part of why Americans dislike and distrust those from the other side of the political aisle is that they hold significant misperceptions about them: individuals think they have much less in common with the other party than they do in reality. But if we correct this false belief, and show people what the parties share (our common bonds), we can lessen partisan animosity and lower the nation's political temperature.

Throughout the book I outline three strategies for doing so. First, our common identities—chief among them our American national identity—can unite us. If Democrats and Republicans see each other as fellow Americans, rather than rival partisans, their attitudes toward the other party improve; the other party goes from a disliked out-group to a liked in-group (this is an application of the Common In-group Identity Model; see Gaertner and Dovidio 2000). Using a set of original experiments, as well as natural experiments resulting from the July 4 holiday and the 2008 Summer Olympics, I show that priming national identity improves attitudes toward the other party, though with some caveats about that effectiveness in 2020 and beyond that I return to below.

But our American national identity is not the only common identity we share. I started with American identity because it is a strong and salient identity that binds us together across parties—indeed, it is one of the most salient identities among all Americans (Theiss-Morse 2009), and it has been shown to ameliorate other cross-group tensions (e.g., Transue 2007). There are, however, other identities that cross the partisan divide, and the same theoretical logic suggests that they too should lessen partisan animus. I test this more general claim using sports fandom, and find that this too mitigates animus: when individuals find out that someone roots for their favorite team, but is from the other party, they like and respect them much more than they otherwise would. Other identities—not just our national identity—can help to bridge the partisan divide.

Second, cross-party friendships can lessen partisan animus. While it is true that most social networks are relative homophilous with respect to partisanship, they are not completely so—in large-scale national surveys, I found that approximately 8 in 10 Americans know and respect someone from the other party. These are most typically friends, but they also include family members, coworkers, and neighbors. Further, these people are often closer to the center of our social networks than to the periphery, so these are not merely occasional contacts, but rather people we see as important to our everyday lives. When we remember that these individuals that we know and respect are part of the other party, we come to see it differently—it is not just the stereotypes and caricatures depicted in the media; it contains our friends, family, and community members as well. As a result, animus toward the other party falls. Consistent with my theoretical account, these effects are especially large when the cross-party friend is a close friend, and when the individuals discuss politics with each other. Bridging the political divide with a friend, family member, or colleague—or at least disagreeing without becoming disagreeable—lessens animosity.

Third, civil cross-party dialogue also mitigates affective polarization. Normally, because we carry around inaccurate partisan stereotypes about the other party, we think that we have nothing in common with them, and they are a distant and unreasonable other. But when we have a civil exchange with them, we realize that we share values and common ground with them, and they are not the negative "other" we perceived them to be—"they" are more like "us" than we had realized. Using data from an original lab-in-the-field experiment, I show that bringing Democrats and Republicans together for a cross-party dialogue reduces partisan animus quite dramatically.

Reducing affective polarization is an important end goal in and of itself, but in chapter 2 I explained why there should also be several downstream effects on other attitudes and behaviors. Three such effects occur here. First, perceived polarization—the extent to which people think the electorate is divided—will decrease. Perceived polarization drives animosity by making people think they have less in common with the other party than they do, but heightened animosity also makes us think the electorate is even more divided than it is—partisan animosity and perceived polarization feed on one another. When animus falls, and individuals see the other party less as a disliked other, they have less incentive to perceive it as very ideologically distant from themselves. As a result, when affective polarization falls, so too does perceived polarization.

Second, individuals will also become less likely to follow political cues and adopt their party's position on the issues. Affective polarization heightens people's sensitivity to both their own party's cues and the opposing party's cues, so as animus rises, so too does cue-taking (Druckman et al. 2021). In contrast, when animosity falls, and people are less sensitive to party cues, then cue-taking will fall as well, as I show using two experiments. This, in turn, has important implications for our understanding of the relationship between affective and ideological polarization. Partisan cue-taking is a primary mechanism driving partisan sorting, as well as ideological polarization more generally (Lenz 2012; Levendusky 2009; Levendusky 2010): affective polarization increases ideological polarization through this cue-taking mechanism. Prior work emphasized how ideological polarization—particularly at the elite level—contributed to affective polarization (Rogowski and Sutherland 2016; Webster and Abramowitz 2017). This work shows that the converse is also true—affective polarization contributes to ideological polarization by changing our receptivity to partisan cues. Put slightly differently, affective polarization and ideological polarization are endogenous to one another, and the two concepts cannot be fully disentangled (see also Druckman et al. 2021).

Third, reducing affective polarization also heightens partisan ambivalence. When partisan animus falls, individuals will have more positive feelings about the other party, and fewer negative thoughts about them, so they come to see them in a more balanced light. Rather than just seeing their own party as good and the other party as bad, they have a more complex and nuanced view of them. This is a particularly important finding, as such ambivalence helps to vitiate partisan motivated reasoning (Lavine, Johnston, and Steenbergen 2012), with broader implications that I explain below.

Taken together, these results demonstrate that it is indeed possible to reduce partisan animus in the mass public, and when we do so, a number of other consequences follow. In the remainder of the chapter, I discuss several implications for political science, before turning my attention to thinking about the lessons for more practical everyday politics and then offering some closing thoughts. In so doing, I also emphasize some of the limitations of these findings and important topics for future work.

Affective Polarization Is More Malleable Than We Think

The findings throughout the book show that affective polarization can be mitigated, at least in some circumstances. While it is not possible to eliminate partisan animosity, my findings demonstrate that we can reduce it by using what Americans share across the partisan divide. But the fact that these strategies work highlights that animus is not as ingrained in ordinary voters as we might think just from reading political media or scrolling through Twitter.

There is a parallel here to the literature on ideological polarization. Based on what the media report, it might seem as if people are irrevocably divided and polarized. But when we look closer at attitudinal data, we see that this is incorrect: most Americans are more centrist, and less certain of their views, than it seems at first glance (Fowler et al. forthcoming). While some voters are polarized, it is primarily those who are most active and engaged (Abramowitz 2010). There is a parallel lesson here about affective polarization. While the media make it seem as if ordinary partisans are on the brink of a civil war, this is incorrect. Most people have negative perceptions of partisan stereotypes, but not of ordinary citizens (Druckman et al. 2022b), and in many contexts, animus is far more muted than we would assume (Klar, Krupnikov, and Ryan 2018; Lelkes and Westwood 2017; Westwood, Peterson, and Lelkes 2019). As Hersh (2019, 34) puts it, "in real life, we don't shout at people, penalize them, or treat them badly because they support the other party." My results here reinforce this point. If simple psychological primes can lessen partisan animus, then that tells us something about its durability. This does not mean we should ignore partisan animosity—far from it. But it does mean that we should think carefully about how our own measurement of it might help to exaggerate it (see also Druckman et al. 2022b).

There is also a lesson about the centrality of partisanship to people's lives. For a small set of individuals—political scientists included—partisanship and politics sit at the center of our identities. But for most people, this is not what defines them: as I showed in chapter 1, it is people's personal and familial ties that are most central to them, not their political views. For most Americans, politics remains a sideshow in the great circus of life, as Dahl (1961) so eloquently put it many decades ago. Given this, it is perhaps not that surprising that affective polarization can be mitigated in the ways I document here. As I explain below, recognizing that not everyone is intensely partisan is a good thing rather than a bad thing.

THE PERSONAL IS A BRIDGE TO THE POLITICAL

Arguably the core lesson of my argument is that our personal ties offer us a route to improve our politics. In the experiments I analyze here, I build on the common bonds between Democrats and Republicans—be they a shared identity, a friendship, or a discussion—to show how to lessen animus. But these personal ties have political ramifications. It is not simply that thinking about a cross-party friendship makes you like that friend more, or that a dialogue with the other party improves your opinion of your interlocutors. Rather, these treatments make respondents like Democrats or Republicans *as a whole* more, so there is generalization to the entire group. They also trust the other party more, and they are more willing to interact with them in a wide variety of different settings. The trust point is a particularly important finding, as that underlines a key political ramification of affective polarization. Affective polarization hollows out trust in government (Hetherington and Rudolph 2015), but my findings show that these treatments improve such trust, often by striking amounts. To be clear, in no experiment do my treatments cause everyone to fully trust the other party, but they certainly trust it more, and that increased trust matters, especially in an age with so many significant governance challenges.

There's another subtle, but important, point here. In chapter 3, in the sports fandom experiment, I asked respondents to evaluate a particular individual, and then varied that person's partisanship and favorite sports team. But even in the least-liked condition—when the person was from the other party and was not a fan of the respondents' favorite team—the average feeling thermometer rating was 54 degrees. This is quite a bit higher than the rating for the other party as a whole in any of the other experiments, which is often around 20–30 degrees. This is not just an artifact of this one experiment: Orr and Huber (2020) report an equivalent pattern—see especially their table 2 and figure 5. People feel much less animus toward an individual from the other side of the aisle than they do toward the party as a whole, reinforcing a methodological point made by Druckman and Levendusky (2019). But this matters substantively as well: exploiting this fact, we can build on warm feelings toward people from the other party to help improve attitudes toward the party more generally. Rather than trying to make Republicans like "Democrats" as a collective, try just getting them to like a few individual Democrats and build from there. Let the personal be a bridge to the political.

An earlier, failed effort to reduce partisan animosity also reinforces this point. While the strategies I used in this book lessen animus, in an earlier paper I found examples of strategies that did not: in particular, having individuals list things they liked about the other party (Levendusky 2018b). My hope in that study was that people would reflect on the fact that they like particular individuals from the other party, or the way in which they handled particular issues or crises. Instead, most respondents reacted with notable vitriol, and said that they liked nothing about the other party. From their responses, it seems that they envisioned "the party" as its key leaders and policies (Jacobson 2019; Druckman and Levendusky 2019). But as I discussed in chapter 4, when they were pushed to think about cross-party friendships respondents reacted much more positively, and saw the other party in a new light. If we start with national politics (or prime people, even inadvertently, to think about national politics), then anger and animus are the result. But if we encourage people to see things through a new lens, then they behave quite differently.

My findings also underscore the fact that once we have opened with the personal, we need to bring in politics to uncover any common ground that might exist, or at least the ability to disagree without being disagreeable. The results about cross-party friendship in chapter 4 speak to this point: it is those friendships where the pairs discuss politics that work most effectively to re-duce animosity. It is that political engagement with the other side that is cru-cial, even if we might need something apolitical to start off the conversation.

In turn, this has implications for future studies of political discussion, building on the work I did in chapter 5, where I gave subjects a strong prompt grounded in politics. But it also suggests that perhaps a more effective strat-egy in the future would be to first have participants talk about something personal and apolitical to build trust with one another, and then discuss a political topic to get the crucial stereotype disconfirming evidence that comes from political conversation. An important topic for future work, then, is test-ing these sorts of insights to better understand how to help Americans bridge the partisan gap.

THE IMPORTANCE OF THE DOWNSTREAM CONSEQUENCES OF AFFECTIVE POLARIZATION

The finding that there are strategies that can reduce affective polarization is important in and of itself. But the downstream effects of these shifts also have important implications for our politics. Take, for example, the effects on per-ceived polarization. Reducing perceived polarization is important not only for correcting a perceptual bias, but because it also changes the message vot-ers send to elites. If the mass public is divided and polarized with no common ground, there is little incentive for elites to support the "spirit of compromise" (Gutmann and Thompson 2012)—efforts to build bipartisan solutions and find common ground. Indeed, part of the reason why elites do not compro-mise or look for common ground much of the time is that key voting blocs do not want that (Harbridge and Malhotra 2011). But if voters understood that there was common ground between the parties, at least on some issues, then their message to elites might be somewhat different, focused more on coming together to solve problems. Indeed, while not a cure-all for elite polarization (such a thing does not exist), one positive outgrowth of this could be voters demanding more compromise and consensus, rather than rallying for more grandstanding and political hardball (see also Wolak 2020).

Reducing affective polarization highlights the deep connection between ideological polarization, party sorting, and affective polarization, as I discussed above. But my findings also explain why ideological polarization and party sorting have a larger effect on affective polarization than affective polarization has on them. Affective polarization heightens ideological polarization and sorting through cue-taking, but cue-taking is predominantly concentrated among those with more cognitive resources (Bang-Peterson et al. 2013; Bakker, Lelkes, and Malka 2020). This helps to explain why these concepts are only weakly empirically related (Lelkes 2018). Reducing affective polarization will lessen ideological polarization, but only to a very modest degree. Even more important is the realization that the two are fully endogenous to one another.

The effects on cue-taking, as well as the effects on partisan ambivalence, point to a broader implication—reducing affective polarization reduces partisan motivated reasoning more generally. This is perhaps the most important downstream benefit of these efforts—helping citizens to become more objective in how they perceive the political world.

Given the difficulty of reducing partisanship's effects on voters' psychology (i.e., Druckman 2012), this is no small feat. Getting citizens to perceive the political world more objectively is hard: "Perhaps, then, there is some way to prompt citizens . . . to make better political judgements on a more regular basis. Unfortunately, we do not see how in practice this can be done" (Lavine, Johnston, and Steenbergen 2012, 222). Indeed, because partisanship, and the accompanying group-centrism, sits so powerfully at the core of our political identities, we naturally want to see our party as good and the other side as bad. But if we can break this way of thinking, then citizens can escape this trap, and can more objectively evaluate the evidence at hand.

This also suggests another insight into motivated reasoning more generally. Previous strategies to mitigate motivated reasoning focus on heightening accuracy motivations (Bolsen, Druckman, and Cook 2014; Mullinix 2018) or prompting greater reflection (Arceneaux and Vander Wielen 2017). The difficulty, however, is that we rarely have incentives to pursue accuracy and reflection in politics, even if they are unquestionably good things. My results suggest a slightly different pathway forward—reducing the centrality of partisanship as a motivation. When we reduce animus, we also reduce the power of partisanship to skew how we perceive the political world, and the effects extend even more broadly than we might expect. Exploring the robustness of this general finding is an important area for future research.

Fascinatingly, several recent studies suggest that reducing affective polarization may not translate into changes in more distant downstream behaviors. In particular, several studies highlight that reducing partisan animosity does not reduce support for anti-democratic attitudes (Broockman, Kalla, and Westwood forthcoming; Voelkel et al. 2021). What explains why these studies find no effect on downstream behaviors, while I find some? I suspect it centers on the nature of the downstream inference, in two ways. First, all of my downstream outcomes are more focused on proximate factors (i.e., perceptions of common ground, cue-taking, etc.). These studies focus on a more distant factor—support for anti-democratic attitudes—by asking respondents whether they would prefer an out-party candidate who respects constitutional safeguards over a same-party candidate who does not (building on the work of Graham and Svolik 2020). Yet all of the treatments used in these studies change how individuals feel toward out-partisans, rather than out-party elites, and scholars know that voters see these as related, but distinct, entities (Druckman and Levendusky 2019). It may be that changing attitudes toward the other party's politicians requires a different strategy; this is an important topic for future research (see, e.g., Voelkel et al. 2022).

Second, these relationships are likely quite subtle and indirect, and hence may be more complicated than they appear at first glance. For example, Druckman et al. (2022a) show that support for democratic norms is related to partisan animus, but the effect is modest, limited to a particular subset of voters, and conditional on the type of norm in question (such norms are related to, but distinct from, support for anti-democratic politicians).[1] As Druckman et al. (2022a) explain, understanding which voters drive these effects is an important dimension of these effects. Understanding the subtlety of these effects—and why, theoretically, they occur—is an important component to the future research agenda in this area.

What Other Strategies Could Work?

Much of the discussion above focuses on the implications of my work for political science theories about citizen decision-making. But there is another set of implications that I need to consider—what do these consequences mean more practically for actual politics? One obvious question to ask is what other strategies could work here. As I noted throughout the book, I focused on a set of interconnected strategies that tackle affective polarization stemming from a common source: misperceptions of how much the parties share in common. But there are many other strategies that could also lessen animosity, and it is worth discussing some of them.

One set of strategies would build quite directly from the approach that I adopted here. My strategies focused on reducing misperceptions about the dissimilarities between the parties, but this same strategy could work in other contexts as well. For example, one could highlight demographic similarities (Ahler and Sood 2018) or similarities in terms of political interest and extremity (Klar, Krupnikov, and Ryan 2018; Druckman et al. 2022b) to reduce animus. This highlights that common bonds can extend even beyond the factors I explored here (on overcoming misperceptions more generally, see Bursztyn and Yang 2021).

Researchers could also help individuals recognize that their identities are complex and multifaceted. As I showed in chapter 3, shared identities—not just as Americans, but also as fans of the same sports teams—can help to bridge the partisan divide. This latter type of explicitly apolitical identity is an especially useful one, as there are many such identities that bring us together across party lines. Democrats and Republicans attend the same colleges and universities, watch the same mainstream TV shows, are fans of the same music groups, and are part of the same community and social groups. Recognizing these bonds helps us see what we share with the other side. I return to this point below, as it highlights the importance of these types of nonpolitical organizations as a means to lessening partisan animus.

But there is a subtler point as well—we all need to recognize the "identity complexity" in ourselves and in one another (Klein 2020). If I told you that someone was a Republican and an evangelical Christian, you would likely get a clear image of that person in your mind, and with it a set of issue positions they would be likely to hold. You might, for example, think that they are likely to not believe in climate change, and to oppose policies designed to address it. But for some evangelicals this is not the case, as they believe the Bible calls on mankind to protect and defend the earth, and such individuals (especially younger ones) are attempting to push the Republican Party to address this issue (Anderson 2020). The groups "Republican," "evangelical," and "climate change believer" might seem not to overlap, but they do. This same pattern is true more generally: we tend to paint all Democrats and Republicans with a broad brush, but those stereotypes are often inaccurate. This reflects social identity complexity: our social groups cross-cut, rather than just reinforce, one another (Rocas and Brewer 2002). While identities have become more aligned over time (Mason 2018), that process remains incomplete. Not all Trump supporters think the election was stolen, and not all Biden supporters want to defund the police; failing to recognize the fact that most people have complicated attitudes obscures the reality of public opinion in America. This sort of identity and attitudinal complexity helps us to realize what we share with the other side, and lessens our animus toward them (Brewer and Pierce 2005). We all contain multitudes, and recognizing this makes us better able to understand others and bridge the partisan divide.

In addition, we could encourage people to de-emphasize *national* politics in their everyday lives. Many who care about politics—myself included—focus most of our efforts on the machinations in Washington, DC. But as Hersh (2019) notes, in the contemporary period this leads us to become political hobbyists—we watch Fox News or MSNBC, write checks to the DNC or RNC, and post about politics on Twitter and Facebook. But what difference does that make? In the end, it is largely sound and fury, signifying nothing—while the decisions McConnell and Biden make are hugely significant, our own contribution is not. Spending time on Facebook, Twitter, and other websites only adds fuel to the fire of polarization by skewing our misperceptions of the other side (Lelkes, Sood, and Iyengar 2017; Settle 2018). Watching cable news or creating a Facebook meme might make us feel better, but it only heightens our in-group identification and riles us up against the other party without actually accomplishing very much. It is the political equivalent of a sugar high: satisfying in the moment, but ultimately unproductive and unhelpful.

This should not be read as discouraging political activity or interest—far from it. If people want to be active, that activity is better directed toward the local or state level (though I have more to say about how we might encourage meaningful *national*-level engagement later in the chapter). While we all constantly glance at our phones for the latest *New York Times* news alert, decisions with much more tangible consequences are being made in state capitals and city governments around the country. Indeed, many decisions—from school funding, to policing and criminal justice, to efforts to fight climate change and boost sustainability—are made primarily at the state and local level, not nationally. Getting involved in your community is a more efficacious strategy to enact political change than is national-level hobbyism.

But there is an even deeper point here. Many issues at the state and especially the local level do not lend themselves to easy ideological stereotyping—they are "more tangible and less symbolic": everyone wants safer streets, good schools, and a robust business community (Klein 2020, 266). Working genuinely in politics at a local level, caring about concrete issues more than the latest manufactured national outrage, would help us to see how we could more directly make a difference in our communities (Hersh 2019). As Hopkins (2018) notes, while there are over 5,000 elected officials in America, only 537 are at the national level. While we should not ignore those 537, we should also pay attention to the many thousands of others as well.

There's also a corollary to this local engagement piece: Americans should consume more local media. There are more political media than ever before, but they nearly all focus on national politics inside the Beltway; few, if any, of them devote any attention at all to state and local politics. This matters not only because it affects vote choice (Moskowitz 2021; Darr, Hitt and Dunaway 2018), but also because it can affect levels of affective polarization. Darr, Hitt, and Dunaway (2021) report on what happened when the *Palm Springs Desert Sun* stopped printing national politics editorials or letters to the editor for one month in 2019, instead shifting its attention to state and local issues. As a result, the paper's readers became less affectively polarized: local news is about less polarizing and partisan topics, and gets covered with less inflammatory rhetoric, so readers feel less animosity toward the other side. Not only would more local news help to lower the political temperature, it would also keep us all better informed about our local communities, a positive good in and of itself (Hayes and Lawless 2021).

We could also encourage individuals to engage in community-building activities independent of politics, but have them do so (unknowingly) with members of the other party. So, for example, individuals could work to solve a problem (say, a set of puzzles) in cross-party groups. Solving the problem collaboratively would allow them to bond and form positive associations with one another without realizing that they come from different parties (this is akin to the "fast friends" protocol in psychology; see Aron et al. 1997). Afterward, subjects could be informed that they came from different parties, and the bonds formed through the common activity would help to tamp down partisan animus. In short, the initial activity helps people to realize what they have in common, and that they can get along, and the partisan divisions should then not seem such an overwhelming divide (this is similar to the argument that national service would reduce polarization; see Mason and Liu 2019; Ignatius 2020; Holloway 2021).

On a more informal level, we could help individuals understand the true heterogeneity of their partisan networks. A generation of social network studies have demonstrated that we *think* our networks are much more homophilous than they are in reality, as we tend to project our own opinions onto others (Huckfeldt and Sprague 1987). Even our online social networks are more heterogeneous than they might seem at first glance, with much more exposure to cross-cutting opinions than the narrative about echo chambers would suggest (Messing and Westwood 2012; Goel, Mason, and Watts 2010). If we realized that our online and offline social networks really were quite diverse—that our dog walker is a Republican, or our next-door neighbor is a Democrat—then we would get a more accurate picture of the other party.

If we genuinely heard from the other party—instead of just from the loudest and most strident voices in the room—then we would likely perceive the other party more positively.[2]

Fifth, one could also prime a set of civic ideals surrounding non-partisanship and accuracy. Mullinix (2018) shows that priming a sense of civic duty reduces the effect of partisanship on decision-making, presumably by reminding them of the ideals of impartiality (i.e., looking at evidence evenhandedly and triggering our desire to form accurate opinions). This, in effect, reminds people that American politics has norms of respecting opinions from both sides of the aisle, listening carefully, compromising, and so forth (Gutmann and Thompson 2012). Triggering those norms would likely reduce animus toward the other party as well (see also Mullinix and Lythgoe forthcoming). Relatedly, Wojcieszak, Winter, and Yu (2020) show that priming open-mindedness (a willingness to hear the other side) reduces partisan selective exposure and affective polarization. Reminding Americans that a part of our civic culture involves transcending partisanship can be a good thing.

Finally, there are two entirely separate sets of strategies that one could use that work from different theoretical starting points. First, all of the strategies discussed in this book focus on reducing out-group animus. But another strategy would be to try to decrease in-group identification—to find ways of making people see the downside of their own party, to remind them of when its leaders are embroiled in scandal, when it performs poorly, and so forth (see Lavine, Johnston, and Steenbergen 2012; Klar 2014). While that strategy might work, it also has the potential to backfire and even increase out-party animus: because many people are somewhat ambivalent about their own party, they engage in a "lesser of two evils" defense to justify their identification with it (Groenendyk 2012). Scholars who wish to use this sort of route will need to think through this issue carefully.

Second, all of the strategies here focus on changing how ordinary citizens behave. But of course, another strategy would be to think about how elite-level changes can lessen animus. One example of that would be to highlight successful bipartisan legislation, such as the First Step Act of 2018, which was a bipartisan effort to reform the criminal justice system. While such examples are not as common as they once were, they do still exist, and bipartisanship remains a strategy in Congress (Harbridge 2015; Curry and Lee 2020). Reminding individuals of these sorts of bipartisan policy successes can help them to see that even the party elites can bridge the divide, which should in turn lower their animus toward the other party (Bolsen, Druckman, and Cook 2014). Of course, one could—correctly—note that Americans are treated daily with more partisan elite communications, so the effects of this sort of treatment are likely to be extremely muted (this is a classic "pre-treatment" effect; see Druckman and Leeper 2012). This makes me skeptical that this is right approach to reducing animosity. Ultimately, change at the elite level requires more fundamental structural alterations (for a discussion of this point, see Azari and Hetherington 2016).[3]

To be clear, these strategies are—again—just the tip of the iceberg, and no doubt there are myriad others that could work just as well, if not better, than any I have discussed here (for more discussion of other possible strategies, see Hartman et al. 2022). There is, no doubt, more to the story.

Can These Strategies Work in the Real World?

The other obvious question—beyond asking whether other strategies can work at all—is asking how well any of these strategies work in the "real world" outside the context of a survey or lab-in-the-field experiment. To be clear, none of these is any sort of magic spell—we cannot simply sprinkle in a few references to American identity and expect partisan animus to fade into the ether. For example, as I explained in chapter 3, presidents do try to appeal to our national identity to rally the public and move us to action. But except in extraordinary circumstances—say, like the aftermath of 9/11 or Hurricane Katrina—the effect is quite muted, precisely because it gets interpreted through the lens of partisan politics. The blame for that failure, however, lies much more with elites, who have systematically chosen to prioritize political gain over problem solving (see also Lee 2016). If we want a wholesale change in our politics, it is political elites who need to lead the way.

But that does not absolve ordinary voters of the need to act. Encouraging respectful and civil discussion across party lines with a goal of mutual understanding is a good first step. This is what a host of organizations are attempting to do, from Unify America, to Braver Angels (originally Better Angels), to Living Room Conversations, to Younify, to ListenFirst, to the Bridge Alliance, just to name a few (Graham 2018; for efforts to evaluate these sorts of programs, see Baron et al. 2021; Fishkin et al. 2021).[4] Doing so also helps citizens to find their own voices and show them what they can do to solve problems in their own communities (see the discussion in Hersh 2019, 208).

This also suggests an important point about civics education in America. For generations, civics education has focused on teaching people "civic skills" about how to vote and how to participate in politics more generally, but my results show that we've overlooked an important part of this skill set: teaching people how to have productive conversations around political topics. There are a variety of dimensions to this, including the structure and civility I discuss above, as well as other skills such as asking probing questions about others' viewpoints (Kalla and Broockman 2020; Voelkel, Ren, and Brandt 2021), focusing on personal experiences to explain why they hold the positions they do (Kubin et al. 2021), and being open to opposing viewpoints (Yeomans et al. 2020). Part of being a citizen in a democracy is learning how to converse civilly and productively across lines of difference, to see politics as about dialogue and not just conflict. Learning how we can engage with each other to seek out commonalities, but also not lose our individual differences, is crucial, and it is something sorely missing from society, as evidenced by the organizations above. But that makes it more rather than less important that we learn how to have these conversations collectively.

Of course, such conversations are difficult, and that's why most Americans try to avoid them. The literature on political discussion and deliberation is replete with evidence about how uncomfortable this type of discussion makes people, and how much they want to avoid it (see, among many others, Mutz 2006; Settle and Carlson 2019). Indeed, in data gathered by the Pew Research Center, nearly 60 percent of Americans have little confidence that their fellow citizens can have civil discussions across lines of political difference (Rainie, Keeter, and Perrin 2019). To be sure, cross-party dialogue contains within it the seeds of *potential* discomfort. But the key word there is potential, and how we have that conversation shapes whether that discomfort emerges. Indeed, the reality is that many of these conversations are much more enjoyable than people imagine (Dorison, Minson, and Rogers 2019). But this also highlights another point: part of why we fear them is because when we are asked if we want to talk to someone from the other party, we imagine a stereotype, not a real person. Actual conversations—which typically are much more productive—are also more pleasant. As the evidence in chapter 5 suggests, once people have this sort of discussion, and it goes well, they are more willing to engage in such interactions in the future (see also Levendusky and Stecula 2021). Little by little, people can be convinced that they need not fear all cross-party conversations.

Another way of encouraging such conversations is fostering the type of cross-cutting social institutions that allow us to build apolitical bonds across lines of difference. Calls for these organizations are nothing new, and a whole generation of scholarship has investigated their decline. While the Kiwanis Club and the Rotary Club may no longer be what they once were, other groups—from hobby groups, to choirs, to gardening clubs, to coffee klatches—allow us the opportunity to build such ties. Precisely because they are apolitical, they allow individuals to build social ties and friendships before politics is brought into the mix, and they therefore help to foster the sorts of bonds that can reduce animus. Indeed, ties that bind us in some other way—like sports and entertainment—are often an excellent pathway to bringing together diverse voices (Wojcieszak and Mutz 2006). I am far from the first to call for a strengthened civil society; indeed, there is a cottage industry of scholarly work encouraging precisely that. But this work highlights the crucial role that such outlets play in exposing us to those who are unlike us. They allow us to form apolitical bonds over time that, as they deepen, can help us overcome political divides.[5]

Anyone who has spent any amount of time on social media discussing politics (or, really, discussing anything at all) might be scratching their head and asking if I'm on some powerful psychotropic drugs after reading the previous few paragraphs. Political discussions there rarely improve attitudes; if anything, they deepen animus and hostility (Bail et al. 2018; Settle 2018). But this is why social media harm our politics more than they help it. These outlets feature the loudest voices shouting for attention in the most extreme fashion. It is worth remembering that Twitter, Facebook, and so on are most assuredly not real life. As just one example, only slightly more than one in five Americans uses Twitter, and 10 percent of Twitter users are responsible for 97 percent of political tweets (Pew Research Center 2019b). This implies that almost all political conversation on Twitter comes from slightly more than 2 percent of the public! Other social media sites are not quite so lopsided, but they still feature the loudest voices in the room: 70 percent of Americans never or rarely post about politics on social media; only 10 percent do so often, and they are more extreme (McClain 2021; McClain et al. 2021). Political conversations on social media are awful in no small part because they draw disproportionately on the loudest, most extreme, and most confrontational voices out there.

Online social media coarsen our politics in part because they lack the face-to-face norms of civility that undergird everyday political dialogue. Normally, there are norms of civility and politeness that make it possible for us to discuss difficult issues, and there are social sanctions that punish those who violate these norms (van Kleef et al. 2015). Lacking those norms, the online environment seems to illustrate that incivility simply begets more incivility (Kim et al. 2021). Part of the reason why online discourse is so nasty is that it is much easier to yell at a screen than it is to say the same thing to someone's face—it is easier to rage at a disembodied "other" than at an actual person sitting across from you (for an interesting first-person account of this effect, see Glass 2015). Put simply, "when it comes to bridging differences, in-person contact really helps" (Heller 2021).[6]

Does that mean social media can only worsen our politics and not improve it? No, it can improve it, but not in its current form. One shift is the need to adopt stronger norms of civility for these sorts of conversations—norms that focus not just on politeness, but on the dimension of civility I discussed in chapter 2: the idea that we should engage with the other side's arguments carefully and seriously, rather than in a more superficial way.

A second way forward comes from Bail (2021). He reports on the results of an experiment where users could engage in anonymous conversations with one another on controversial topics (immigration and gun control). The idea was that people would put their ideas before their arguments, since they would not see the other person's partisanship, age, race, gender, and so forth (conversation partners were given androgynous pseudonyms when using the platform). The results show that these conversations moderated attitudes, and mitigated animus toward the opposing party (Bail 2021, 122–27). This reflects the tenets that I discussed in earlier chapters: individuals trying to genuinely understand one another, rather than just scoring political points. Undoubtedly, there is much more to be done to study social media and limit its polarizing impact, and no doubt scholars will make important advances in the years to come. Online discussion can mitigate animus and enrich our politics, but to do that it needs to more closely resemble face-to-face interaction and not simply become a shouting match.[7]

This also highlights two things that such conversation asks of us: to speak thoughtfully, but also to listen well. Scholars have spent a great deal of time considering the thoughtful speech part of the equation, discussing the need to "talk with each other in a way that heals, not in a way that wounds" (Obama 2011)—trying to persuade, and put our best arguments forward, but doing so with an eye to other's positions as well (see also Harrison 2020). There is, indeed, a whole body of work on deliberation and persuasion that seeks to do exactly that. But the second part—the need to listen well—is no less important, and often gets overlooked (Dobson 2012). Barber (1984) argues that, just as we need to try and persuade others, we need to listen to others' efforts to persuade us—what he calls "mutualistic listening":

> "I will listen" means . . . not that I will scan my adversary's position for weaknesses and potential trade-offs, nor even (as the minimalist will think) that I will tolerantly permit him to say whatever he chooses. It means, rather, "I will put myself in his place, I will try to understand, I will strain to hear what makes us alike, I will listen for a common rhetoric evocative of a common purpose or a common good." (175)

Note that this conception of listening has both a positive and a negative component: we will not look solely to undermine our opponents, or even to abandon our position, but rather will try to find a position of mutual understanding and compromise (see also Gutmann and Thompson 2012). This is why the sort of canvassing discussed in Kalla and Broockman (2020) works—people listen, and try to see the other person's point of view, and they realize what they actually have in common. Persuading someone requires helping them see why they want to change, not why *you* think they should change. Speaking in the aftermath of the shooting of Arizona Congresswoman Gabby Giffords, President Obama invoked this point quite eloquently, asking us to "listen to each other more carefully, to sharpen our instincts for empathy and remind ourselves of all the ways that our hopes and dreams are bound together" (Obama 2011). Thinking of how we can genuinely listen to what those across the political aisle are saying is an important habit to develop.[8]

American Identity and the Quest for a More Perfect Union

In chapter 3, I found that while American identity still reduced partisan animosity in 2020, it did so primarily for White and Republican respondents; the prime was less effective for non-White and Democratic individuals. Does this mean that American identity no longer bridges the divide: is it now just one more symbol of our divided republic, much like the debates over whether to display the American flag (Nir 2021)? The answer is no—American identity can still be a common bond, but its role is now more complicated than it was in the past.

There are two different ways in which American identity can build bridges in the contemporary era. First, one could prime American identity in a completely apolitical manner. This could be done, as I suggested in chapter 3, by having subjects watch the movie *Miracle*, for example, which depicts the US men's ice hockey team's victory over the heavily favored USSR team in the 1980 Olympic semifinals, or perhaps footage of some of Simone Biles's record-setting gymnastics routines. The event need not be a sporting event; the point is simply that it primes American identity in an apolitical context. The obvious non-sports example used to be the July 4 holiday, but after President Trump celebrated the day with a military parade in 2019 and a de facto campaign rally in 2020, it lost some of its unifying force. In 2021, President Biden held a more muted celebration of the holiday, consistent with concerns about the virus, but the lingering shadow of the pandemic, and its attendant politicization and polarization, likely curbed its ability to serve as a mechanism to bridge the divide. Once a symbol like July 4 becomes politicized, its ability to serve as an apolitical cue wanes.

But there is still a common basis for American identity. Despite their many differences, Democrats and Republicans are still proud and grateful to be

American, and still agree on the core ideas and elements of civic engagement that undergird American life (Hawkins and Raghuram 2020; see also the data presented in chapter 1). The disagreement is about how we can best realize those ideals, and how we tell the story of America. This is perhaps our oldest and most enduring debate; it is reflected in the contradiction embedded in our very founding documents. All men are created equal, yet slavery is the nation's original sin; Jefferson's ability to think and write the stirring rhetoric in the Declaration of Independence was made possible by the stinging lash of the overseer's whip. American identity encompasses both the promise and the peril of what this nation has meant for more than two centuries. Speaking at his inauguration, President Biden (2021) highlighted this paradox:

> Our history has been a constant struggle between the American ideal that we're all created equal and the harsh, ugly reality that racism, nativism, fear, and demonization have long torn us apart. The battle is perennial. Victory is never assured. Through the Civil War, the Great Depression, World War, 9/11, through struggle, sacrifice, and setbacks, our "better angels" have always prevailed. In each of these moments, enough of us came together to carry all of us forward. And, we can do so now.

This is the tension highlighted by those who had a negative view of their American identity in 2020: the failures of systemic racism, of police brutality, of inequality and so forth, the ways in which our past and present are sources of shame more than of pride. This is perhaps the deepest, and truest, form of American identity—the recognition that America is imperfect, and yet is worth striving for. As Huntington (1983, 262) famously put it, "critics say that America is a lie because its reality falls so far short of its ideals. They are wrong. America is not a lie; it is a disappointment. But it can be a disappointment only because it is also a hope." The sentiment was put more poetically by James Thompson, a young Black cafeteria worker from Wichita, Kansas, on the eve of World War II. Noting that he would go to fight for and return home to a segregated nation that would deny him his political equality and his full humanity, he wrote that "I love America and am willing to die for the America I know will someday become a reality" (Johnson 2020).

Striving to ensure that America does the hard work of living up to its founding ideals is not easy, and it is never without controversy. Indeed, part of the debate is over what those ideals *are*, and not just whether we live up to them (Smith 1997). But most Americans embrace our "greatest professed commitments, to liberty and justice for all" (Smith 1983, 228) and share a desire to embody the best of the founding ideals.[9] As Steven Smith (2021, 154) notes, taking pride in one's American identity requires recognizing this struggle: it "does not allow complacency or self-satisfaction with what we are but, to the contrary, entails a lively awareness of our present imperfections and our failures to live up to what we might become." To do this, we must be frank about where the nation has succeeded, but also—and more importantly—where it has failed, most notably in its failure to address the legacy of slavery and racism. To do less than this—and particularly to ignore our failures—is to ignore the lessons of our past, and to fail to live up to our American ideals.

But this also lays bare what we owe one another as fellow citizens, in two profound ways. First, we owe each other equal treatment as citizens:

> In this huge, sprawling nation, teeming with ethnic, religious, cultural, and ideological variety, there is one thing that binds all Americans together. And that is, we are all Americans, all citizens of the same republic, all bound by the same laws that all of us have at least some power to shape and to change. We share full and equal membership in one body politic, and we therefore owe all our fellow members the mutual respect that this common equal status entails. To be good citizens, we should treat all Americans, even those with whom we have political differences, as our civic and political equals. (Lindsey 2021)

Müller (2021) summarizes this more succinctly when he notes that in a democracy, "no distinction is drawn between first- and second-class citizens"—we are all equal by virtue of our citizenship (see also Allen 2014). This means that we must genuinely listen and hear one another, and realize that in a diverse and pluralistic democracy others will disagree with us, and that is a good thing, not a bad thing—it reflects the real and genuine differences between the parties. Politics does not promise us an idyll where we all agree; instead it offers us a system for self-government, a "legitimate forum for the harsh clashes that may be necessary for progress" (Osnos 2020). The price of living in a pluralistic society is discord and some level of partisan animosity. But the promise of it is that we also have mechanisms for coping with, and managing, that conflict.

This helps us to see that rather than competing teams, we are all members of the same American team who alternate playing on the field and cheering from the bench (Lindsey 2021). We must practice what Sabl (2005) calls "democratic sportsmanship," and recognize that we are all working toward the same goals, albeit from slightly different angles. As President Biden put it on the one-year anniversary of the January 6 insurrection, "you can't love your country only when you win"—we all must work together to fully achieve our nation's founding ideals (Biden 2022). In a country that is more closely divided than deeply divided (Fiorina, Abrams, and Pope 2005), small shifts in opinion swing elections and the control of government. But neither side is close to winning all-out control in the ways seen in earlier eras (Ansola-behere, Rodden, and Snyder 2006), so finding ways to work together toward common ends is a valuable goal. For if the nation fails, we all fail, red and blue, Democrat and Republican alike.

Indeed, there is a parallel here to the literature on legislating. Much of the focus in Washington, DC, in recent years has been on unilateral behavior (through executive orders and other types of presidential action) or partisan lawmaking (where one party uses tools like the budget reconciliation process to enact policy with little to no input from the other side). Partisan, rather than bipartisan, policy is seemingly the order of the day. To be sure, partisan pathways have yielded important policy changes in recent years. But as Curry and Lee (2020) note, *contra* our expectations, this is the exception, not the norm: most lawmaking remains bipartisan, not least the significant COVID-19 relief bills that passed in 2020. Indeed, in recent years many lower-profile, but still quite significant, legislative achievements were passed this way, from the Every Student Succeeds Act (revamping K-12 education policy), to the Support Act (to revamp and expand opioid treatment options), to the First Step Act (reforming criminal justice), to the No Surprises Act (which banned out-of-network charges from medical providers), and many others. As Bazelon and Yglesias (2021) note, getting policy passed this way requires not framing the "issue as a 'win' for your party; talk about it as a common-sense reform. Do the work of trying to find and convince people across the ideological spectrum that it's a good idea and that it's in their interest to support it." Our system of governance requires finding compromise and common ground, and progress comes from coming together, not fracturing apart.

One could easily counter-argue that this necessarily trims the sails of what the parties can achieve, at least legislatively; big challenges require big solutions. Few would disagree, but the point is that the system cannot enact those solutions at the moment. What it *is* capable of delivering is these small-bore (or perhaps smaller-bore) solutions. The parallel in the public is that it may not be possible to bridge the gap on every issue, but there are cases where compromise and coming together is possible, and finding those pathways is worthwhile. There will be profound differences on some issues in the public, especially high-profile issues. But that does not mean that common ground can never be found.

But this also highlights the second, and even more important, implication of this conception of American identity: what it places out of bounds. If we treat each other as civic and political equals, then efforts that deny one another's political and legal standing are necessarily illegitimate. So, for example, efforts that deny the legacies of slavery and racial discrimination, or seek to restrict the franchise and political voice of our fellow citizens, or undermine the legitimacy of our democratic institutions, are not acceptable. Treating one another as equals requires recognizing that we all have a right to sit at the table, but rejecting that fundamental truth is grounds for excluding those voices from the political realm, akin to Popper's (1945) paradox of tolerance. One could rightly note that such ideas have often been part of our political culture. But this line of argument shows why they had no legitimate place then, and they have no legitimate place moving forward. Encouraging dialogue and debate, then, is not a reason to accept bigotry, intolerance, and other ideas that reject our equality with one another; it is a reason to reject those forces (see also Keith and Danisch 2020). There are some divides that cannot be bridged, and recognizing that some debates are not legitimate is part of a healthy democratic culture.

This sets up American identity as a profoundly powerful force for unity in the longer term, but as a force for division and dissensus in the shorter term. We all understand and share some of the most important core values; we have differences about how best to realize them and how to tell our national story. There will be clashes over how to right the wrongs our nation has perpetuated for centuries, as these are hard problems with no easy answers. The path forward is not an easy one, but it is the one we must all travel together.

DID 2020 AND JANUARY 6 CHANGE EVERYTHING?

I finished the initial draft of the book in fall 2020, just as the campaign between Trump and Biden was coming to a close. Like many in our profession, I expected Trump to try to cast some doubt on the election, and I expected some angry tweets and a few lawsuits if he lost, but I thought that would be the end of it. I was profoundly wrong. Despite the fact that academic experts (Eggers, Garro, and Grimmer 2021), security experts (Tucker and Bajak 2020), state election officials (Corasaniti, Epstein, and Rutenberg 2020), and the Department of Justice (Balsamo 2020) all found no evidence of voter fraud—even when pressed to do so by the president (Benner 2021)—President Trump and his allies continued to repeat the lie that Biden stole the election. This mendacity tragically culminated in the attack on the US Capital on January 6. Not only that: some Republicans attempted to downplay the severity of this attack in the weeks and months that followed by saying that the insurrectionists were Antifa members pretending to be Trump supporters (Grynbaum, Alba, and Epstein 2021), or that the insurrection was a peaceful protest (Fandos 2021). We also know that Trump's allies in Congress and elsewhere coordinated to help perpetrate those tragic events, even when they knew the underlying claims of voter fraud were false (Clark, Berzon, and Berg 2022). Do these lies render compromise and coming together beyond the pale?

In many ways, this event is really just an extension of the debate I discussed above about the role of race in American history. Throughout the campaign, Trump's arguments about voter fraud centered on plurality-Black cities such as Philadelphia, Detroit, and Atlanta, implicitly linking race with voter fraud. Support for the storming of the Capitol is strongly correlated with concerns about demographic and cultural change in America, better known as status threat (Annenberg IOD Collaborative 2023). The January 6 insurrection was, in no small part, about America's transition toward becoming a truly multiracial democracy, perhaps best symbolized by the insurrectionists carrying the Confederate battle flag inside the US Capitol, achieving what Jefferson Davis and Robert E. Lee never could. This attack on our democratic institutions is a way of attacking the equality and legitimacy of our fellow citizens, and as such, sits outside the bounds of legitimate debate. To again quote President Biden, "Those who stormed this Capitol and those who instigated and incited and those who called on them to do so held a dagger at the throat of America, at American democracy" (Biden 2022). Such attacks cannot be tolerated, as they are an attack on the legitimacy of our system, and an attack on our political equality as citizens. There *is* a path forward toward healing, but it recognizes the lies and falsehoods that led to that day. It punishes those who assaulted our democracy, and ensures that it cannot happen ever again. There can be legitimate grievances aired, but it must be clear that violence, mob rule, and efforts to undermine the legitimacy of the system are beyond the pale.

This underscores two important points. First, January 6 is largely a consequence of elite cue-taking. Ordinary Republican voters did not spontaneously decide that the election was illegitimate; they did so because Republican elites, led by President Trump, told them that for months on end despite the lack of valid evidence to support their claims. Belief in election fraud did not spring into being fully formed, like Athena from the head of Zeus; it emerged from trusted elites telling people that the election was stolen *ad nauseam*. Indeed, in the panel data reported by the Annenberg IOD Collaborative (2023), in spring 2020 Democrats and Republicans were equally confident that the election would be free and fair; they only diverged after President Trump began to question the election's legitimacy. Republican elites bear most of the blame, and therefore the central solution to the problem will lie with them as well. The types of mass public solutions I discuss in this book are an important first step, but to truly solve the problem, elite-level changes are needed.

This does not mean dialogue necessarily ceases, though. There is little to be gained by trying to have Biden and Trump supporters debate the events of January 6; that will only serve to harden the battle lines. After all, this isn't an issue on which compromise is really possible: "there isn't really any middle ground on overthrowing the government" (Williamson 2021). But a different approach—one that, say, asked them to begin with what they *disliked* about their party or its standard bearer, or what their candidate did that disappointed them—could well yield more fruitful and productive conversations, as it would ask people to dialogue in a way that opens up space for conversation, rather than foreclosing it. It would recognize the identity complexity we all have, and that we can support a political candidate without endorsing many of their positions. Treating each other as political equals requires that both sides make a good faith effort to see where some possible common ground might be found.

Responsible Partisanship, Participation, and Citizenship

Perhaps most profoundly, these findings suggest that we should rethink what we ask of political parties, and of citizens, along several different dimensions. One of the oldest calls to improve American politics is the call for "responsible" parties: strong, ideologically coherent parties that offer voters a clear choice at the ballot box (APSA Committee on Political Parties 1950; Ranney 1951). Such parties are indeed essential to democracy, for they allow us to hold parties accountable for what government actually does (Fiorina 1980). In many ways, the last few decades seem to have given us exactly that: regardless of what else one can claim, it is hard to say that today's political parties do not offer voters a clear choice. Likewise, no one would argue that partisanship does not powerfully shape how voters behave. From this perspective, perhaps we got what the reformers recommended, and have found it wanting.

But this is not quite right, as our contemporary system falls short of what reformers wanted. The partisan spirt that animates voters is not terribly responsible—it "sends partisans into action for the wrong reasons" and gives them "a desire for victory that exceeds their desire for the greater good" (Mason 2018, 6). This strong but irresponsible partisanship then partners with hollow parties: parties that are adept at raising ever increasing sums of money, and enforcing discipline in Congress, but little else (Schlozman and Rosenfeld 2019; see also Azari 2016). This is problematic because these hollow parties can do little to drive change and to channel this spirit in constructive directions. Partisanship drives behavior, but parties are ill equipped to harness it.

The parties' voter outreach strategy highlights this mismatch. Parties are quite adept at mobilizing voters—their strategies can, quite literally, bring millions of additional citizens into the electorate via their get-out-the-vote efforts (McKenna and Han 2015; Enos and Fowler 2018). But the engagement ends there, and voters are never asked to do anything beyond showing up at the polls. The one effort to do this—when Obama for America became Organizing for America—largely died on the vine. Having turned voters out in ever greater numbers, the parties do nothing to have them contribute to policy change (by, say, contacting and putting pressure on members of Congress, attending town halls, etc.). In short, mass partisanship is a way of winning elections, but not of governing. We have substituted electoral participation and shouting on social media for actual civic participation, and our nation—and our politics—is poorer for it.

What, then, can I recommend? Perhaps most importantly, the answer is not some sort of mythical anti-partisanship or independence—parties are too important, and too fundamental, to our democracy for this to work. The point is to recognize the value of parties and partisanship, while also mitigating the extreme partisan animus that has infected our politics. This involves thinking about a more *productive* partisanship. This would entail the parties engaging voters more meaningfully, and helping them to see how to produce policy, not just win an election. Why is this more productive? Simply put, because policy change requires compromise and consensus building, what Gutmann and Thompson (2012, 100) call "mutual sacrifice," which is the ability to "adjust principles to improve the status quo"; this is also central to the idea of treating one another as political equals discussed above. Seeing that there are ways to come together to make people's lives better is the goal of government—that is how we promote the general welfare and secure the blessings of liberty. But doing that requires us not only to hold firm to our convictions, but also to recognize where progress might be made—in short, to both realize the value of our own party's ideals, and also recognize that governing involves compromise and a willingness to accept that no one has a monopoly on truth. Rather than mobilizing based on fear of the other side, parties would mobilize around the hard work of improving citizens' lives—justifying themselves through reason-giving, rather than just demonizing the opposition and saying that "chaos" will reign if the other party wins.

The goal of such partisanship is not to erase the differences between parties—far from it. Indeed, the whole point of parties is that Democrats and Republicans have different policies rooted in different philosophies about the world, and differences between them are a good thing, not a bad thing. As Muirhead (2014, 256) notes, "what vital democratic politics needs is . . . deeper clarity about the public choices that cannot be avoided." At its best, partisanship is a mechanism for clarifying such choices—as Rosenblum (2011, 302) argues, parties draw "lines of division" and clarify what is at stake in a given conflict. Such contrasts help partisans recognize not just the strength of their own party's program, but also its weaknesses, developing what Muirhead (2014, 257) calls "negative capacity," the ability to accept that one's own side's ideas might be incomplete or lacking.[10] This is what a focus on governing gives partisans: the ability to advocate for their views while recognizing that improving the status quo might also necessitate compromise.

This highlights a third, and perhaps most important, point. Much as civic education should teach us how to have productive conversations with those who are different from us, it should also educate us all on the value of parties and partisanship, and their vital role in American politics. The anti-party tradition in America is strong, as Rosenblum (2008) notes—it can hardly be any other way in a nation resting on Madisonian principles where the first president warned of the dangers of partisanship in perhaps his most famous public address. Yet parties are, simply put, indispensable for democracy, as scholars dating back to Schattschneider (1942) have noted, but that point rarely penetrates the public consciousness. Civic education could teach all citizens that parties are what make mass democracy possible:

> Party antagonism focuses attention on problems, information, and interpretation are brought out, stakes are delineated, points of conflict and commonality are located, the range of possibilities is winnowed, and relative competence on different matters is up for judgement. . . . Shaping conflict is what partisans do, and it will not be done, certainly not regularly and reasonably coherently in the way representative democracy requires, without them. (Rosenblum 2011, 301)

Parties structure political competition and make it possible for ordinary voters to actually participate in politics (Sniderman and Levendusky 2007). They do this by articulating a vision and principles of what those conflicts are, and how they are related to more fundamental values that underlie their philosophies. It is in outlining this vision of the good society, and this connection to more fundamental principles—what Muirhead (2014) calls "high partisanship"—that reminds us all of the essential role of parties and partisanship. One could, quite rightly, note that modern parties are failing at this task, and our reality is quite distant from this ideal. But in emphasizing the disjuncture between reality and the ideal, it would help us all to see what we can strive toward, and perhaps help us overcome some of what ails our politics.

But any such reforms bring with them a potential downside. The anger and animus of affective polarization leads citizens to participate in the political process (Huddy, Mason, and Aarøe 2015; Webster 2020). A different sort of partisanship—one that shows them that the other side might have some worthwhile ideas—exposes them to opposing arguments, and potentially makes them less likely to participate (Mutz 2006; Lavine, Johnston, and Steenbergen 2012). But perhaps this is not such a bad thing. Participation itself is not some unalloyed good; rather, the goal of participation is to have government policy reflect the public's preferences. One would struggle to make the case that government policy today does that, and that the shouting and vitriol improve our democracy. As numerous scholars note, we need citizens to be open-minded and willing to change their attitudes, their vote choice, and even their partisanship in response to changing circumstances—otherwise, accountability is a hollow concept (Mason 2018; Lavine, Johnston, and Steenbergen 2012). The sort of closed-minded tribalism promoted by affective polarization—what Mason (2018, 126) calls "blind activism"—is not especially helpful. But a more productive partisan engagement might be, by helping people see how to engage in governance, rather than just electioneering.

This also underscores the role of civic organizations in helping to bring voters into the political process more fully (Han 2014; Han 2017). Getting citizens to see how to be more meaningfully engaged in their democracy might also bring individuals who feel disengaged from the process back into the public sphere. If it is about something other than just winning the next election, citizens might become less cynical and be more willing to take part in our democracy. Participation and partisanship are means, not ends; they are ways to have the government function more effectively and more accurately reflect the public's preferences. That, ultimately, should be our collective aim.

These arguments also call for us to rethink our conceptions of what "good" citizenship means. For decades, scholars have debated what opinions *should* look like. While that is always a fraught discussion, the consensus—to the extent that there is one—is that such opinions should reflect what Mansbridge (1983) terms "enlightened preferences," essentially the preferences one would hold in a world of perfect information (see also Lau and Redlawsk's 1997 conception of "correct voting," which draws on the same normative ideal, as well as Althaus 1998 and Fishkin 1995 for related ideas). But achieving this is quite hard, if not effectively impossible for most citizens most of the time. But the work here suggests a new standard—we want opinions that reflect genuine engagement with different viewpoints and carefully consider the evidence at hand (see also Druckman 2012). This asks citizens to avoid the types of partisan motivated reasoning that plague contemporary political decision-making, and instead to truly listen to different viewpoints. Note that this goal is also implicit in a more responsible conception of partisanship: by engaging with the other side, it asks citizens to recognize what the other party might have to offer and to try to find a way to come together to compromise. Even if we cannot get to our enlightened preferences—or simply consider a way of understanding that counterfactual scenario—hearing and thinking about the other side provides us with a more achievable, but still laudable, goal.

In the end, the reader might be disappointed that none of the things I propose here will transform American politics. I can offer no grand strategy to eliminate polarization, and frankly, neither can anyone else. It is unclear what such a strategy would even look like beyond some sort of realignment that altered the dimensions of political competition. But at some level, that's also the point. Yes, fixing polarization in some macro sense requires structural changes to politics from elites. But from a more realistic perspective, this is what we can actually do in the here and now.

There is no *deus ex machina* to resolve this conflict, and as long as elites think it is in their interest to foment animosity, they will do so, as we have seen again and again in recent years. But to accept that elites are largely to blame does not absolve us all as citizens of the responsibility to do something about our body politic; rather, it leads us to work across the divide to build bridges and a common future. If we the people accept that there are things we can do, we can rise to the challenge. Working together, there is no doubt that ordinary citizens can do just that.

Acknowledgments

Finishing a book and reflecting back on the process provides a rare moment of academic happiness. It gives you the opportunity to step back, think about those who helped along the way, and thank them for their contributions. First, I owe a special thanks to Neil Malhotra and Yotam Margalit. The genesis of this project came in conversation with them, and though our eventual collaboration took a very different turn, I am indebted to them for prompting me to think along these lines. If that's where the project began, it ended with Elias Dinas and Miriam Golden. They invited me to visit the European University Institute, where I put the finishing touches on this manuscript while staring out my office window at the Tuscan countryside. They helped guide me through the process of living in Italy, and helped me find my own small piece of *la dolce vita*. A thousand thanks are not enough for the kindness and hospitality they showed me. I also thank the Tuesday visiting fellows lunch group—Dietlind, Jason, Johannes, and Carles—for providing a stimulating intellectual and social environment.

But in the process of writing a book, you end up indebted to many people, not just a few. Those who commented on the project at various stages in its development improved the final product tremendously. I thank John Bullock, Dan Hopkins, Kathleen Hall Jamieson, Yph Lelkes, Michele Margolis, Marc Meredith, Diana Mutz, Rune Slothuus, Rogers Smith, Paul Sniderman, and Sean Westwood, as well as seminar participants at the International Society of Political Psychology, the University of California, Berkeley, Brigham Young University, Florida State University, and Stanford University for many thoughtful comments along the way. I also thank Penn's PORES program for providing the research assistants who helped me throughout this project. I owe a special thanks to the four scholars who participated in a book manuscript workshop in August 2020: Jamie Druckman, Marc Hetherington, Howie Lavine, and Linda Tropp; their generosity and insights made the book markedly stronger than it otherwise would have been. Indeed, Jamie not only read and commented on the book manuscript for the conference, but—as always—provided other incredibly insightful comments along the way. Over the years, Paul Sniderman has given me many invaluable pieces of advice, but his best piece of advice was telling me many years ago that I needed to get to know Jamie. I also owe Dom Stecula and my fantastic research assistants— Leah, Liza, and Natalie—many thanks for helping me carry out the discussion experiments presented in chapter 5; and I owe Adam Berinsky, Sara Doskow, and Chuck Meyers thanks for helping me find a home (again!) at the University of Chicago Press.

But my deepest thanks goes to the Annenberg Public Policy Center (APPC) and its director, Kathleen Hall Jamieson. Through the Stephen and Mary Baran Chair in the Institutions of Democracy, the APPC provided the resources needed to carry out the studies described in this book. At the APPC, because of the generosity of the Annenbergs' gift, individuals have the ability to name their own chair. When I found out that I'd been given a chair there—after the initial shock wore off—I spent days racking my brain about what name to pick. My initial idea was to honor one of my academic forebears, but after going through dozens of them, none of them felt right. With all due respect to Phil Converse, Paul Lazarsfeld, and other giants of the field, none of them had much to do with me or who I was as a scholar. Instead, I wanted to honor those much closer to home—people who died before I was born, but who shaped my life in incalculable ways. Stephen and Mary Baran, like the children of so many immigrants at the turn of the last century, left school at an early age to go and join the workforce. But they instilled a love of learning in their daughter and granddaughter, who in turned passed it on to me, and made what came later possible. At times when I am depressed about the state of American democracy, I think back to all it has given to my family and countless others, and realize that we must all work together to ensure that it can continue to do so for generations to come.

Data Sources Used

This appendix gives the full question wording and response options for each of the original datasets used throughout the book. Details on each sample are provided in the chapters.

American Identity Experiment (chapter 3)

For full details, see the supplemental appendix to Levendusky 2018a.

American Identity Experiment under Trump (chapter 3)

We'd like you to read a brief article that recently appeared in the news. Please read it carefully, and then we'll ask you a few about it.

To give you time to read the article, the "next screen" button will not appear right away. When you are ready to begin reading the article, please click to advance to the next screen.

[RANDOMLY ASSIGN SUBJECTS TO T0, T1, OR T2.]

[IF T0, SHOW:]

WHY IS *KEEPING UP WITH THE KARDASHIANS* ENDING?

After fourteen years and twenty seasons, *Keeping Up with the Kardashians* is coming to an end. On Tuesday, Kim Kardashian announced on Instagram that her family had made "the difficult decision" to move on and that the long-running reality TV show would air its final episodes in 2021. She thanked her fans and loyal viewers, saying "I wouldn't be where I am today" without them and the series.

But what Kim didn't reveal is exactly why she and her siblings had decided now was the best moment to walk away from the lucrative franchise. According to sources who spoke with *Page Six*, it was simply that the family wanted to end on a "high note," adding, "It was a good time to end." A source who spoke to *Entertainment Tonight* more or less confirmed that reasoning, saying, "There was no big reason why the family decided to end *KUWTK*; it was a mutual decision. The kids who started the show now have their own kids and it's getting very hard to film all together or get enough footage separately. The family is grateful for their time and is happy they have all of these memories filmed for the rest of their lives. The family wanted time to focus more on their family and future projects and the show is a major job that takes up a lot of time."

They also added that despite the rumors, it is "not true" that Kris Jenner will be joining *The Real Housewives of Beverly Hills*. Rich Greenfield had another take on the decision, telling the *LA Times*, "Obviously they bring their own audience like nobody else, and they have an ability to monetize like nobody else in all sorts of different ways. If you're the Kardashians, you realize your audience is watching less and less TV every day." Thanks to the show, Kylie Jenner has amassed 195 million Instagram followers and Kim 188 million. It also helped them launch their beauty brands to massive success, making them both billionaires. But regardless of the real reason why it's over, Kim wrote on her Instagram, "This show made us who we are and I will be forever in debt to everyone who played a role in shaping our careers and changing our lives forever."

[New Screen]

How often do you see articles like this in the news?

1. Very often
2. Somewhat often
3. Not too often
4. Never

[New Screen]

When you go out to restaurants, what types of restaurants do you prefer and why? Please explain briefly in the space below.

[MEDIUM TEXTBOX]

[IF T1, SHOW:]

AMERICA: WHAT MAKES IT GREAT

The Declaration of Independence, whose signing we celebrate every July 4th, established America as one of the first representative democracies in the world. As we begin America's 239th year, we wanted to reflect on some of the factors that continue to make America a great nation. Here are some of the top reasons we love America.

INNOVATION—Edison, Gates, Jobs: they and we are known for thinking outside the box. As a people, we create and innovate; we don't wait for others, then appropriate their creations. From search engines to social networks—Google, Yahoo, Twitter and Facebook—it all started here.

TECHNOLOGY—From cotton gin to light bulb, records to movies, rockets to Internet, the gadgets and discoveries originating from the US have changed the world, and continue to do so today.

DIVERSITY—"Give me your tired, your poor, your huddled masses yearning to breathe free. . . ." So says the inscription on the Statue of Liberty in the middle of New York Harbor. We are a nation of immigrants whose spirit of hard work and desire for a better life have been a hallmark since the first settlers arrived here more than 400 years ago.

ECONOMY—Despite the spotlight on China and other Asian countries, the United States still possesses the world's richest economy and consumer base— larger than Japan, Germany, China and Great Britain combined. The economy of a single US state—California—would be among the top 10 economies in the world if it were a country.

INDIVIDUAL SPRIT VS. CLASS SYSTEM—Unlike other countries such as India, China or much of Europe, where one's station in life is determined by a caste system, government monolith or an outdated monarchy, in America you are free to carve out your own destiny. Wealth carries huge influence, but unlike most countries, where one's fate is determined by others, in the US you are free to chart your own course.

TOLERANCE—While other cultures in Syria, Iraq and Africa are slaughtering each other in the name of religion, in America Jews, Catholics, Sikhs, Protestants, Hindus, Muslims—and atheists—live and work together in peace.

ENTREPRENEURSHIP—The US, by far, has more self-made millionaires and billionaires proportionally than anywhere in the world. Much has been said of late about the rapid rise of a millionaire class in China and Vietnam. But that's still—pardon the cliche—a drop in the ocean.

INSTITUTIONS AND LAW—We are a nation of laws and equality under the law; those laws provide stability, continuity, structure and protect against intellectual theft.

EDUCATION—Students from everywhere in the world come here for their education, not the opposite.

ENTERTAINMENT—OK, we didn't invent classical music, but we created Dixieland, ragtime, jazz, swing, big band, bluegrass, Hawaiian, pop, rock 'n' roll, hiphop, rap and even disco; then there's radio, television, movies, video games, hula hoops, Hollywood and Disneyland.

NATURAL BEAUTY—From the California coast, through the Rocky Mountains to the forests of Maine and Vermont, and including our national parks, we are a nation of contrasts, with two oceans, numerous lakes and rivers, gargantuan mountains, vast plains and spacious deserts, all with their individual charm.

GENEROSITY—Americans are the most generous nation in terms of donating to charities, both in total dollars given and total hours. No other nation has America's generosity of spirit and willingness to help their fellow man.

ENDURANCE—After 238 years, we are still here in, basically, the same form. No nation in modern times has come close when it comes to longevity. And that goes for our human life span—longer than anywhere else but Okinawa.

STANDARD OF LIVING—The highest in the world; nothing more to be said.

[New Screen]

In the article you just read, the article gave a number of reasons why many people love America and think it is a great country. Now we'd like to know what you think. What do you think is the most important reason people like America and are proud to be an American?

You should try your best to be as thorough and convincing [*sic*], because we want to use these answers to explain to people who have never been to America why Americans are proud of their country.

Please take your time and do not rush. To help with that, the next screen arrow will not appear for a few moments to give you time to write out your answer.

[MEDIUM TEXTBOX]

[IF T2, SHOW:]

9/11 REMINDS US OF AMERICAN UNITY

All of us, those who remember where we were, carry a little bit of that morning with us each and every day moving forward.

If you were an adult on September 11, 2001, chances are good that you remember exactly where you were that morning. You remember looking up at the sweet blue sky above you knowing that it was full of ash and smoke in New York City, Washington, DC, and a field in Pennsylvania. We who lived it share that pain; we remember those who died, as well as those who survived. All of us carry a little bit of that morning with us each and every day.

This is not the time to forgo our solemn celebrations of this event. We promised the first responders, the families, and the friends of the 2,977 Americans who died in the terrorist attacks that day that we would "never forget." We stood strong as a united people following that awful day and showed our deep gratitude to the police, firefighters, and military every chance we could. We worked together to find our common purpose. We volunteered, we helped one another, and we improved our communities. We found that we were not so different, and that we were united by the common bond of being Americans.

September 11th, 9/11, or Patriot Day—whatever you want to call it, we as Americans need it. We need that reminder, that common bond of united suffering, to remind us that we are one people—we are Americans. Even those who don't remember it for themselves, it is still their shared history. Let's not wait until the next tragedy to remember that more unites us than divides us. Look to your neighbor, to your coworker, to your family member and make a conscious effort to look more for the good than the bad. Look past our differences to find what we share in common. Give grace to those who need it, and make sure you extend that to yourself as well. We are Americans. And like World War II in the 1940s, like the Cold War in the 20th century, we will overcome and triumph. It will take all of us now, just like it did then.

[New Screen]

Think back to the days immediately following 9/11, and think about how Americans came together to help one another. How did that coming together and unity make you feel? If you do not remember that day yourself, think about what others have told you about that event, and what you learned in school about it, and how learning about it made you feel. Please take your time and do not rush. To help with that, the next screen arrow will not appear for a few moments to give you time to write out your answer.

[MEDIUM TEXTBOX]

[ALL SUBJECTS ANSWER:]

I'd like to get your feelings toward some groups or individuals who are in the news these days. Below, you'll see the name of a group next to a feeling thermometer. Ratings between 50 and 100 degrees mean that you feel favorably and warm toward that group; ratings between 0 and 50 degrees mean that you don't feel favorably toward that group. You would rate the person at the 50 degree mark if you don't feel particularly warm or cold toward the group.

Please use the feeling thermometer to indicate your feeling toward the following groups.

What about the $OUTPARTY?

[HORIZONTAL SCALE 0–100]

What about the $INPARTY?

[HORIZONTAL SCALE 0–100]

Now we'd like to know more about what you think about $OUTPARTY.[1] Below, we've given a list of words that some people might use to describe them. For each item, please indicate how well you think it applies to $OUT-PARTY: not at all well, not too well, somewhat well, very well, or extremely well.

Grid Items:
A. Patriotic
B. Intelligent
C. Honest
D. Open-minded
E. Generous
F. Hypocritical
G. Selfish
H. Mean

Response Options:
1. Not at all well
2. Not too well
3. Somewhat well
4. Very well
5. Extremely well

How much of the time do you think you can trust $OUTPARTY to do what is right for the country?

1. Almost never
2. Once in a while
3. About half the time
4. Most of the time
5. Almost always

Please indicate whether you agree or disagree with these items using the scale provided.

The religion of Islam supports acts of violence.

1. Strongly agree
2. Somewhat agree
3. Neither agree nor disagree
4. Somewhat disagree
5. Strongly disagree

The religion of Islam is Anti-American.

1. Strongly agree
2. Somewhat agree
3. Neither agree nor disagree
4. Somewhat disagree
5. Strongly disagree

Sports Fandom Experiment (chapter 3)

Generally speaking, I think of myself as:

1. Democrat
2. Independent
3. Republican

[If Democrat/Republican:]
Would you call yourself a strong $PARTY or a not so strong $PARTY?

1. Strong $PARTY
2. Not so strong $PARTY

[If Independent:]
Do you think of yourself as closer to the Democratic Party or the Republican Party?

1. Closer to the Democratic Party
2. Closer to the Republican Party

Which of the following teams is your favorite professional football team?
[Respondents see a list of all NFL teams]
How important is being a $TEAM fan to you?

1. Extremely important
2. Very important
3. Somewhat important
4. Not too important
5. Not at all important

How well does the term "$TEAM fan" describe you?

1. Extremely well
2. Very well
3. Somewhat well
4. Not too well
5. Not at all well

To what extent do you see yourself as a typical $TEAM fan?

1. A great deal
2. A fair amount
3. Somewhat

4. Not too much
5. Not at all

When talking about $TEAM fans, how often do you say "we" instead of "they"?

1. Always
2. Most of the time
3. Sometimes
4. Not too often
5. Never

You are a $TEAM fan. Why is being a fan of the $TEAM important to you? Please take a moment and write your answer in the box below. Please explain your reasoning, as we want to explain to people who are not sports fans why fans think rooting for their team is important. To give you time to think, the "next screen" button will not appear for a few moments.

[Respondents are shown a brief text box]

How often do you go to the movies?

1. Very often
2. Somewhat often
3. Not too often
4. Not at all often

When you go to the movies, what types of films do you like to see? Please write your answer in the box below.

[Respondents are shown a brief text box]

Think about the next place you would like to go on vacation. Which of the following best describes that location?

1. A beach, lake, or island
2. A mountain
3. A theme or amusement park, such as Walt Disney World
4. A city, such as New York, Paris, or London
5. Somewhere else

Now we would like to get your feelings toward people you might meet on any [sic] everyday basis, and then we'll ask you to rate them on several different dimensions. Suppose you met someone who is a $AGE year old $RACE $GENDER. This person is also a [$INPARTY/$OUTPARTY/(Blank)] and a [$TEAM/(blank)] fan.[2]

We'd like you to rate your feelings towards this person using something we call the feeling thermometer. Ratings between 50 degrees and 100 degrees mean that you feel favorable and warm toward the person. Ratings between 0 degrees and 50 degrees mean that you don't feel favorable toward the person and that you don't care too much for that person. You would rate the person at the 50 degree mark if you don't feel particularly warm or cold toward the person.

How would you rate someone who was a $AGE year old $RACE $GENDER who is also a $INPARTY and a $TEAM fan?

[0–100 SLIDER]

Suppose you met someone who is a $AGE year old $RACE $GENDER. This person is also a $INPARTY and a $TEAM fan.

How much of the time do you think you can trust this person to do what is right for the country?

1. Almost always
2. Most of the time
3. About half the time
4. Once in a while
5. Almost never

Suppose you met someone who is a $AGE year old $RACE $GENDER. This person is also a $INPARTY and a $TEAM fan.

Below, we've given a list of words that some people might use to describe others. For each item, please indicate how well you think it applies to this person: not at all well; not too well; somewhat well; very well; or extremely well.

Grid Items:
I. Patriotic
J. Intelligent
K. Honest
L. Open-minded
M. Generous
N. Hypocritical
O. Selfish
P. Mean

Response Options:
1. Not at all well
2. Not too well
3. Somewhat well
4. Very well
5. Extremely well

Pew American Trends Data (chapter 4)

In politics today, do you consider yourself a:

1. Republican
2. Democrat
3. Independent
4. Something else

[Ask if Independent or Something Else:]
As of today do you lean more to . . .

1. The Republican Party
2. The Democratic Party

[Ask if Republican/Democrat:]
Do you identify with the [Republican/Democratic] Party . . .

1. Strongly
2. Not strongly

We'd like to get your feelings toward a number of groups in the US on a "feeling thermometer." A rating of zero degrees means you feel as cold and negative as possible. A rating of 100 degrees means you feel as warm and positive as possible. You would rate the group at 50 degrees if you don't feel particularly positive or negative toward the group.

How do you feel toward:

Republicans
Democrats
Hillary Clinton
Bernie Sanders
Ted Cruz
John Kasich
Donald Trump[3]

Overall, would you say the $OUTPARTY has . . .

1. A lot of good ideas
2. Some good ideas
3. A few good ideas
4. Almost no good ideas

AmeriSpeak Cross-Party Friendship Experiment (chapter 4, chapter 6)

Generally speaking, I think of myself as a:

1. Democrat
2. Republican
3. Independent

[IF D/R:]
Would you call yourself a strong $PARTY or a not very strong $PARTY?

1. Strong $PARTY
2. Not very strong $PARTY

[IF IND/OTHER:]
Would you think of yourself as closer to the Democratic Party or the Republican Party?

1. Closer to the Democratic Party
2. Closer to the Republican Party

[RANDOMLY ASSIGN SUBJECTS TO TREATMENT OR CONTROL.]
[IF CONTROL:]
How often do you go to the movies?

1. Very often
2. Somewhat often
3. Not too often
4. Not at all

When you go to the movies, what types of movies do you like to see, and why? Please explain briefly in the space below.

Think about the next place you would like to go on vacation. Which of these best describes that destination?

1. A beach, lake, or island
2. A mountain
3. A theme or amusement park, such as Walt Disney World
4. A city, such as New York or Paris
5. Somewhere else

[IF TREATMENT:]
Although you are a $PARTY, you likely know people who are $OUTPARTY. Think about one such $OUTPARTY that you like and respect a great deal. This

person could be a friend, relative, neighbor, coworker, or just someone that you know. Please explain why you feel this way about this person.

Please think about the answer carefully, and then write it in the space below in as much detail as you would like. To give you time to reflect on your answer, the "Continue" button will not appear for a few moments.

[MEDIUM TEXTBOX]

How often do you talk about politics with this person?

1. Very frequently
2. Somewhat frequently
3. Not too frequently
4. Not at all frequently

We'd like to get your feelings toward some groups or individuals who are in the news these days. Below, you'll see the name of a group next to a feeling thermometer. Ratings between 50 and 100 degrees mean that you feel favorably and warm toward that group; ratings between 0 and 50 degrees mean that you don't feel favorably toward that group. You would rate the person at the 50 degree mark if you don't feel particularly warm or cold toward the group.

Please use the feeling thermometer to indicate your feeling toward the following groups.

What about the $OUTPARTY?

[HORIZONTAL SCALE 0–100]

What about the $INPARTY?

[HORIZONTAL SCALE 0–100]

In general, how much common ground is there between Democrats and Republicans?

1. A great deal
2. A fair amount
3. Some
4. Not too much
5. None at all

How often do you think Democrats and Republicans agree on the issues of the day?

1. All the time
2. Most of the time
3. Sometimes
4. Not too often
5. Never

Now we'd like to know more about what you think about $OUTPARTY. Below, we've given a list of words that some people might use to describe them. For each item, please indicate how well you think it applies to $OUTPARTY: not at all well, not too well, somewhat well, very well, or extremely well.

Grid Items:
Q. Patriotic
R. Intelligent
S. Honest
T. Open-minded
U. Generous
V. Hypocritical
W. Selfish
X. Mean

Response Options:
11. Not at all well
12. Not too well
13. Somewhat well
14. Very well
15. Extremely well

How much of the time do you think you can trust $OUTPARTY to do what is right for the country?

6. Almost never
7. Once in a while
8. About half the time
9. Most of the time
10. Almost always

Many cities are discussing proposals that would channel urban growth toward cities' centers. They would do this by prohibiting development outside of a growth boundary. Democrats typically favor these proposals to limit urban development, and Republicans typically oppose them. What do you think: do you support or oppose creating boundaries that limit urban growth?

1. Strongly support boundaries to urban development (i.e., clear limits to urban development)
2. Mildly support boundaries to urban development
3. Neither oppose nor favor boundaries to urban development
4. Mildly oppose boundaries to urban development
5. Strongly oppose boundaries to urban development (i.e., no limits to urban development)

A class-action lawsuit is when a group of people come together to sue a company for a faulty product or an unfair policy. Congress has recently considered legislation that would limit class-action lawsuits, with Republicans supporting such limits on class-action lawsuits and Democrats opposing them. What do you think: do you support or oppose limiting class-action lawsuits?

1. Strongly support limits on class-action lawsuits
2. Mildly support limits on class-action lawsuits
3. Neither oppose nor favor limits on class-action lawsuits
4. Mildly oppose limits on class-action lawsuits
5. Strongly oppose limits on class-action lawsuits

Bovitz Cross-Party Friendship Experiment (chapter 4, chapter 6)

Generally speaking, I think of myself as a:

1. Democrat
2. Republican
3. Independent

[IF DEMOCRAT/REPUBLICAN:]
Would you call yourself a strong $PARTY or a not very strong $PARTY?

1. Strong $PARTY
2. Not very strong $PARTY

[IF INDEPENDENT OR IS SKIPPED:]
Would you think of yourself as closer to the Democratic Party or the Republican Party?

1. Closer to the Democratic Party
2. Closer to the Republican Party

[RANDOMIZE SUBJECTS INTO $T1 = 0$ OR $T1 = 1$. IF $T1 = 0$, SHOW:]
How often do you go to the movies?

5. Very often
6. Somewhat often
7. Not too often
8. Not at all

When you go to the movies, what types of movies do you like to see, and why? Please think about the answer carefully, and then write it in the space below in as much detail as you would like. To give you time to reflect on your answer, the "Continue" button will not appear for a few moments.

[MEDIUM TEXTBOX]

Think about the next place you would like to go on vacation. Which of these best describes that destination?

6. A beach, lake, or island
7. A mountain
8. A theme or amusement park, such as Walt Disney World
9. A city, such as New York or Paris
10. Somewhere else

[IF T1 = 1, SHOW:]

Although you are $PARTY, you likely know people who are $OTHER-PARTY. Think about one such $OTHERPARTY that you like and respect a great deal. This person could be a friend, relative, neighbor, coworker, or just someone that you know. Please explain why you feel this way about this person.

Please think about the answer carefully, and then write it in the space below in as much detail as you would like. To give you time to reflect on your answer, the "Continue" button will not appear for a few moments.

[MEDIUM TEXTBOX]

Which of the following best describes the person you just wrote about?

1. Friend
2. Family member
3. Coworker
4. Neighbor
5. Someone else [text box for explanation]

How close are you to that person?

1. Extremely close
2. Very close
3. Somewhat close
4. Not too close
5. Not at all close

[ALL SUBJECTS ANSWER THE FOLLOWING QUESTIONS:]
[Show on screen:]

Now we'd like to ask for your opinion about a few issues that have recently been in the news. There are no right or wrong answers, we simply want to know what you think.

[New screen:]

A class-action lawsuit is when a group of people come together to sue a company for a faulty product or an unfair policy. Congress has recently considered legislation that would limit class-action lawsuits, with Republicans supporting such limits on class-action suits and Democrats opposing them. What do you think: do you support or oppose limiting class-action lawsuits?

1. Strongly support limits on class-action lawsuits
2. Somewhat support limits on class-action lawsuits
3. Neither oppose nor favor limits on class-action lawsuits
4. Somewhat oppose limits on class-action lawsuits
5. Strongly oppose limits on class-action lawsuits

Congress has recently considered legislation to allow more citizens to vote by mail, rather than needing to visit a polling place on Election Day to cast their ballot, with Democrats supporting this legislation and Republicans opposing it. What do you think: do you support or oppose allowing more citizens to vote by mail?

1. Strongly support allowing more citizens to vote by mail
2. Somewhat support allowing more citizens to vote by mail
3. Neither support nor oppose allowing more citizens to vote by mail
4. Somewhat oppose allowing more citizens to vote by mail
5. Strongly oppose allowing more citizens to vote by mail

Congress has recently considered legislation to expand the use of nuclear power plants to generate electricity, with Republicans supporting this and Democrats opposing it. What do you think: do you support or oppose expanding the use of nuclear power plants to generate electricity?

1. Strongly support expanding the use of nuclear power plants to generate electricity
2. Somewhat support expanding the use of nuclear power plants to generate electricity
3. Neither support nor oppose expanding the use of nuclear power plants to generate electricity
4. Somewhat oppose expanding the use of nuclear power plants to generate electricity
5. Strongly oppose expanding the use of nuclear power plants to generate electricity

Now we'd like to get your feelings toward some groups or individuals who are in the news these days. Below, you'll see the name of a group next to a feeling thermometer. Ratings between 50 and 100 degrees mean that you feel favorably and warm toward that group; ratings between 0 and 50 degrees mean that you don't feel favorably toward that group. You would rate the person at the 50 degree mark if you don't feel particularly warm or cold toward the group.

What about the $OUTPARTY?

[SLIDER 0–100]

What about the $INPARTY?

[SLIDER 0–100]

How much of the time do you think you can trust the $OUTPARTY Party to do what is right for the country?

1. Almost never
2. Once in a while
3. About half the time
4. Most of the time
5. Almost always

You might have some favorable thoughts or feelings about the $OUTPARTY Party. Or you might have unfavorable thoughts or feelings about the $OUTPARTY Party. Or you might have some of each. We would like to ask you first about any thoughts or feelings you might have about the $OUTPARTY Party. Then, in a moment, we'll ask you some separate questions about any unfavorable thoughts or feelings you might have.

First, do you have any favorable thoughts or feelings about the $OUTPARTY Party?

1. Yes
2. No

[IF YES:]

How favorable are your favorable thoughts or feelings about the $OUTPARTY Party?

1. Extremely favorable
2. Very favorable
3. Moderately favorable
4. Slightly favorable

Do you have any unfavorable thoughts or feelings about the $OUTPARTY Party?

1. Yes
2. No

[IF YES:]

How unfavorable are your unfavorable thoughts or feelings about the $OUTPARTY Party?

1. Extremely unfavorable
2. Very unfavorable
3. Moderately unfavorable
4. Slightly unfavorable

You might have some favorable thoughts or feelings about the $INPARTY Party. Or you might have unfavorable thoughts or feelings about the $IN-PARTY Party. Or you might have some of each. We would like to ask you first about any thoughts or feelings you might have about the $INPARTY Party. Then, in a moment, we'll ask you some separate questions about any unfavorable thoughts or feelings you might have.

First, do you have any favorable thoughts or feelings about the $INPARTY Party?

1. Yes
2. No

[IF YES:]
How favorable are your favorable thoughts or feelings about the $IN-PARTY Party?

1. Extremely favorable
2. Very favorable
3. Moderately favorable
4. Slightly favorable

Do you have any unfavorable thoughts or feelings about the $INPARTY Party?

1. Yes
2. No

[IF YES:]
How unfavorable are your unfavorable thoughts or feelings about the $INPARTY Party?

1. Extremely unfavorable
2. Very unfavorable
3. Moderately unfavorable
4. Slightly unfavorable

Cross-Party Discussion Experiment (chapter 5)

Generally speaking, which of the options below best describes your partisan identification?

1. Strong Democrat
2. Weak Democrat
3. Leaning Democrat
4. Independent
5. Leaning Republican
6. Weak Republican
7. Strong Republican

Which point on this scale best describes your political views?

1. Very liberal
2. Mostly liberal
3. Somewhat liberal
4. Moderate
5. Somewhat conservative
6. Mostly conservative
7. Very conservative

In general, how interested are you in politics?

1. Not at all interested
2. Not too interested
3. Somewhat interested
4. Very interested
5. Extremely interested

What is the highest level of education you have completed?

1. Less than high school
2. High school graduate
3. Some college
4. 4-year college degree
5. Advanced degree

What is your estimate of your family's annual household income (before taxes)?

1. Less than $30,000
2. $30,000–$69,000

3. $70,000–$99,999
4. $100,000–$200,000
5. More than $200,000

Which of the following do you consider to be your primary racial or ethnic group?

1. White
2. African-American
3. Asian-American
4. Hispanic
5. Native American
6. Other

What is your age?

1. 18–24
2. 25–34
3. 35–50
4. 51–65
5. Over 65

Are you male or female?

1. Male
2. Female

How often do you participate in political activities (e.g., working on a campaign, attending a rally)?

1. Never
2.
3.
4. A few times a year
5.
6.
7. Weekly

About how many days a week, on average, do you talk about politics with your family and/or friends?

1. Never
2. 1 day a week
3. 2 days a week
4. 3 days a week
5. 4 days a week
6. 5 days a week

7. 6 days a week
8. Every day

For the text of the news articles subjects read, or the full instructions, please see Levendusky and Stecula (2021).

POST-TEST ITEMS:

We'd like to get your feelings toward some of our political leaders and other groups who are in the news these days. We'll ask you to do that using a 0 to 100 scale that we call a feeling thermometer. Ratings between 50 degrees and 100 degrees mean that you feel favorable and warm toward the person. Ratings between 0 degrees and 50 degrees mean that you don't feel favorable toward the person and that you don't care too much for that person. You would rate the person at the 50 degree mark if you don't feel particularly warm or cold toward the person. Using that 0 to 100 scale, how would you rate each of the following groups or people below?

[SHOW A SLIDER FOR EACH GROUP BELOW:]

The Democratic Party
The Republican Party

How comfortable are you having a political discussion with a $OUTPARTY?

1. Extremely comfortable
2. Somewhat comfortable
3. Not too comfortable
4. Not at all comfortable

How comfortable are you having neighbors on your street who are $OUTPARTY?

1. Extremely comfortable
2. Somewhat comfortable
3. Not too comfortable
4. Not at all comfortable

How comfortable are you having close personal friends who are $OUTPARTY?

1. Extremely comfortable
2. Somewhat comfortable
3. Not too comfortable
4. Not at all comfortable

Suppose one of your children was getting married. How would you feel if he or she married a $OUTPARTY?

1. Extremely upset
2. Somewhat upset
3. Not too upset
4. Not at all upset

How much of the time do you think you can trust the $OUTPARTY to do what is right for the country?

1. Almost never
2. Once in a while
3. About half the time
4. Most of the time
5. Almost always

Below, we've given a list of words that some people might use to describe individuals. For each item, please indicate how well you think it applies to $OUTPARTY: extremely well, very well, somewhat well, not too well, or not at all well.

Grid Items:
A. Patriotic
B. Intelligent
C. Honest
D. Open-minded
E. Generous
F. Hypocritical
G. Selfish
H. Mean

Response Options:
1. Extremely well
2. Very well
3. Somewhat well
4. Not too well
5. Not at all well

Notes

Chapter One

1. Unsurprisingly, core values such as egalitarianism and moral traditionalism—which are closely linked to issue positions (Jacoby 2006)—also shape affective polarization (Enders and Lupton 2021).

2. Consistent with this assertion, ratings of Biden and Trump in 2020 look more like ratings of Obama and Romney in 2012 than they do like ratings of Clinton and Trump in 2016 (restricting 2012 and 2016 to online respondents). Indeed, Republicans rate Trump (on average) 14 degrees more warmly in 2020 than they did in 2016. This suggests that Clinton and Trump's unique unpopularity in 2016 did drag down same-party feeling thermometer ratings in 2016, but this represents more of an aberration than a shift in the longer-term trend.

3. The reader might wonder if there are partisan differences in these patterns. While there are differences in the levels (on balance, Republicans have liked their own party less and the other party more), the patterns over time are the same: stability for same-party ratings, a decline for other-party ratings.

4. While on balance affective polarization has some negative effects, there are some positive benefits to it, most notably an increase in correct voting (Pierce and Lau 2019).

5. Subsequent debates over masking and vaccines only reinforce this point.

6. Some might wonder why I do not include support for partisan violence in this list (Kalmoe and Mason 2022). While that is an important topic, it is only modestly related to animosity; indeed, as Uscinski et al. (2021) explain, such attitudes are at least as much about antiestablishment sentiments as they are about partisan animus (see also Annenberg IOD Collaborative 2023).

7. The survey also asks about the importance of religious identity, and unsurprisingly, there is a large and statistically significant difference between the parties here. But given the religious/religiosity sorting that has taken place in recent years (Margolis 2018; Campbell, Layman, and Green 2020), this is hardly noteworthy.

8. For the cross-tabs from the survey, see https://www.rd.com/wp-content/uploads/2020/06/Readers-Digest_More-in-Common-American-Unity-Survey.pdf.

9. For the cross-tabs from the Hidden Common Ground project, see https://www.publicagenda.org/wp-content/uploads/2020/09/HCG-Economic-Opportunity-Inequality.pdf.

Chapter Two

1. There are a number of additional psychological dispositions that also affect individuals' level of affective polarization. These include, but are not limited to, their level of authoritarianism (Hetherington and Weiler 2009; Luttig 2017; Johnston 2018), their propensity to moralize (Garrett and Bankert 2020), their level of self-monitoring (Weber and Klar 2019), their need for affect and/or need for cognition (Arceneaux and Vander Wielen 2017), their intellectual humility (Bowes et al. 2020), and so forth. While these individual-level patterns are interesting, they are orthogonal to my purpose here, though an interesting future project would be to consider how shifting these traits could lower levels of partisan animus. For one example of how to use these sorts of psychological correlations to reduce partisan animosity, see Wojcieszak, Winter, and Yu (2020).

2. Individuals engage in this sort of reasoning because keeping a differential between the liked in-group and the disliked out-group helps to maintain positive self-image and self-esteem (Hogg and Abrams 1988, see esp. chapter 4).

3. A related puzzle is why partisan animosity is rooted in out-group animus, rather than in-group favoritism, which is the typical mechanism driving this sort of social identity–driven animosity (Brewer 1999). This is a fascinating question, but it is less relevant to the discussion here, though this broader question deserves more careful study.

4. By elites, I mean elected officials who have control over policy—most notably, presidents and members of Congress. There is clear evidence that these individuals have polarized ideologically in recent decades (McCarty 2019). Similarly, there is also clear evidence that partisan activists have polarized (Layman et al. 2010). These groups sit in contrast to the mass public, where there is much less evidence showing ideological polarization (Fiorina 2017).

5. The quote comes from Thomas Dewey, the former New York governor and 1944 Republican Party presidential nominee, as quoted in Klein (2020, 5).

6. In addition, the parties in Congress have become uncivil to one another over time. Both elite incivility and elite ideological divergence fuel affective polarization (Skytte 2021).

7. Further, as Hall (2019) notes, moderate candidates—even though they have an electoral edge—are less likely to run today than they were in the past. This further polarizes elites, as moderate candidates are not even running for office, often leaving voters with a choice between two extremist candidates (see also Thomsen 2017). Likewise, as Drutman (2020) notes, the winner-take-all nature of our elections also serves to exacerbate these trends.

8. Relatedly, the parties now are divided not just on economic issues, but on a whole host of economic, cultural, and racial issues (Layman and Carsey 2002; Hare forthcoming). The rise of these non-economic dimensions—where compromise is more difficult—further fuels elite polarization and animosity (Hetherington and Weiler 2009).

9. In reality, most social networks are more heterogeneous with respect to partisanship than we realize, but because of projection (Huckfeldt and Sprague 1987), as well as social conformity (Cowan and Baldassarri 2018), most people exaggerate the degree of partisan similarity. This distinction has important implications, which I explain later in the chapter.

10. Unsurprisingly, those who are more active on social media say it is a way for them to express their opinions (McClain et al. 2021): 77 percent of highly active Twitter users say that they use Twitter as a way to express their opinions, versus only 29 percent of low activity Twitter users. But as Bail (2021) shows, because people are selective about what they show online, the opinions they express are designed to present a slanted—and more extreme—version of their political selves.

11. Of course, there are still other techniques scholars have used to reduce animosity. For example, scholars might prime open-mindedness (Wojcieszak, Winter, and Yu 2020) or intellectual humility (Bowes et al. 2020; Stanley, Sinclair, and Seli 2020), or have respondents read about warm interpersonal relationships between politicians (Huddy and Yair 2021). For an overview of various tactics that have been used, see Hartman et al. (2022).

12. This is not the first application of this model to political science: Kam and Ramos (2008) use it to study presidential approval, and Transue (2007) uses it to study racial tolerance. Reid (2012) uses a similar argument (though a slightly different theoretical model) to show effects on hostile media bias. Here, I extend these arguments by using it to study affective polarization.

13. Another possible mechanism is that that interacting with an out-party friend with whom you are close makes you think of the other party as part of your in-group via self-expansion theory (Page-Gould et al. 2010; Aron, Aron, and Smollan 1992). Differentiating among these exact mechanisms is not per se the goal here, though in chapter 4, when I analyze these data, I talk about the extent to which the data are consistent with different potential theoretical accounts.

14. Perhaps not surprisingly, while cross-party marriages are rare (only 6 percent of marriages cross party lines), those individuals are less affectively polarized than other Americans (Fisk and Fraga 2020).

15. Indeed, perspective-getting works both ways: the listener benefits from hearing the new perspective, and the speaker benefits by feeling like they are being heard by someone from the other side of the political divide (Bruneau and Saxe 2012).

16. Allport's (1954) text argued that these conditions were essential for contact to reduce between-group animus. Later studies, however, argue that they are not required, but simply make such contact more effective (Pettigrew and Tropp 2006; though see Paluck, Green, and Green 2019).

17. Gerber and Green (2002) introduce the idea of "downstream" benefits of experimentation: the idea that experimental interventions can have indirect effects on other outcomes of interest beyond the main dependent variables (see also Klar 2014). Here, I use it in this sense: while the main focus of the study is on reducing affective polarization, the treatments used to do so will also affect other attitudes.

18. The theoretical logic here assumes that the parties signal opposite preferences from one another: Democrats are pro-choice, Republicans are pro-life; Democrats want to increase fuel economy standards, Republicans want to lower them; etc. Given the contemporary logic of American politics, this is often, but not always, the case. What the logic of the argument predicts in other cases, such as when the cue is more one-sided (i.e., only one party is really talking about an issue), is less clear; I leave that topic for future research.

19. While the 1959 volume is the classic statement of the argument, Bogardus's original work was done in the 1920s; see Wark and Galliher (2007).

20. An example of a treatment that is designed to reduce same-party support would be to ask respondents to list several things they did not like about their own party (see, e.g., Klar 2014).

Chapter Three

1. This figure excluded the roughly 7 percent of subjects who wrote gibberish (random nonsense text strings) or otherwise did not respond to the prompt (writing "nice survey," "this is good," etc.), though I include these respondents in the subsequent analyses in this chapter.

2. Whether or not the American Dream is *actually* achievable (Chetty et al. 2016), most Americans continue to believe in it (Younis 2019).

3. To ensure that subjects in the treatment condition had, in fact, reported higher levels of American identity, the study contained a manipulation check battery asking subjects to report how strongly they identified as Americans, using the items from Huddy, Mason, and Aarøe 2015 (i.e., how well does the term "American" describe you, when you talk about Americans do you use "we" rather than "they," etc.). The treatment strengthened American identity: on a 1 (low) to 5 (high) scale, American identity grew from 4.3 in the control condition to 4.4 in the treatment condition, a statistically significant increase ($p < 0.01$).

4. The limitation, of course, is that perhaps I simply do not have large enough sample sizes to detect such heterogeneity, as the experiments were designed to have enough power to detect the main effects, rather than interactive effects. I leave exploring this sort of heterogeneity for future studies.

5. In an earlier publication (Levendusky 2018a), I note that the effects of the American identity prime are much stronger for positive traits (like intelligent) than for negative traits (like mean), but I could not offer a theoretical explanation as to why. Mullinix and Lythgoe (forthcoming) show that because of our innate negativity bias, it is easier to manipulate positive trait ratings than negative ones, which may well explain the gap. This is an area ripe for future exploration.

6. Brandt and Turner-Zwinkels (2020) attempted to replicate this effect in 2019, and found a null effect. But their study suffers from a number of significant limitations, most notably being dramatically under-powered, as well as using a single item from the social distance scale, which, as Druckman and Levendusky (2019) show, is a measure of affective polarization distinct from those I use here. Further, to celebrate the day, President Trump held a large military parade, which potentially changed the meaning of the day for respondents in that year.

7. I thank Omer Yair for suggesting this analysis.

8. In a similar vein, Depetris-Chauvin, Durante, and Campante (2020) show that during international competition, national football team wins increase national identity and reduce ethnic violence in sub-Saharan Africa.

9. I used the same stimulus to prime American national identity, but I used a new control group article. When I had initially done the original experiments, I used an article on a New Mexico cat library that allowed office workers to borrow a kitten to play with in their office (Mackie 2015). But given the COVID-19 pandemic, and the fact that people were (by and large) not working in their offices in fall 2020 when I conducted the experiment, I thought this might come across as very strange. Given this, I substituted an article on the end of the popular reality TV show, *Keeping Up with the Kardashians* (Kirkpatrick 2020).

10. https://news.gallup.com/poll/116677/presidential-approval-ratings-gallup-historical-statistics-trends.aspx.

11. One concern with using a prime that asks subjects to remember the time around 9/11 would be that it would prime Islamophobia, which increased in the wake of the attacks (Panagopoulos 2006). To test for this, I included a set of items from the Islamophobia scale developed by Lee et al. (2009). I found no detectable increase in Islamophobia as a result of either treatment in the sample as a whole, or in either party or racial group.

12. That is, $H_0: \beta_{american} = \beta_{9/11}$.

13. That is, testing the null hypothesis: $H_0: \beta_{treat} + \beta_{treat^*dem} = 0$, or the equivalent one for non-white respondents.

14. There is also evidence that sports fandom might also be able to reduce prejudice; see Alrababa'h et al. (2021).

15. To identify professional football fans, at the end of an earlier study I included a set of questions measuring team fandom. I focused on football fans because professional football is—by far—the most popular sport in the US (Norman 2018).

16. I also re-estimated these models interacting the treatment conditions with strength of fandom, on the expectation that those who were more attached to their team might display larger effects. The effects of this interaction were quite muted, but this may well reflect the fact that I only included those who were already sports fans in the sample, so there was limited variation in strength of fandom in my sample.

17. Further, invoking Americanness can also lead to more animosity toward non-Americans (Wojcieszak and Garrett 2018), though it may be possible to temper this by reminding subjects of America's legacy of accepting immigrants (Williamson et al. 2021).

Chapter Four

1. The data used here are waves 15 and 16 of Pew's American Trends Panel. Full question wording for all items can be found in the data appendix.

2. Because I count partisan leaners as partisans, I increase the fraction of the public that has cross-party friendships relative to the Pew Research Center (2016) report, which counts only strong and weak partisans as partisans in its analysis. This coding choice does not change the substantive conclusions that I draw from this analysis, as Pew Research Center (2016) also shows that those with cross-party friendships report lower levels of partisan animus.

3. Following Pew Research Center (2016), I analyze the effect of cross-party friendships on feeling thermometer ratings of the other party. This is a slightly odd choice, however, in that the feeling thermometer ratings were asked in wave 15, while the cross-party friendship item was included in wave 16, approximately one month later. Because social networks are stable over a one-month period, this should not pose an analytical problem. As a robustness check, I also examined the effect of cross-party friendships on candidate feeling thermometers, since wave 16 included feeling thermometer ratings of Bernie Sanders, Hillary Clinton, John Kasich, Ted Cruz, and Donald Trump, the candidates then seeking their party's 2016 nomination. The results of this candidate-centered analysis are substantively identical to the party analysis I present here; see the appendix to this chapter for the results.

4. Given this finding, I re-analyzed the Pew data to see if there were heterogeneous treatment effects: perhaps the effects of cross-party friendship are weaker for strong partisans or ideologues. This analysis, however, yielded null results, as even for this sub-population the more cross-party friendships respondents had, the less affectively polarized they were (though again, all of the usual treatment vs. selection caveats apply, as well as concerns about a lack of statistical power to detect this sort of heterogeneity). Likewise, given concerns about racial homophily in friendship networks, I also searched for heterogeneous effects by race, given the strong correlation between race and partisanship in America (White and Laird 2020). While non-White Americans are less likely to have cross-party friends, there is no evidence of heterogeneous treatment effects.

5. Here, slightly more respondents—approximately 85 percent—gave a valid response to the prompt, suggesting that the 81 percent figure in the AmeriSpeak study is not an aberration.

6. Though one respondent did name the singer—and onetime presidential candidate—Kanye West.

7. The only difference is that here I used the original battery from Garrett et al. (2014), which used "patriotic" rather than "American." Otherwise, the batteries are identical.

8. The discussion in this chapter centers a cognitive account of these effects: cross-party friendship changes how individuals see the other party. An alternative mechanism is that the treatment changes the respondent's motivation in answering the question. By asking about cross-party friendships, I might disrupt a type of partisan cheerleading: normally, people will see the feeling thermometer and other types of affective polarization measures as an opportunity to engage in expressive responding (i.e., signaling their commitment to their party by saying something negative about the other party). This is, of course, possible. But this cannot fully explain these effects because of the findings I presented earlier in the Pew data. There, I find that those who have more cross-party friendships have lower levels of out-party animus. If the story were simply motivational, then the number of friends should not matter (since it is just about changing people's propensity to engage in partisan cheerleading). This suggests that the effects are more likely to be due to the fact that people with more cross-party friends think about the party differently (i.e., they have more information at hand that disconfirms their negative view of the other side). In the end, one cannot really separate out these effects fully, but the data suggest that this is not simply a story about cheerleading. I thank a reviewer for this insightful comment.

9. This effect—where evaluations of one person change evaluations of an entire group—is known as an assimilation effect (i.e., you assimilate your positive views of the friend into the assessment of the larger group). This occurs in a number of other contexts as well (see, e.g., Henderson-King and Nisbett 1996; Hamill, Wilson, and Nisbett 1980). Of course, not all situations generate assimilation effects; some generate contrast effects (when one does not generalize from the individual to the group; see Schwarz and Bless 1992). The classic exemplar of this is someone who claims that they cannot be a racist because they have a Black friend; Herschel Walker provided such an illustration for Donald Trump at the 2020 Republican National Convention. So why does a cross-racial friend generate a contrast effect, but a cross-party friend an assimilation effect? Fully fleshing out this distinction is beyond the scope of this study, but I suspect it partially depends on the durability of these stereotypes, as well as the conversations that occur in the different types of friendships. Most people have stereotypes of the other party, but they are rather fluid, as my experiments illustrate. In contrast, their views of racial minorities are more fixed, due in large part to prejudice. The stereotype disconfirming evidence of an out-party friend therefore confronts a lower barrier to attitude change than for a cross-racial friend. Indeed, because of the durability of prejudice, and the difference in social standing between White and Black Americans, cross-racial friendships often do not reduce racial animus (Jackman and Crane 1986). Further, to the extent that cross-racial friendships do not discuss the problems of racism, and the lived experiences of Black Americans encountering this racism, they are unlikely to break down this prejudice. I thank an anonymous reviewer for raising this point.

Chapter Five

1. There are a number of thoughtful critiques of the structure of political discussion and deliberation, paying special attention to the role of inequalities of power due to factors like race and gender (e.g., Lupia and Norton 2017; Karpowitz and Mendelberg 2014). But these studies ultimately want to mitigate such inequality, rather than do away with political discussion altogether.

2. In the experiment, subjects were also assigned to a third condition of homogeneous political discussion (i.e., discussion with others from only their own party). The goal of that condition was to see if such discussions heightened affective polarization, consistent with arguments

that homogeneous discussions prime social identity (Isenberg 1986). Because this is less relevant for my purposes here, I omit those subjects from the discussion in this chapter. Full results are in Levendusky and Stecula (2021), but I note that such partisan homogeneous discussion had only very weak effects, largely because subjects came into the study quite affectively polarized (and so there was almost certainly a ceiling effect).

3. The sample is 63% white, 55% female, 26% student-aged, 26% very interested in politics, 47% with a college degree, and 29% making at least $100,000 per year. This skew toward higher political interest, income, and education is typical of such non-random samples (i.e., Druckman, Levendusky, and McClain 2018).

4. Due to variation in the number of subjects who came to a particular session, and the need to form discussion groups with partisan balance, not all groups have exactly 4 subjects. All heterogeneous discussion groups have either 4 or 6 subjects, again with an equal number of Democrats and Republicans in each group—4-person groups have 2 Democrats and 2 Republicans, and 6-person groups have 3 Democrats and 3 Republicans (as in the other experiments in the book, partisan leaners are treated as partisans). Control groups vary between 3 and 7 subjects per group, and we found no heterogeneous treatment effects based on group size (see the appendix to Levendusky and Stecula 2021).

5. We conducted our study in 28 experimental sessions over a nine-month period. Because there could be differences across sessions (given who showed up, timing effects, etc.), I include fixed effects for sessions here to control for such differences (see Gerber and Green 2012). Including or excluding them has no effect on the substantive results.

6. Here, I analyzed the social distance items as an index, since they all scale together ($\alpha = 0.8$). Analyzing the items separately produced the same substantive results.

7. In chapter 3, I also used another common identity—shared sports team fandom—to examine whether other identities could reduce affective polarization. But because the target of evaluation is different in that experiment—a particular person, rather than the other party—it does not make sense to compare it to the other results here.

8. Another possibility is that the heterogeneous discussion condition article helped to prime these norms as well, as it emphasized areas of consensus and common ground between the parties.

Chapter Six

1. In Levendusky and Stecula (2021), using the discussion data examined in chapter 5, we argue that perception of common ground is a mechanism driving those effects, rather than a downstream consequence. Ultimately, differentiating these two pathways (treatment → common ground → lessened animus vs. treatment → lessened animus → common ground) is not possible without additional, more complicated data. And indeed, as I argued in chapter 2, perceived polarization is likely both a cause and a consequence of partisan animosity.

2. Some subjects were also randomly assigned to be asked about whether we should expand concealed carry laws, but there was an error in how that item was administered to respondents, so I drop it from the analysis here. So for some respondents, I have their opinion only on one item (the class action lawsuit item), not two. Because this is random, it reduces my power, but otherwise does not affect the experiment.

3. For the Bovitz data, in the control condition, the figures are 24% adopt the other party's position, 22% adopt the scale midpoint, and 54% adopt their party's position. In the treatment condition, the figures are 23%, 26%, and 50%.

4. All subjects were asked about the other party first, and then completed the battery about their own party second.

5. To use the language of Lavine, Johnston, and Steenbergen (2012), the treatment increases identity-conflicting responses, ones that cut against the norm (driven by the greater number of positive thoughts about the other party).

Chapter Seven

1. Consistent with this finding, in the American identity experiment I conducted in 2020 I included a short battery to measure out-party spite, building on the work on Moore-Berg et al. (2020). I wanted to test whether lowering out-party animus lowered spite, but it did not. Of course, interpreting this null effect is complicated by the fact that the treatment only lowered animus among Republican/White subjects (see chapter 3), but even looking only at these groups, I find no effects.

2. One might ask then why we do not know most people's partisanship, and why we might often misperceive it. The reason is relatively straightforward: most people do not begin conversations by talking about their partisanship, in part because they think it will cause trouble (Cowan and Baldassarri 2018). Instead, they try to make a good impression by discussing other topics, as politics is a topic most people would rather avoid (Klar and Krupnikov 2016; Krupnikov and Ryan 2022).

3. The essays in Persily (2015) highlight just how difficult it will be to reduce animosity at the elite level, as the book offers few workable solutions to reduce animus (reflecting the fact that few of them likely exist). Indeed, the only published mechanism for reducing animosity by focusing on elite politics comes from Huddy and Yair (2021), who show that highlighting warm personal relationships between the party leaders (Schumer and McConnell in the Senate) reduces animus.

4. Partnering with these sorts of groups will also be vital to testing the types of interventions in the "real world" that I discuss here. Of course, that brings with it a separate set of challenges centered around the different needs of researchers and practitioners (for more discussion of the challenges of scaling such efforts, see Al-Ubaydli et al. 2021).

5. This might also help individuals learn to frame their arguments in ways that are more receptive to the other side (Feinberg and Willer 2019).

6. Further, those who are the least civil are simply more visible online: you can only shout at someone in person if you are physically in the same space, but shout on Facebook and the whole world can hear you. So even if they are few in number, they *seem* more prevalent online (see Bor and Bang-Peterson 2022). A small subset of trolls are responsible for most attacks online on Reddit (Kumar et al. 2018), highlighting that small numbers of people are the ones doing much of the damage in our online spaces.

7. Allcott, Braghieri et al. (2020) show that when people are paid to deactivate their Facebook accounts, partisan animus falls, but so too does factual political knowledge. This suggests a tough trade-off with efforts to limit the polarizing effects of social media, since doing so may also limit political knowledge.

8. For an empirical effort to measure listening in the context of difficult political conversations, see Eveland et al. (2020).

9. I say the best of the founding ideals because, as Smith (1997) and others note, many in the founding era—and subsequent periods—saw racial and gender discrimination as American "ideals."

10. This is likely why intellectual humility helps to lessen animus (Bowes et al. 2020). Realizing what we don't know is an important step to helping foster a recognition that perhaps the other party might have some good ideas.

Appendix

1. Here and throughout the data appendix, I use $OUTPARTY to refer to those from the other party. So, for example, if a Democrat reads the item, they will be asked "Now we'd like to know more about what you think about Republicans."

2. All respondents see someone who is the same age range, gender, and race. The treatments consist of whether they are told the person's partisanship (same party, other party, not given) and their favorite sports team (same as respondent, or not given).

3. As I noted in the text, Pew asked the party feeling thermometer items in wave 15, and the remaining items in wave 16.

Bibliography

Abramowitz, Alan. 2010. *The Disappearing Center: Engaged Citizens, Polarization, and American Democracy*. New Haven, CT: Yale University Press.

Abramowitz, Alan, and Kyle Saunders. 2008. "Is Polarization a Myth?" *Journal of Politics* 70 (2): 542–55.

Abramowitz, Alan, and Steven Webster. 2016. "The Rise of Negative Partisanship and the Nationalization of U.S. Elections in the 21st Century." *Electoral Studies* 41 (March): 12–22.

———. 2018. "Negative Partisanship: Why Americans Dislike Parties but Behave Like Rabid Partisans." *Political Psychology: Advances in Political Psychology* 39 (S1): 119–35.

Achen, Christopher, and Larry Bartels. 2016. *Democracy for Realists: Why Elections Do Not Produce Responsive Government*. Princeton, NJ: Princeton University Press.

Ahler, Douglas, and Gaurav Sood. 2018. "The Parties in Our Heads: Misperceptions about Party Composition and their Consequences." *Journal of Politics* 80 (3): 964–81.

Allcott, Hunt, Levi Boxell, Jacob Conway, Matthew Gentzkow, Michael Thaler, and David Yang. 2020. "Polarization and Public Health: Partisan Differences in Social Distancing During the Coronavirus Pandemic." *Journal of Public Economics* 191 (November): 104254.

Allcott, Hunt, Luca Braghieri, Sarah Eichmeyer, and Matthew Gentzkow. 2020. "The Welfare Effects of Social Media." *American Economic Review* 110 (3): 629–76.

Allen, Danielle. 2014. *Our Declaration: A Reading of the Declaration of Independence in Defense of Equality*. New York: Liveright Publishing.

Allport, Gordon. 1954. *The Nature of Prejudice*. Reading, MA: Addison-Wesley Publishing.

Alrababa'h, Ala', William Marble, Salma Mousa, and Alexandra Siegel. 2021. "Can Exposure to Celebrities Reduce Prejudice? The Case of Mohamed Salah on Islamophobic Behaviors and Attitudes." *American Political Science Review* 115 (4): 1111–28.

Althaus, Scott. 1998. "Information Effects in Collective Preferences." *American Political Science Review* 92 (3): 545–58.

Al-Ubaydli, Omar, Min Sok Lee, John List, Claire Mackevicus, and Dana Suskind. 2021. "How Can Experiments Play a Greater Role in Public Policy? Twelve Proposals from an Economic Model of Scaling." *Behavioural Public Policy* 5 (1): 2–49.

Anderson, Ericka. 2020. "I'm a Conservative Christian Environmentalist. No, That's Not an Oxymoron." *New York Times*, 7 August.

Annenberg IOD Collaborative. 2023. *Democracy Amid Crises: Polarization, Pandemic, Protests, and Persuasion.* New York: Oxford University Press.

Ansolabehere, Stephen, Jonathan Rodden, and James M. Snyder. 2006. "Purple America." *Journal of Economic Perspectives* 20 (2): 97–118.

APSA Committee on Political Parties. 1950. "Toward a More Responsible Two-Party System: A Report of the Committee on Political Parties." *American Political Science Review* 44 (3, Supplement): 1–96.

Arceneaux, Kevin, and Ryan Vander Wielen. 2017. *Taming Intuition: How Reflection Minimizes Partisan Reasoning and Promotes Democratic Accountability.* New York: Cambridge University Press.

Armaly, Miles, and Adam Enders. 2021. "The Role of Affective Orientations in Promoting Perceived Polarization." *Political Science Research and Methods* 9 (3): 615–26.

Aron, Arthur, Elaine Aron, and Danny Smollan. 1992. "Inclusion of Other in the Self Scale and the Structure of Interpersonal Closeness." *Journal of Personality and Social Psychology* 63 (4): 596–612.

Aron, Arthur, Edward Melinat, Elaine Aron, Robert Vallone, and Renee Bator. 1997. "The Experimental Generation of Interpersonal Closeness: A Procedure and Some Preliminary Findings." *Personality and Social Psychology Bulletin* 23 (4): 363–77.

Associated Press. 2021. "Many Value Democratic Principles, but Few Think Democracy Is Working Well These Days." Press release, 8 February. https://bit.ly/3miW2nD, last accessed December 2021.

Azari, Julia. 2016. "Weak Parties and Strong Partisanship Are a Bad Combination." *Vox*, 3 November. https://www.vox.com/mischiefs-of-faction/2016/11/3/13512362/weak-parties-strong-part isanship-bad-combination.

Azari, Julia, and Marc Hetherington. 2016. "Back to the Future? What the Politics of the Late Nineteenth Century Can Tell Us about the 2016 Election." *The Annals of the American Academy of Political and Social Science* 667 (1): 92–109.

Bafumi, Joseph, and Michael Herron. 2010. "Leapfrog Representation and Extremism: A Study of American Voters and Their Members in Congress." *American Political Science Review* 104 (3): 519–42.

Bail, Christopher. 2021. *Breaking the Social Media Prism: How to Make Our Platforms Less Polarizing.* Princeton, NJ: Princeton University Press.

Bail, Christopher, Lisa Argyle, Taylor Brown, John Bumpus, Haohan Chen, M. B. Fallin Hunzaker, Jaemin Lee, Marcus Mann, Friedolin Merhout, and Alexander Volfovsky. 2018. "Exposure to Opposing Views on Social Media Can Increase Polarization." *Proceedings of the National Academy of Sciences* 115 (37): 9216–21.

Baker, Peter. 2020a. "George W. Bush Calls for End to Pandemic Partisanship." *New York Times*, 3 May.

———. 2020b. "For Trump, It's Not the United States, It's Red and Blue States." *New York Times*, 17 September.

Bakker, Bert, Yphtach Lelkes, and Ariel Malka. 2020. "Understanding Partisan Cue Receptivity: Tests of Predictions from the Bounded Rationality and Expressive Utility Models." *Journal of Politics* 82 (3): 1061–77.

Balsamo, Michael. 2020. "Disputing Trump, Barr Says No Widespread Election Fraud." *AP News*, 1 December. https://apnews.com/article/barr-no-widespread-election-fraud-b1f1488796c9 a98c4b1a9061a6c7f49d.

Bang-Peterson, Michael, Martin Skov, Søren Serritzlew, and Thomas Ramsey. 2013. "Motivated Reasoning and Political Parties: Evidence for Increased Processing in the Face of Party Cues." *Political Behavior* 35 (4): 831–54.

Bankert, Alexa. 2021. "Negative and Positive Partisanship in the 2016 Presidential Elections." *Political Behavior* 43 (4): 1467–85.

Barasz, Kate, Tami Kim, and Ioannis Evangelidis. 2019. "I Know Why You Voted for Trump: (Over)Inferring Motives Based on Choice." *Cognition* 188 (July): 85–97.

Barber, Benjamin. 1984. *Strong Democracy: Participatory Politics for a New Age*. Berkeley: University of California Press.

Bardon, Aurélia, Matteo Bonotti, Steven Zech, and William Ridge. Forthcoming. "Disaggregating Civility: Politeness, Public-Mindedness, and Their Connection." *British Journal of Political Science*.

Barlow, Fiona Kate, Winnifred Louis, and Miles Hewstone. 2009. "Rejected! Cognitions of Rejection and Intergroup Anxiety as Mediators of the Impact of Cross-Group Friendships on Prejudice." *British Journal of Social Psychology* 48 (3): 389–405.

Baron, Hannah, Robert Blair, Donghyun Danny Choi, Laura Gamboa, Jessica Gottleib, Amanda Lee Robinson, Steven Rosenzweig, Megan Turnbull, and Emily West. 2021. "Can Americans Depolarize? Assessing the Effects of Reciprocal Group Reflection on Partisan Polarization." Unpublished manuscript, University of Pittsburgh.

Bartels, Larry. 1993. "Messages Received: The Political Impact of Media Exposure." *American Political Science Review* 87 (2): 267–85.

Bazelon, Simon, and Matthew Yglesias. 2021. "The Rise and Fall of Secret Congress." *Slow Boring*, 21 June. https://www.slowboring.com/p/the-rise-and-importance-of-secret?s=r.

Benner, Katie. 2021. "Trump Pressed Justice Department to Declare Election Results Corrupt, Notes Show." *New York Times*, 30 July.

Berry, Jeffery, and Sarah Soberaj. 2014. *The Outrage Industry: Political Opinion Media and the New Incivility*. New York: Oxford University Press.

Beyond Conflict. 2020. "America's Divided Mind: Understanding the Psychology that Drives Us Apart." June. https://beyondconflictint.org/wp-content/uploads/2020/06/Beyond-Conflict-America_s-Div-ided-Mind-JUNE-2020-FOR-WEB.pdf.

Bialik, Kristen, and A. W. Geiger. 2016. "Republicans, Democrats Find Common Ground on Many Provisions of Health Care Law." Pew Research Center report, 8 December. https://www.pewresearch.org/fact-tank/2016/12/08/partisans-on-affordable-care-act-provisions/.

Biden, Joseph. 2020. "Transcript of President-Elect Joe Biden's Victory Speech." *AP News*, 7 November.

———. 2021. "Inaugural Address by President Joseph R. Biden, Jr." *The White House*, press release, 21 January. https://www.whitehouse.gov/briefing-room/speeches-remarks/2021/01/20/inaugural-address-by-president-joseph-r-biden-jr/.

———. 2022. "Remarks by President Biden to Mark One Year Since the January 6th Deadly Assault on the U.S. Capitol." *The White House*, press release, 6 January. https://www.whitehouse.gov/briefing-room/speeches-remarks/2022/01/06/remarks-by-president-biden-to-mark-one-year-since-the-january-6th-deadly-assault-on-the-u-s-capitol/.

Bigler, Rebecca, and Julie Milligan Hughes. 2010. "Reasons for Skepticism about the Efficacy of Simulated Social Contact Interventions." *American Psychologist* 65 (2): 132–33.

Bisgaard, Martin. 2015. "Bias Will Find a Way: Economic Perceptions, Attributions of Blame, and Partisan-Motivated Reasoning during Crisis." *Journal of Politics* 77 (3): 849–60.

———. 2019. "How Getting the Facts Right Can Fuel Partisan Motivated Reasoning." *American Journal of Political Science* 63 (4): 824–39.

Bogardus, Emory. 1959. *Social Distance*. Los Angeles: The University of Southern California Press.

Boisjoly, Johanne, Greg Duncan, Michael Kremer, Dan Levy, and Jacque Eccles. 2006. "Empathy or Antipathy? The Impact of Diversity." *American Economic Review* 96 (5): 1890–1905.

Bolsen, Toby, James Druckman, and Fay Lomax Cook. 2014. "The Influence of Partisan Motivated Reasoning on Public Opinion." *Political Behavior* 36 (2): 235–62.

Bonos, Lisa. 2020. "Strong Views on Trump Can Be a Big Dating Dealbreaker." *Washington Post*, 7 February.

Bor, Alexander, and Michael Bang-Peterson. 2022. "The Psychology of Online Political Hostility: A Comprehensive, Cross-National Test of the Mismatch Hypothesis." *American Political Science Review* 116 (1): 1–18.

Bougher, Lori. 2017. "The Correlates of Discord: Identity, Issue Alignment, and Political Hostility in Polarized America." *Political Behavior* 39 (3): 731–62.

Bowes, Shauna, Madeline Blanchard, Thomas Costello, Alan Abramowitz, and Scott Lilienfeld. 2020. "Intellectual Humility and Between-Party Animus: Implications for Affective Polarization in Two Community Samples." *Journal of Research in Personality* 88 (October): 103992.

Boxell, Levi, Matthew Gentzkow, and Jesse Shapiro. 2017. "Greater Internet Use Is Not Associated with Faster Growth in Political Polarization among US Demographic Groups." *Proceedings of the National Academy of Sciences* 114 (40): 10612–17.

Braley, Alia, Gabriel Lez, Dhaval Adjodah, Hossein Rahnama, and Alex Pentland. 2021. "The Subversion Dilemma: Why Voters Who Cherish Democracy Vote It Away." Unpublished manuscript, University of California Berkeley.

Brandt, Mark, and Felicity Turner-Zwinkels. 2020. "No Additional Evidence that Proximity to the July 4th Holiday Affects Affective Polarization." *Collabra: Psychology*, 29 July. https://doi.org/10.1525/collabra.368.

Brenan, Megan. 2019. "American Pride Hits New Low; Few Americans Proud of Political System." *Gallup News*, 2 July. https://news.gallup.com/poll/259841/american-pride-hits-new-low-few-proud-political-system.aspx.

Brewer, Marilynn. 1999. "The Psychology of Prejudice: Ingroup Love or Outgroup Hate?" *Journal of Social Issues* 55 (3): 429–44.

Brewer, Marilyn, and Kathleen Pierce. 2005. "Social Identity Complexity and Outgroup Tolerance." *Personality and Social Psychology Bulletin* 31 (3): 428–37.

Bright Line Watch. 2021. "Tempered Expectations and Hardened Divisions a Year into the Biden Presidency." November. http://brightlinewatch.org/tempered-expectations-and-hardened-divisions-a-year-into-the-biden-presidency/.

Broockman, David, Joshua Kalla, and Sean Westwood. Forthcoming. "Does Affective Polarization Undermine Democratic Norms or Accountability? Maybe Not." *American Journal of Political Science*.

Bruneau, Emile, and Rebecca Saxe. 2012. "The Benefits of 'Perspective Giving' in the Context of Intergroup Conflict." *Journal of Experimental Social Psychology* 48 (4): 855–66.

Bullock, John, Donald Green, and Shang Ha. 2010. "Yes, But What's the Mechanism? (Don't Expect an Easy Answer)." *Journal of Personality and Social Psychology* 98 (4): 550–58.

Bullock, John, Alan Gerber, Seth Hill, and Gregory Huber. 2015. "Partisan Bias in Factual Beliefs about Politics." *Quarterly Journal of Political Science* 10 (4): 519–78.

Burgees, Diana, Michelle van Ryn, John Dovidio, and Somnath Saha. 2007. "Reducing Racial Bias among Health Care Providers: Lessons from Social-Cognitive Psychology." *Journal of General Internal Medicine* 22 (6): 882–87.

Bursztyn, Leonardo, and David Yang. 2021. "Misperceptions about Others." National Bureau of Economic Research Working Paper #29168.

Busby, Ethan. 2021. *Should You Stay Away from Strangers? Experiments on the Political Consequences of Intergroup Contact.* Cambridge Elements in Experimental Political Science. New York: Cambridge University Press.

Caluwaerts, Didier, and Min Reuchamps. 2014. "Does Inter-Group Deliberation Foster Inter-Group Appreciation? Evidence from Two Experiments in Belgium." *Politics* 34 (2): 101–15.

Campbell, David, Geoffrey Layman, and John Green. 2020. *Secular Surge: A New Fault Line in American Politics.* New York: Cambridge University Press.

Carey, John M., Gretchen Helmke, Brendan Nyhan, Mitchell Sanders, and Susan Stokes. 2019. "Searching for Bright Lines in the Trump Presidency." *Perspectives on Politics* 17: 699–718.

Carlin, Ryan, and Gregory Love. 2018. "Political Competition, Partisanship, and Interpersonal Trust in Electoral Democracies." *British Journal of Political Science* 48 (1): 115–39.

Carlson, Taylor, and Jaime Settle. 2021. "What Goes Without Saying: Navigating Political Discussion in America." Unpublished manuscript, Washington University, St. Louis, MO.

Cassese, Erin. 2021. "Partisan Dehumanization in American Politics." *Political Behavior* 43 (1): 29–50.

Chen, M. Keith, and Ryne Rohla. 2018. "The Effects of Partisanship and Political Advertising on Close Family Ties." *Science* 360 (6392): 1020–24.

Chetty, Raj, David Grusky, Maximilian Hell, Nathaniel Hendren, Robert Manduca, and Jimmy Narang. 2016. "The Fading American Dream." *Science* 356 (6336): 398–406.

Chong, Dennis, and James Druckman. 2007. "Framing Public Opinion in Competitive Democracies." *American Political Science Review* 101 (4): 637–55.

Chotiner, Isaac. 2019. "The Disturbing, Surprisingly Complex Relationship between White Identity Politics and Racism." *New Yorker*, 19 January.

Citrin, Jack, Cara Wong, and Brian Duff. 2001. "The Meaning of American National Identity." In *Social Identity, Intergroup Conflict, and Conflict Reduction*, ed. Richard Ashmore, Lee Jussim, and David Wilder. New York: Oxford University Press.

Clark, Doug Bock, Alexandra Berzon, and Kirsten Berg. 2022. "Building the 'Big Lie': Inside the Creation of Trump's Stolen Election Myth." *ProPublica*, April 26. https://www.propublica.org/article/big-lie-trump-stolen-election-inside-creation#1319228.

Cobern, Trasa. 2020. "9/11 Reminds Us of American Unity." *Texas Scorecard*, 11 September. https://texasscorecard.com/commentary/cobern-9-11-reminds-us-of-american-unity/.

Coe, Kevin, Kate Kenski, and Stephen Rains. 2014. "Online and Uncivil? Patterns and Determinants of Incivility in Newspaper Website Comments." *Journal of Communications* 64 (4): 658–79.

Cohn, Nate, and Kevin Quealy. 2019. "The Democratic Electorate on Twitter Is Not the Actual Democratic Electorate." *New York Times*, 9 April.

Corasaniti, Nick, Reid Epstein, and Jim Rutenberg. 2020. "The Times Called Election Officials in Every State: No Evidence of Voter Fraud." *New York Times*, 10 November.

Cottingham, Marci. 2012. "Interaction Ritual Theory and Sports Fans: Emotion, Symbols, and Solidarity." *Sociology of Sport Journal* 29 (1): 168–85.

Cowan, Sarah, and Delia Baldassarri. 2018. "'It Could Turn Ugly': Selective Disclosure of Attitudes in Political Discussion Networks." *Social Networks* 52 (1): 1–17.

Crisp, Richard, and Miles Hewstone. 2000. "Crossed Categorization and Intergroup Bias: The Moderating Roles of Intergroup and Affective Context." *Journal of Experimental Social Psychology* 36 (4): 357–83.

Crisp, Richard, Miles Hewstone, and Mark Rubin. 2001. "Does Multiple Categorization Reduce Intergroup Bias?" *Personality and Social Psychology Bulletin* 27 (1): 76–89.

Crisp, Richard, and Rhiannon Turner. 2009. "Can Imagined Interactions Produce Positive Perceptions? Reducing Prejudice through Simulated Social Contact." *American Psychologist* 64 (4): 231–40.

Curry, James, and Frances Lee. 2020. *The Limits of Party: Congress and Lawmaking in a Polarized Era.* Chicago: University of Chicago Press.

Dach-Gruschow, Karl, and Yin Yi Hong. 2006. "The Racial Divide in Response to the Aftermath of Katrina: A Boundary Condition of the Common Ingroup Identity Model." *Analyses of Social Issues and Public Policy* 6 (1): 125–41.

Dahl, Robert. 1961. *Who Governs? Democracy and Power in an American City.* New Haven, CT: Yale University Press.

Darr, Joshua, Matthew Hitt, and Johanna Dunaway. 2018. "Newspaper Closure Polarizes Voting Behavior." *Journal of Communication* 68 (6): 1007–28.

———. 2021. *Home Style Opinion: How Local News Can Slow Polarization.* Cambridge Elements in Politics and Communication. New York: Cambridge University Press.

Davies, Kristin, Linda Tropp, Arthur Aron, Thomas Pettigrew, and Stephen Wright. 2011. "Cross-Group Friendships and Intergroup Attitudes: A Meta-Analytic Review." *Personality and Social Psychology Review* 15 (4): 332–51.

Dawsey, Josh. 2018. "Trump Derides Protections for Immigrants from 'Shithole' Countries." *Washington Post,* 12 January.

Deichert, Maggie, Stephen Goggin, and Alexander Theodoridis. 2019. "God, Sex, and *Especially* Politics: Disentangling the Dimensions of Discrimination." Unpublished manuscript, Vanderbilt University.

Delli-Carpini, Michael, Fay Cook, and Larry Jacobs. 2004. "Public Deliberation, Discursive Participation, and Citizen Engagement: A Review of the Empirical Literature." *Annual Review of Political Science* 7 (1): 315–44.

Dennis, J. Michael. 2018. "Technical Overview of the AmeriSpeak Panel, NORC's Probability-Based Household Panel." NORC at the University of Chicago, Technical Report, 6 February. https://www.norc.org/PDFs/AmeriSpeak%20Technical%20Overview%202015%2011%2025 .pdf.

Depetris-Chauvin, Emilio, Ruben Durante, and Filipe Campante. 2020. "Building Nations through Shared Experiences: Evidence from African Football." *American Economic Review* 110 (5): 1572–1602.

Dessel, Adrienne. 2010. "Effects of Intergroup Dialogue: Public School Teachers and Sexual Orientation Prejudice." *Small Group Research* 41 (5): 556–92.

Devos, Thierry, and Mahzarin Banaji. 2005. "American = White?" *Journal of Personality and Social Psychology* 88 (3): 447–66.

Dobson, Andrew. 2012. "Listening: The New Democratic Deficit." *Political Studies* 60 (4): 843–59.

Dorison, Charles, Julia Minson, and Todd Rogers. 2019. "Selective Exposure Partly Relies on Faulty Affective Forecasts." *Cognition* 188 (July): 98–107.

Druckman, James. 2012. "The Politics of Motivation." *Critical Review: A Journal of Politics and Society* 24 (2): 199–216.

Druckman, James, Samara Klar, Yanna Krupnikov, Matthew Levendusky, and John Barry Ryan. 2021. "Affective Polarization, Local Contexts and Public Opinion in America." *Nature Human Behaviour* 5 (1): 28–38.

———. 2022a. "(Affective) Polarization in America: When It Matters Politically and When It Does Not." Unpublished manuscript, Northwestern University.

———. 2022b. "(Mis-)Estimating Affective Polarization." *Journal of Politics* 84 (2): 1106–17.

Druckman, James, and Thomas Leeper. 2012. "Learning More from Political Communication Experiments: Pretreatment and Its Effects." *American Journal of Political Science* 56 (4): 875–96.

Druckman, James, and Matthew Levendusky. 2019. "What Do We Measure When We Measure Affective Polarization?" *Public Opinion Quarterly* 83 (1): 114–22.

Druckman, James, Matthew Levendusky, and Audrey McLain. 2018. "No Need to Watch: How the Effects of Partisan Media Can Spread via Inter-Personal Discussions." *American Journal of Political Science* 62 (1): 99–112.

Druckman, James, Erik Peterson, and Rune Slothuus. 2013. "How Elite Partisan Polarization Affects Public Opinion Formation." *American Political Science Review* 107 (1): 57–79.

Drutman, Lee. 2020. *Breaking the Two-Party Doom Loop: The Case for Multiparty Democracy in America*. New York: Oxford University Press.

Dryzek, John. 2005. "Deliberative Democracy in Divided Societies." *Political Theory* 33 (2): 218–42.

Dvorak, Petula. 2020. "Our Brief Moment of National Unity After the 9/11 Attack Was Just That—Brief. Can We Ever Get It Back?" *Washington Post*, 10 September.

Edy, Jill. 2006. *Troubled Pasts: News and the Collective Memory of Social Unrest*. Philadelphia: Temple University Press.

Eggers, Andrew, Haritz Garro, and Justin Grimmer. 2021. "No Evidence for Systematic Voter Fraud: A Guide to Statistical Claims about the 2020 Election." *Proceedings of the National Academy of Sciences* 118 (45): e2103619118.

Elling, Agnes, Ivo Van Hilvoorde, and Remko Van Den Dool. 2014. "Creating or Awakening National Pride through Sporting Success: A Longitudinal Study on Macro Effects in the Netherlands." *International Review for the Sociology of Sport* 49 (2): 129–51.

Enders, Adam, and Robert Lupton. 2021. "Value Extremity Contributes to Affective Polarization in the U.S." *Political Science Research and Methods* 9 (4): 857–66.

Engelhardt, Andrew, and Stephen Utych. 2020. "Grand Old (Tailgate) Party? Partisan Discrimination in Apolitical Settings." *Political Behavior* 42 (3): 769–89.

Enos, Ryan, and Anthony Fowler. 2018. "Aggregate Effects of Large-Scale Campaigns on Voter Turnout." *Political Science Research and Methods* 6 (4): 733–51.

Eveland, William, Kathryn Coduto, Osei Appiah, and Olivia Bullock. 2020. "Listening During Political Conversations: Traits and Situations." *Political Communication* 37 (5): 656–77.

Falce, Lori. 2020. "The People We Were on 9/11." *Tribune-Review* (western Pennsylvania), 10 September.

Fandos, Nicholas. 2021. "Why Jim Banks and Jim Jordan Were Blocked from the Capitol Riot Panel." *New York Times*, 21 July.

Feinberg, Matthew, and Robb Willer. 2019. "Moral Reframing: A Technique for Effective and Persuasive Communication across Political Divides." *Social and Personal Psychological Compass* 13 (12): e12501.

Finkel, Eli, Christopher Bail, Mina Cikara, Peter Ditto, Shanto Iyengar, Samara Klar, Lilliana Mason, et al. 2020. "Political Sectarianism in America." *Science* 370 (6516): 533–36.

Fiorina, Morris. 1980. "The Decline of Collective Responsibility in American Politics." *Daedalus* 109 (3): 25–45.

———. 2017. *Unstable Majorities: Polarization, Party Sorting and Political Stalemate*. Stanford, CA: Hoover Institution Press.

Fiorina, Morris, Samuel Abrams, and Jeremy Pope. 2005. *Culture War? The Myth of a Polarized America*. New York: Pearson Longman.

———. 2008. "Polarization in the American Public: Misconceptions and Misreadings." *Journal of Politics* 70 (2): 556–60.

Fishkin, James. 1995. *The Voice of the People: Public Opinion and Democracy*. New Haven, CT: Yale University Press.

Fishkin, James, Alice Su, Larry Diamond, and Norman Bradburn. 2021. "Is Deliberation an Antidote to Extreme Partisan Polarization: Reflections on 'American in One Room.'" *American Political Science Review* 115 (4): 1464–81.

Fisk, Colin, and Bernard Fraga. 2020. "'Til Death Do Us Part(isanship): Voting and Polarization in Opposite-Party Marriages." Democracy Fund Voter Study Group report, August. https://www.voterstudygroup.org/publication/til-death-do-us-partisanship.

FixUS. 2020. "Divided Nationally, United Locally: FixUS Focus Groups Explore What Values Unite and Divide Us." FixUS report, accessed December 2021. https://img1.wsimg.com/blobby/go/170f220a-55db-44b3-84d9-5662ed7d6605/FixUS_Focus_Group_Report.pdf.

———. 2021. "Progress Report: December 2021." FixUS report, accessed December 2021. https://fixusnow.org/fixus-2021-report.

Fowler, Anthony, Seth Hill, Jeff Lewis, Chris Tausanovitch, Lynn Vavreck, and Christopher Warshaw. Forthcoming. "Moderates." *American Political Science Review*.

Fowler, Luke, Jaclyn Kettler, and Stephanie Witt. 2020. "Democratic Governors Are Quicker in Responding to the Coronavirus than Republicans" *The Conversation*, 6 April. https://theconversation.com/democratic-governors-are-quicker-in-responding-to-the-coronavirus-than-republicans-135599.

Freeder, Sean. 2020. "Malice and Stupidity: Outgroup Motive Attribution and Affective Polarization." Unpublished manuscript, University of North Florida.

Friedman, Will, and David Schleifer. 2021. "America's Hidden Common Ground on Overcoming Divisiveness." Public Agenda report, April. https://www.publicagenda.org/wp-content/uploads/2021/04/HCG-Overcoming-Divisiveness-2021.pdf.

Gabriel, Trip. 2019. "Ahead of Debates, Pennsylvania Democrats Want Candidates to Stress Pragmatism." *New York Times*, 30 July.

Gaertner, Samuel, and John Dovidio. 2000. *Reducing Intergroup Bias: The Common Ingroup Identity Model*. Philadelphia: Psychology Press.

Gaertner, Samuel, Jeffrey Mann, Audrey Murrell, and John Dovidio. 1989. "Reducing Intergroup Bias." *Journal of Personality and Social Psychology* 57 (2): 239–49.

Gainesville Times. 2020. "We Must Find [*sic*] Resolve and Unity We Had After 9/11 if America Is to Shine Bright Again." 11 September.

Gardiner, Aidan. 2020. "'There Are Too Many Minefields': Readers on Swiping and Dating in the Trump Era." *New York Times*, 25 January.

Gardner, James. 1995. "Shut Up and Vote: A Critique of Deliberative Democracy and the Value of Talk." *Tennessee Law Review* 63 (2): 421–52.

Garrett, Kristin, and Alexa Bankert. 2020. "The Moral Roots of Partisan Division: How Moral Conviction Heightens Affective Polarization." *British Journal of Political Science* 50 (2): 621–40.

Garrett, R. Kelly, Shira Gvirsman, Benjamin Johnson, Yariv Tsfati, Rachel Neo, and Aysenur Dal. 2014. "Implications of Pro- and Counter-attitudinal Information Exposure for Affective Polarization." *Human Communication Research* 40 (3): 309–32.

Gelman, Andrew, and Hal Stern. 2006. "The Difference Between 'Significant' and 'Not Significant' Is Not Itself Statistically Significant." *American Statistician* 60 (4): 328–31.

Gerber, Alan, and Donald Green. 2002. "The Downstream Benefits of Experimentation." *Political Analysis* 10 (4): 394–402.

———. 2012. *Field Experiments: Design, Analysis, and Interpretation.* New York: W. W. Norton and Company.

Gift, Karen, and Thomas Gift. 2015. "Does Politics Influence Hiring? Evidence from a Randomized Experiment." *Political Behavior* 37 (3): 653–75.

Glass, Ira, producer. 2015. "If You Don't Have Anything Nice to Say, SAY IT IN ALL CAPS." *This American Life* (podcast), 23 January. https://www.thisamericanlife.org/545/if-you-dont -have-anything-nice-to-say-say-it-in-all-caps.

Goel, Sharod, Winter Mason, and Duncan Watts. 2010. "Real and Perceived Agreement in Social Networks." *Journal of Personality and Social Psychology* 99 (4): 611–21.

Gollwitzer, Anton, Cameron Martel, William Brady, Philip Pärnamets, Isaac Freedman, Eric Knowles, and Jay Van Bavel. 2020. "Partisan Differences in Physical Distancing Are Linked to Health Outcomes During the COVID-19 Pandemic." *Nature Human Behaviour* 4 (11): 1186–97.

Goren, Paul, Christopher Federico, and Miki Caul Kittilson. 2009. "Source Cues, Partisan Identities, and Political Value Expression." *American Journal of Political Science* 53 (4): 805–20.

Goya-Tocchetto, Daniela, Aaron Kay, Heidi Vuletich, Andrew Vonasch, and Keith Payne. 2022. "The Partisan Trade-Off Bias: When Political Polarization Meets Policy Trade-Offs." *Journal of Experimental Social Psychology* 98 (January): 104231.

Graham, David. 2018. "The Bipartisan Group That's Not Afraid of Partisanship." *The Atlantic,* 29 December. https://www.theatlantic.com/politics/archive/2018/12/better-angels-affective -polarization-political-divide/578539/.

Graham, Matthew, and Milan Svolik. 2020. "Democracy in America? Partisanship, Polarization, and the Robustness of Support for Democracy in the United States." *American Political Science Review* 114 (2): 392–409.

Groenendyk, Eric. 2012. "Justifying Party Identification: A Case of Identifying with the 'Lesser of Two Evils.'" *Political Behavior* 34 (3): 453–75.

———. 2018. "Competing Motives in a Polarized Electorate: Political Responsiveness, Identity Defensiveness, and the Rise of Partisan Antipathy." *Political Psychology: Advances in Political Psychology* 39 (S1): 159–71.

Groenendyk, Eric, and Yanna Krupnikov. 2021. "What Motivates Reasoning? A Theory of Goal-Dependent Political Evaluation." *American Journal of Political Science* 65 (1): 180–96.

Groenendyk, Eric, Michael Sances, and Kirill Zhirkov. 2020. "Intraparty Polarization in American Politics." *Journal of Politics* 82 (4): 1616–20.

Grynbaum, Michael, Davey Alba, and Reid Epstein. 2021. "How Pro-Trump Forces Pushed a Lie About Antifa at the Capitol Riot." *New York Times,* 1 March.

Gutmann, Amy, and Dennis Thompson. 1996. *Democracy and Disagreement*. Cambridge, MA: Harvard University Press.

———. 2012. *The Spirit of Compromise: Why Governing Demands It and Campaigning Undermines It*. Princeton, NJ: Princeton University Press.

Hall, Andrew. 2019. *Who Wants to Run: How the Devaluing of Political Office Drives Polarization*. Chicago: University of Chicago Press.

Hamil, Ruth, Timothy DeCamp Wilson, and Richard Nisbett. 1980. "Insensitivity to Sample Bias: Generalizing from Atypical Cases." *Journal of Personality and Social Psychology* 39 (4): 578–89.

Han, Hahrie. 2014. *How Organizations Develop Activists: Civic Associations and Leadership in the 21st Century*. New York: Oxford University Press.

———. 2017. "Want Gun Control? Learn from the NRA." *New York Times*, 4 October.

Harbridge, Laurel. 2015. *Is Bipartisanship Dead? Policy Agreement and Agenda Setting in the House of Representatives*. New York: Cambridge University Press.

Harbridge, Laurel, and Neil Malhotra. 2011. "Electoral Incentives and Partisan Conflict in Congress: Evidence from Survey Experiments." *American Journal of Political Science* 55 (3): 494–510.

Hare, Christopher. Forthcoming. "Constrained Citizens? Ideological Structure and Conflict Extension in the US Electorate, 1980–2016." *British Journal of Political Science*.

Harrison, Brian. 2020. *A Change Is Gonna Come: How to Have Effective Political Conversations in a Divided America*. New York: Oxford University Press.

Harrison, Brian, and Melissa Michelson. 2017. *Listen, We Need to Talk: How to Change Attitudes about LGBT Rights*. New York: Oxford University Press.

Hart, P. Sol, Sedona Chinn, and Stuart Soroka. 2020. "Politicization and Polarization in COVID-19 News Coverage." *Science Communication* 42 (5): 679–97.

Hartman, Rachel, Will Blakey, Jake Womick, Chris Bail, Eli Finkel, Hahrie Han, John Sarrouf, Juliana Schroeder, Paschal Sheeran, Jay Van Bavel, Robb Willer, and Kurt Gray. 2022. "Interventions to Reduce Political Animosity: A Systematic Review." Unpublished manuscript, PsyArXiv, 17 February; last updated 18 July. doi:10.31234/osf.io/ha2tf.

Hawkins, Stephen, and Taran Raghuram. 2020. "American Fabric: Identity and Belonging." More in Common report, December. https://www.moreincommon.com/media/s5jhgpx5/more incommon_americanfabricreport.pdf.

Hayes, Danny, and Jennifer Lawless. 2021. *News Hole: The Demise of Local Journalism and Political Engagement*. New York: Cambridge University Press.

Healy, Andrew, Neil Malhotra, and Cecelia Hyunjung Mo. 2010. "Irrelevant Events Affect Voters' Evaluations of Government Performance." *Proceedings of the National Academy of Sciences* 107 (29): 12804–9.

Heere, Bob, and Jeffrey James. 2007. "Stepping Outside the Lines: Developing a Multi-Dimensional Team Identity Scale Based on Social Identity Theory." *Sports Management Review* 10 (1): 65–91.

Heller, Nathan. 2021. "In a Divided Country, Communal Living Redefines Togetherness." *New Yorker*, 5 July.

Henderson-King, Eaaron, and Richard Nisbett. 1996. "Anti-Black Prejudice as a Function of Exposure to the Negative Behavior of a Single Black Person." *Journal of Personality and Social Psychology* 71 (4): 654–64.

Henninger, Annie. 2011. "Whatever Happened to 9/11?" *Wall Street Journal*, 8 September.

Hersh, Eitan. 2019. *Politics Is for Power: How to Move Beyond Political Hobbyism, Take Action, and Make Real Change.* New York: Scribner.

Hersh, Eitan, and Matthew Goldenberg. 2016. "Democratic and Republican Physicians Provide Different Care on Politicized Health Issues." *Proceedings of the National Academy of Sciences* 114 (42):11811–16.

Hetherington, Marc. 2004. *Why Trust Matters.* Chicago: University of Chicago Press.

Hetherington, Marc, and Thomas Rudolph. 2015. *Why Washington Won't Work: Polarization, Political Trust, and the Governing Crisis.* Chicago: University of Chicago Press.

Hetherington, Marc, and Jonathan Weiler. 2009. *Authoritarianism and Polarization in America.* New York: Cambridge University Press.

Hewstone, Miles, and Rupert Brown. 1986. "Contact Is Not Enough: An Intergroup Perspective on the 'Contact Hypothesis.'" In *Contact and Conflict in Intergroup Encounters,* ed. Miles Hewstone and Rupert Brown. Oxford, UK: Basil Blackwell.

Hill, Seth, and Chris Tausanovitch. 2015. "A Disconnect in Representation? Comparison of Trends in Congressional and Public Polarization." *Journal of Politics* 77 (4): 1058–75.

Hogg, Michael, and Dominic Abrams. 1988. *Social Identifications: A Social Psychology of Intergroup Relations and Group Processes.* New York: Routledge.

Holloway, Jonathan. 2021. "To Unite a Divided America, Make People Work for It." *New York Times,* 2 July.

Homola, Jonathan, Natalie Jackson, and Jeff Gill. 2016. "A Measure of Survey Mode Differences." *Electoral Studies* 44 (December): 255–74.

Hopkins, Daniel. 2018. *The Increasingly United States: How and Why American National Behavior Nationalized.* Chicago: University of Chicago Press.

Huber, Gregory, and Neil Malhotra. 2017. "Political Homophily in Social Relationships: Evidence from Online Dating Behavior." *Journal of Politics* 79 (1): 269–83.

Huckfeldt, Robert, Paul Johnson, and John Sprague. 2004. *Political Disagreement: The Survival of Diverse Opinions within Communication Networks.* New York: Cambridge University Press.

Huckfeldt, Robert, and John Sprague. 1987. "Networks in Context: The Social Flow of Political Information." *American Political Science Review* 81 (4): 1197–1216.

Huddy, Leonie, and Nadia Khatib. 2007. "American Patriotism, National Identity, and Political Involvement." *American Journal of Political Science* 51 (1): 63–77.

Huddy, Leonie, Lilliana Mason, and Lene Aarøe. 2015. "Expressive Partisanship: Campaign Involvement, Political Emotion, and Partisan Identity." *American Political Science Review* 109 (1): 1–17.

Huddy, Leonie, and Omer Yair. 2021. "Reducing Affective Polarization: Warm Group Relations or Policy Compromise?" *Political Psychology* 42 (2): 291–309.

Huntington, Samuel. 1983. *American Politics: The Promise of Disharmony.* Cambridge, MA: Harvard University Press.

Ignatius, David. 2020. "Congress's Bipartisan National Service Bill Would Be a Powerful Tonic for What's Ailing America." *Washington Post,* 8 July.

Isenberg, Daniel. 1986. "Group Polarization: A Critical Review and Meta-Analysis." *Journal of Personality and Social Psychology* 50 (6): 1141–51.

Iyengar, Shanto, Tobias Konitzer, and Kent Tedin. 2018. "The Home as Political Fortress: Family Agreement in an Era of Polarization." *Journal of Politics* 80 (4): 1326–38.

Iyengar, Shanto, and Masha Krupenkin. 2018. "The Strengthening of Partisan Affect." *Political Psychology: Advances in Political Psychology* 39 (S1): 201–18.

Iyengar, Shanto, Yphtach Lelkes, Matthew Levendusky, Neil Malhotra, and Sean Westwood. 2019. "The Origins and Consequences of Affective Polarization in the United States." *Annual Review of Political Science* 22 (1): 129–46.

Iyengar, Shanto, Gaurav Sood, and Yphtach Lelkes. 2012. "Affect, Not Ideology: A Social Identity Perspective on Polarization." *Public Opinion Quarterly* 76 (3): 405–31.

Iyengar, Shanto, and Sean Westwood. 2015. "Fear and Loathing Across Party Lines: New Evidence on Group Polarization." *American Journal of Political Science* 59 (3): 690–707.

Jackman, Mary, and Marie Crane. 1986. "'Some of My Best Friends Are Black': Interracial Friendship and Whites' Racial Attitudes." *Public Opinion Quarterly* 50 (4): 459–86.

Jacobson, Gary. 2006. *A Divider, Not a Uniter: George W. Bush and the American People.* New York: Longman.

———. 2019. *Presidents and Parties in the Public Mind.* Chicago: University of Chicago Press.

Jacoby, William. 2006. "Value Choice and American Public Opinion." *American Journal of Political Science* 50 (3): 706–23.

Jamieson, Kathleen Hall, and Bruce Hardy. 2012. "What Is Civil Engaged Argument and Why Does Aspiring to It Matter?" *PS: Political Science and Politics* 45 (3): 412–15.

Jamieson, Kathleen Hall, et al. 2017. "The Political Uses and Abuses of Civility and Incivility." In *The Oxford Handbook of Political Communication*, ed. Kate Kenski and Kathleen Hall Jamieson, 205–18. New York: Oxford University Press.

Jefferson, Thomas. 1800. "Letter from Thomas Jefferson to William Hamilton, 22 April 1800." In *Papers of Thomas Jefferson* 31,533–35. https://tjrs.monticello.org/letter/1325.

Johnson, Theodore. 2020. "The Challenge of Black Patriotism." *New York Times*, 18 November.

Johnston, Christopher. 2018. "Authoritarianism, Affective Polarization, and Economic Ideology." *Political Psychology: Advances in Political Psychology* 39 (S1): 219–38.

Johnston, Richard. 2008. "Modeling Campaign Dynamics on the Web in the 2008 National Annenberg Election Study." *Journal of Elections, Public Opinion, and Parties* 18 (4): 401–12.

Judd, Charles, David Kenny, and Jon Krosnick. 1983. "Judging the Positions of Political Candidates: Models of Assimilation and Contrast." *Journal of Personality and Social Psychology* 44 (5): 952–63.

Kahan, Daniel. 2010. "Fixing the Communication Failure." *Nature* 463 (January 20): 296–97.

Kalla, Joshua, and David Broockman. 2020. "Reducing Exclusionary Attitudes through Interpersonal Conversation: Evidence from Three Field Experiments." *American Political Science Review* 114 (2): 410–25.

———. Forthcoming a. "Voter Outreach Campaigns Can Reduce Affective Polarization among Implementing Political Activists." *American Political Science Review.*

———. Forthcoming b. "Which Narrative Strategies Durably Reduce Prejudice? Evidence from Field and Survey Experiments Support the Efficacy of Perspective-Getting." *American Journal of Political Science.*

Kalmoe, Nathan, and Lilliana Mason. 2022. *Radical American Partisanship: Mapping Violent Hostility, Its Causes, and the Consequences for Democracy.* Chicago: University of Chicago Press.

Kam, Cindy, and Maggie Deichert. 2020. "Boycotting, Buycotting, and the Psychology of Political Consumerism." *Journal of Politics* 82 (1): 72–88.

Kam, Cindy, and Jennifer Ramos. 2008. "Joining and Leaving the Rally: Understanding the Surge and Decline in Presidential Approval Following 9/11." *Public Opinion Quarterly* 72 (4): 619–50.

Karni, Annie. 2020. "Trump Fuels Culture War Message at Mt. Rushmore." *New York Times*, 3 July.

Karpowitz, Chris, and Tali Mendelberg. 2014. *The Silent Sex: Gender, Deliberation, and Institutions*. Princeton, NJ: Princeton University Press.

Karpowitz, Christopher, and Jeremy C. Pope. 2018. "The American Family Study 2018." Computer file. Released 1 August 2018. Center for the Study of Elections and Democracy, Brigham Young University, Provo, UT. http://csed.byu.edu/american-family-survey/.

Keeter, Scott. 2019. "Growing and Improving the Pew Research Center's American Trends Panel." Pew Research Center, 27 February. https://pewrsr.ch/2wVfy23.

Keith, Bruce, David Magleby, Candice Nelson, Elizabeth Orr, Mark Westlye, and Raymond Wolfinger. 1992. *The Myth of the Independent Voter*. Berkeley: University of California Press.

Keith, William, and Robert Danisch. 2020. *Beyond Civility: The Competing Obligations of Citizenship*. University Park: The Pennsylvania State University Press.

Kiesler, Sara, Jane Siegel, and Timothy McGuire. 1984. "Social Psychological Aspects of Computer-Mediated Communication." *American Psychologist* 39 (10): 1123–34.

Kim, Jin Woo, Andrew Guess, Brendan Nyhan, and Jason Reifler. 2021. "The Distorting Prism of Social Media: How Self-Selection and Exposure to Incivility Fuel Online Comment Toxicity." *Journal of Communication* 71 (6): 922–46.

Kingzette, Jon, James Druckman, Samara Klar, Yanna Krupnikov, Matthew Levendusky, and John Ryan. 2021. "How Affective Polarization Undermines Support for Democratic Norms." *Public Opinion Quarterly* 85 (2): 663–77.

Kirkpatrick, Emily. 2020. "Why Is *Keeping Up with the Kardashians* Ending?" *Vanity Fair*, 9 September.

Klar, Samara. 2014. "Partisanship in a Social Setting." *American Journal of Political Science* 58 (3): 687–704.

———. 2018. "When Common Identities Decrease Trust: An Experimental Study of Partisan Women." *American Journal of Political Science* 62 (3): 610–22.

Klar, Samara, and Yanna Krupnikov. 2016. *Independent Politics: How American Disdain for Parties Leads to Political Inaction*. New York: Cambridge University Press.

Klar, Samara, Yanna Krupnikov, and John Barry Ryan. 2018. "Affective Polarization or Partisan Disdain? Untangling a Dislike for the Opposing Party from a Dislike of Partisanship." *Public Opinion Quarterly* 82 (2): 379–90.

Klein, Ezra. 2020. *Why We're Polarized*. New York: Avid Reader Press.

Kliff, Sarah. 2020. "How Progressives Flipped the Script on Medicaid Expansion." *New York Times*, 4 August.

Klofstad, Casey, Scott McClurg, and Meredith Rolfe. 2009. "Measurement of Political Discussion Networks." *Public Opinion Quarterly* 73 (3): 462–83.

Krupnikov, Yanna, and John Barry Ryan. 2022. *The Other Divide: Polarization and Disengagement in American Politics*. New York: Cambridge University Press.

Kubin, Emily, Curtis Puryear, Chelsea Schein, and Kurt Gray. 2021. "Personal Experiences Bridge Moral and Political Divides Better than Facts." *Proceedings of the National Academy of Sciences* 118 (6): e2008389118.

Kubin, Emily, and Christian von Sikorski. 2021. "The Role of (Social) Media in Political Polarization: A Systematic Review." *Annals of the International Communication Association* 45 (3): 188–206.

Kumar, Srijan, William Hamilton, Jure Leskovec, and Dan Jurafsky. 2018. "Community Interaction and Conflict on the Web." *WWW '18: Proceedings of the 2018 World Wide Web Conference*. https://doi.org/10.1145/3178876.3186141.

Lau, Richard. 1982. "Negativity in Political Perception." *Political Behavior* 4 (4): 353–77.

Lau, Richard, and David Redlawsk. 1997. "Voting Correctly." *American Political Science Review* 91 (3): 585–98.

Lavine, Howard, Christopher Johnston, and Marco Steenbergen. 2012. *The Ambivalent Partisan: How Critical Loyalty Promotes Democracy*. New York: Cambridge University Press.

Layman, Geoffrey, and Thomas Carsey. 2002. "Party Polarization and 'Conflict Extension' in the American Electorate." *American Journal of Political Science* 46 (4): 786–802.

Layman, Geoffrey, Thomas Carsey, John Green, Richard Herera, and Rosalyn Cooperman. 2010. "Activists and Conflict Extension in American Party Politics." *American Political Science Review* 104 (2): 324–46.

Lee, Frances. 2016. *Insecure Majorities: Congress and the Permanent Campaign*. Chicago: University of Chicago Press.

Lee, Frances, and Nolan McCarty. 2019. *Can America Govern Itself?* New York: Cambridge University Press.

Lee, Sherman, Jeffrey Gibbons, John Thompson, and Hussam Timani. 2009. "The Islamophobia Scale: Instrumental Development and Initial Validation." *International Journal for the Psychology of Religion* 19 (2): 92–105.

Leeper, Thomas, and Rune Slothuus. 2014. "Political Parties, Motivated Reasoning, and Public Opinion Formation." *Political Psychology: Advances in Political Psychology* 35 (S1): 129–56.

Lees, Jeffrey, and Mina Cikara. 2020. "Inaccurate Group Meta-Perceptions Drive Negative Out-Group Attributions in Competitive Contexts." *Nature Human Behavior* 4 (2): 279–86.

Leibovich, Mark. 2020. "Trump Turns Shared American Experiences into Us Versus Them." *New York Times*, 26 April.

Lelkes, Yphtach. 2018. "Affective Polarization and Ideological Sorting: A Reciprocal, Albeit Weak, Relationship." *The Forum* 16 (1): 67–79.

———. 2021. "Policy over Party: Comparing the Effects of Candidate Ideology and Party on Affective Polarization." *Political Science Research and Methods* 9 (1): 189–96.

Lelkes, Yphtach, Gaurav Sood, and Shanto Iyengar. 2017. "The Hostile Audience: The Effect of Broadband Access on Partisan Affect." *American Journal of Political Science* 61 (1): 5–20.

Lelkes, Yphtach, and Sean Westwood. 2017. "The Limits of Partisan Prejudice." *Journal of Politics* 79 (2): 485–501.

Lenz, Gabriel. 2012. *Follow the Leader? How Voters Respond to Politicians' Policies and Performance*. Chicago: University of Chicago Press.

Lerman, Amy, Meredith Sadin, and Samuel Trachtman. 2017. "Policy Uptake as Political Behavior: Evidence from the Affordable Care Act." *American Political Science Review* 111 (4): 755–70.

Levendusky, Matthew. 2009. *The Partisan Sort: How Liberals Became Democrats and Conservatives Became Republicans*. Chicago: University of Chicago Press.

———. 2010. "Clearer Cues, More Consistent Voters: A Benefit of Elite Polarization." *Political Behavior* 32 (1): 111–31.

———. 2013. *How Partisan Media Polarize America*. Chicago: University of Chicago Press.

———. 2018a. "Americans, Not Partisans: Can Priming American National Identity Reduce Affective Polarization?" *Journal of Politics* 80 (1): 59–70.

———. 2018b. "When Efforts to Depolarize the Electorate Fail." *Public Opinion Quarterly* 82 (3): 583–92.

————. 2022. "Finding Common Ground: Experimental Efforts to Reduce Partisan Animus." In *Reconsidering Parties and Partisanship*, ed. Christopher Karpowitz and Jeremy Pope. Ann Arbor: University of Michigan Press.

Levendusky, Matthew, and Neil Malhotra. 2016a. "Does Media Coverage of Partisan Polarization Affect Political Attitudes?" *Political Communication* 33 (2): 283–301.

————. 2016b. "(Mis)Perceptions of Partisan Polarization in the American Public." *Public Opinion Quarterly* 80 (S1): 378–91.

Levendusky, Matthew, and Dominik Stecula. 2021. *We Need to Talk: How Cross-Party Dialogue Reduces Affective Polarization*. Elements in Experimental Political Science. New York: Cambridge University Press.

Levitan, Lindsay, and Penny Visser. 2008. "The Impact of the Social Context on Resistance to Persuasion: Effortful versus Effortless Responses to Counter-attitudinal Information." *Journal of Experimental Social Psychology* 44 (3): 640–49.

Levitsky, Steven, and Daniel Ziblatt. 2018. *How Democracies Die*. New York: Penguin Random House.

Lindsey, Brink. 2021. "In Search of Civic Virtue." The Niskanen Center, 11 January. https://www.niskanencenter.org/in-search-of-civic-virtue/.

Lipsitz, Keena, and Grigore Pop-Eleches. 2020. "The Partisan Divide in Social Distancing." Unpublished manuscript, City University of New York, last updated 13 May 2020. Available from Social Science Research Network at https://papers.ssrn.com/sol3/papers.cfm?abstract_id=3595695.

Little, Andrew, Keith Schnakenberg, and Ian Turner. 2022. "Motivated Reasoning and Democratic Accountability." *American Political Science Review* 116 (2): 751–67.

Livingstone, Andrew, Lucía Fernández Rodríguez, and Adrian Rothers. 2020. "'They Just Don't Understand Us': The Role of Felt Understanding in Intergroup Relations." *Journal of Personality and Social Psychology* 119 (3): 633–56.

Lord, Charles, Mark Lepper, and Elizabeth Preston. 1984. "Considering the Opposite: A Corrective Strategy for Social Judgment." *Journal of Personality and Social Psychology* 47 (6): 1231–43.

Lupia, Arthur, and Anne Norton. 2017. "Inequality Is Always in the Room: Language and Power in Deliberative Democracy." *Daedalus* 146 (3): 64–76.

Luttig, Matthew. 2017. "Authoritarianism and Affective Polarization: A New View on the Origins of Partisan Extremism." *Public Opinion Quarterly* 81 (4): 866–95.

Lyons, Jeffrey, and Anand Sokhey. 2017. "Discussion Networks, Issues, and Perceptions of Polarization in the American Electorate." *Political Behavior* 39 (4): 967–88.

MacFarquhar, Neil. 2021. "Sweet Cherries, Bitter Politics: Two Farm Stands and the Nation's Divides." *New York Times*, 6 June.

MacInnis, Cara, and Elizabeth Page-Gould. 2015. "How Can Intergroup Interaction Be Bad If Intergroup Contact Is Good?" *Perspectives on Psychological Science* 10 (3): 307–27.

Mackie, Drew. 2015. "New Mexico 'Cat Library' Allows Office Workers to Check Out Kittens." *People*, 11 June. https://people.com/pets/new-mexico-cat-library-allows-office-workers-to-check-out-kittens/.

MacKuen, Michael, Jennifer Wolak, Luke Keele, and George Marcus. 2010. "Civic Engagements: Resolute Partisanship or Reflective Deliberation." *American Journal of Political Science* 54 (2): 440–58.

Madestam, Andreas, and David Yanagizawa-Drott. 2012. "Shaping the Nation: The Effect of Fourth of July on Political Preferences and Behavior in the United States." Kennedy School Working Paper Series RWP12, Harvard University.

Malhotra, Neil, and Jon Krosnick. 2007. "The Effect of Survey Mode and Sampling on Inferences about Political Attitudes and Behavior: Comparing the 2000 and 2004 ANES to Internet Surveys with Nonprobability Samples." *Political Analysis* 15 (3): 286–323.

Mansbridge, Jane. 1983. *Beyond Adversary Democracy*. Chicago: University of Chicago Press.

———. 1999. "Everyday Talk in the Deliberative System." In *Deliberative Politics: Essays on Democracy and Disagreement*, ed. Stephen Macedo. New York: Oxford University Press.

Margolis, Michele. 2018. *From Politics to the Pews: How Partisanship and the Political Environment Shape Religious Identity*. Chicago: University of Chicago Press.

Martherus, James, Andres Martinez, Paul Piff, and Alexander Theodoridis. 2021. "Party Animals? Extreme Partisan Polarization and Dehumanization." *Political Behavior* 43 (3): 517–40.

Martin, Gregory, and Steven Webster. 2020. "Does Residential Sorting Explain Geographic Polarization?" *Political Science Research and Methods* 8 (2): 215–31.

Mason, Lilliana. 2015. "'I Disrespectfully Agree': The Differential Effects of Partisan Sorting on Social and Issue Polarization." *American Journal of Political Science* 59 (1): 128–45.

———. 2016. "A Cross-Cutting Calm: How Social Sorting Drives Affective Polarization." *Public Opinion Quarterly* 80 (S1): 351–77.

———. 2018. *Uncivil Agreement: How Politics Became Our Identity*. Chicago: University of Chicago Press.

Mason, Lilliana, and Eric Liu. 2019. "How to Fix Polarization: Mandatory National Service." *Politico*, last accessed 16 March 2022. https://www.politico.com/interactives/2019/how-to-fix-politics -in-america/polarization/mandatory-national-service/.

Mason, Lilliana, and Julie Wronski. 2018. "One Tribe to Bind Them All: How Our Social Group Attachments Strengthen Partisanship." *Political Psychology* 39 (S1): 257–77.

McCarty, Nolan. 2019. *Polarization: What Everyone Needs to Know*. New York: Oxford University Press.

McClain, Colleen. 2021. "70% of U.S. Social Media Users Never or Rarely Post or Share about Political, Social Issues." Pew Research Center report, 4 May. https://www.pewresearch.org /fact-tank/2021/05/04/70-of-u-s-social-media-users-never-or-rarely-post-or-share-about -political-social-issues/.

McClain, Colleen, Regina Widjaya, Gonzalo Rivera, and Aaron Smith. 2021. "The Behaviors and Attitudes of U.S. Adults on Twitter." Pew Research Center report, 15 November. https://www .pewresearch.org/internet/2021/11/15/the-behaviors-and-attitudes-of-u-s-adults-on-twitter/.

McClosky, Herbert. 1964. "Consensus and Ideology in American Politics." *American Political Science Review* 58: 361–82.

McConnell, Christopher, Neil Malhotra, Yotam Margalit, and Matthew Levendusky. 2018. "The Economic Consequences of Partisanship in a Polarized Era." *American Journal of Political Science* 62 (1): 5–18.

McGregor, Shannon. 2019. "Social Media as Public Opinion: How Journalists Use Social Media to Represent Public Opinion." *Journalism* 20 (8): 107–86.

McKenna, Elizabeth, and Hahrie Han. 2015. *Groundbreakers: How Obama's 2.2 Million Volunteers Transformed Campaigning in America*. New York: Oxford University Press.

McPherson, Miller, Lynn Smith-Lovin, and James Cook. 2001. "Birds of a Feather: Homophily in Social Networks." *Annual Review of Sociology* 27 (1): 415–44.

Merkley, Eric, Aengus Bridgman, Peter John Loewen, Taylor Owen, Derek Ruths, and Oleg Zhilin. 2020. "A Rare Moment of Cross-Partisan Consensus: Elite and Public Response to the COVID-19 Pandemic in Canada." *Canadian Journal of Political Science / Revue Canadienne de Science Politique* 53 (2): 311–18.

Merkley, Eric, and Dominik Stecula. 2020. "Party Cues in the News: Democratic Elites, Republican Backlash, and the Dynamics of Climate Skepticism." *British Journal of Political Science* 51 (4): 1439–56.

Mernyk, Joseph, Sophia Pink, James Druckman, and Robb Willer. 2022. "Correcting Inaccurate Metaperceptions Reduces Americans' Support for Partisan Violence." *Proceedings of the National Academy of Sciences* 119 (16): e2116851119.

Messing, Solomon, and Sean Westwood. 2012. "Selective Exposure in the Age of Social Media." *Communication Research* 41 (8): 1042–63.

Minozzi, William, Hyujin Song, David Lazer, Michael Neblo, and Katherine Ognyanova. 2020. "The Incidental Pundit: Who Talks Politics with Whom, and Why?" *American Journal of Political Science* 64 (1): 135–51.

Mo, Cecelia Hyunjung, and Katherine Conn. 2018. "When Do the Advantaged See the Disadvantages of Others? A Quasi-Experimental Study of National Service." *American Political Science Review* 112 (4): 721–41.

Moore-Berg, Samantha, Lee-Or Ankori-Karlinsky, Boaz Hameiri, and Emile Bruneau. 2020. "Exaggerated Meta-Perceptions Predict Intergroup Hostility Between American Political Partisans." *Proceedings of the National Academy of Sciences* 117 (26): 14864–72.

Moskowitz, Daniel. 2021. "Local News, Information, and the Nationalization of U.S. Elections." *American Political Science Review* 115 (1): 114–29.

Muirhead, Russell. 2014. *The Promise of Party in a Polarized Age.* Cambridge, MA: Harvard University Press.

Mullen, Brian, and Li-Tze Hu. 1989. "Perceptions of Ingroup and Outgroup Variability: A Meta-Analytic Integration." *Basic and Applied Social Psychology* 10 (3): 233–52.

Müller, Jan-Werner. 2021. "Democracy Means Not Knowing What Comes Next." *New York Times,* 9 December.

Mullinix, Kevin. 2018. "Civic Duty and Political Preference Formation." *Political Research Quarterly* 71 (1): 199–214.

Mullinix, Kevin, and Trent Lythgoe. Forthcoming. "Priming Norms to Combat Affective Polarization." *Political Research Quarterly.*

Mummolo, Jonathan, and Clayton Nall. 2017. "Why Partisans Do Not Sort: The Constraints on Political Segregation." *Journal of Politics* 79 (1): 45–59.

Mummolo, Jonathan, and Erik Peterson. 2019. "Demand Effects in Survey Experiments: An Empirical Assessment." *American Political Science Review* 113 (2): 517–29.

Mutz, Diana. 2002. "Cross-Cutting Social Networks: Testing Democratic Theory in Practice." *American Political Science Review* 96 (1): 111–26.

———. 2006. *Hearing the Other Side: Deliberative versus Participatory Democracy.* New York: Cambridge University Press.

Mutz, Diana, and Jeffrey Mondak. 2006. "The Workplace as a Context for Cross-Cutting Political Discourse." *Journal of Politics* 68 (1): 140–55.

New Yorker. 2018. "The Mind of the Sports Superfan." 1 February. https://www.newyorker.com/sports/sporting-scene/the-mind-of-the-sports-superfan.

Nicholson, Stephen. 2012. "Polarizing Cues." *American Journal of Political Science* 56 (1): 52–66.

Nir, Sarah Maslin. 2021. "A Fourth of July Symbol of Unity that May No Longer Unite." *New York Times*, 3 July.

Noelle-Neumann, Elisabeth. 1974. "The Spiral of Silence: A Theory of Public Opinion." *Journal of Communication* 24 (2): 23–51.

Norman, Jim. 2018. "Football Still Americans' Favorite Sport to Watch." Gallup News, 4 January. https://news.gallup.com/poll/224864/football-americans-favorite-sport-watch.aspx.

Novarro, Len. 2014. "America: What Makes It Great." *The Times of San Diego*, 3 July.

Obama, Barack. 2011. "Remarks by the President at a Memorial Service for the Victims of the Shooting in Tucson, Arizona." *The White House*, press release, 12 January. https://obama whitehouse.archives.gov/the-press-office/2011/01/12/remarks-president-barack-obama -memorial-service-victims-shooting-tucson.

———. 2013. "Remarks by the President on the Reopening of the Government." *The White House*, press release, 17 October. https://obamawhitehouse.archives.gov/the-press-office /2013/10/17/remarks-president-reopening-government.

O'Brien, Sarah. 2017. "Americans Spend $56 Billion on Sporting Events." *CNBC*, 11 September. https://www.cnbc.com/2017/09/11/americans-spend-56-billion-on-sporting-events.html.

Orr, Lilla, and Gregory Huber. 2020. "The Policy Basis of Measured Partisan Animosity in the United States." *American Journal of Political Science* 64 (3): 569–86.

Osnos, Evan. 2020. "Pulling Our Politics Back from the Brink." *New Yorker*, 16 November.

Padgett, Jeremy, Johanna Dunaway, and Joshua Darr. 2019. "As Seen on TV? How Gatekeeping Makes the U.S. House Seem More Extreme." *Journal of Communication* 69 (6): 696–719.

Page-Gould, Elizabeth, Rodolfo Mendoza-Denton, Jan Marie Alegre, and John Oliver Siy. 2010. "Understanding the Impact of Cross-Group Friendship on Interactions with Novel Out-group Members." *Journal of Personality and Social Psychology* 98 (5): 775–93.

Page-Gould, Elizabeth, Rodolfo Mendoza-Denton, and Linda Tropp. 2008. "With a Little Help from My Cross-Group Friend: Reducing Anxiety in Intergroup Contexts through Cross-Group Friendship." *Journal of Personality and Social Psychology* 95 (5): 1080–94.

Paine, Neil, Harry Enten, and Andrea Jones-Rooy. 2017. "How Every NFL Team's Fans Lean Politically." *FiveThirtyEight*, 29 September. https://53eig.ht/2XlobAo.

Pajer, Nicole. 2020. "Can Love Survive This Election?" *New York Times*, 25 August.

Paluck, Elizabeth Levy, Seth Green, and Donald Green. 2019. "The Contact Hypothesis Re-Evaluated." *Behavioral Public Policy* 3 (2): 129–58.

Papacharissi, Zizi. 2004. "Democracy Online: Civility, Politeness, and the Democratic Potential of Online Political Discussion Groups." *New Media and Society* 6 (2): 259–83.

Panagopoulos, Costas. 2006. "Trends: Arab and Muslim Americans and Islam in the Aftermath of 9/11." *Public Opinion Quarterly* 70 (4): 608–24.

Panagopoulos, Costas, Donald Green, Jonathan Krasno, Kyle Endres, and Michael Schwam-Baird. 2020. "Partisan Consumerism: Experimental Tests of Consumer Reactions to Corporate Political Activity." *Journal of Politics* 82 (3): 996–1007.

Parker, Kim, Rich Morin, and Juliana Menasce Horowitz. 2019. "Looking to the Future, Public Sees an America in Decline on Many Fronts." Pew Research Center report, 21 March. https://www.pewresearch.org/social-trends/2019/03/21/public-sees-an-america-in-de cline-on-many-fronts/.

Parker, Michael, and Ronnie Janoff-Bulman. 2013. "Lessons from Morality-Based Social Identity: The Power of Outgroup 'Hate,' Not Just Ingroup 'Love.'" *Social Justice Research* 26 (1): 81–96.

Parsons, Bryan. 2015. "The Social Identity Politics of Peer Networks." *American Politics Research* 43 (4): 680–707.

Pasek, Michael, Lee-Or Ankori-Karlinsky, Alex Levy-Vene, and Samantha Moore-Berg. 2021. "Biased and Inaccurate Meta-Perceptions about Out-Partisans' Support for Democratic Principles May Erode Democratic Norms." Unpublished manuscript, New School for Social Research.

Persily, Nathaniel, ed. 2015. *Solutions to Political Polarization in America.* New York: Cambridge University Press.

Pettigrew, Thomas. 1997. "Generalized Intergroup Contact Effects on Prejudice." *Personality and Social Psychology Bulletin* 23 (2): 173–85.

Pettigrew, Thomas, and Linda Tropp. 2006. "A Meta-Analytic Test of Intergroup Contact Theory." *Journal of Personality and Social Psychology* 90 (5): 751–83.

———. 2008. "How Does Intergroup Contact Reduce Prejudice? Meta-Analytic Tests of Three Mediators." *European Journal of Social Psychology* 38 (6): 922–34.

———. 2011. *When Groups Meet: The Dynamics of Intergroup Contact.* New York: Psychology Press.

Pew Research Center. 2016. "Partisanship and Political Animosity in 2016." Pew Research Center report, 22 June. https://www.pewresearch.org/politics/2016/06/22/partisanship-and-political -animosity-in-2016/.

———. 2017. "The Partisan Divide on Political Values Grows Even Wider." Pew Research Center report, 5 October. https://www.pewresearch.org/politics/2017/10/05/the-partisan-divide -on-political-values-grows-even-wider/.

———. 2019a. "Public Highly Critical of the State of Political Discourse in the U.S." Pew Research Center report, 19 June. https://www.pewresearch.org/politics/2019/06/19/public -highly-critical-of-state-of-political-discourse-in-the-u-s/.

———. 2019b. "National Politics on Twitter: Small Share of U.S. Adults Produce Majority of Tweets." Pew Research Center report, 23 October. https://www.pewresearch.org/politics /2019/10/23/national-politics-on-twitter-small-share-of-u-s-adults-produce-majority-of -tweets/#national-politics-tweets.

———. 2019c. "Partisan Antipathy: More Intense, More Personal." Pew Research Center report, 10 October. https://www.pewresearch.org/politics/2019/10/10/partisan-antipathy-more-intense -more-personal/.

———. 2020. "Amid Campaign Turmoil, Biden Holds Wide Leads on Coronavirus, Unifying the Country." Pew Research Center report, 9 October. https://www.pewresearch.org /politics/2020/10/09/amid-campaign-turmoil-biden-holds-wide-leads-on-coronavirus -unifying-the-country/.

———. 2021. "Biden Viewed Positively on Many Issues, But Public Is Less Confident He Can Unify Country." Pew Research Center report, 11 March. https://www.pewresearch.org/poli tics/2021/03/11/biden-viewed-positively-on-many-issues-but-public-is-less-confident-he -can-unify-country/.

Pierce, Douglas, and Richard Lau. 2019. "Polarization and Correct Voting in U.S. Presidential Elections." *Electoral Studies* 60 (August): 102048.

Poole, Keith, and Howard Rosenthal. 1984. "The Polarization of American Politics." *Journal of Politics* 46 (4): 1061–79.

Popper, Karl. 1945. *The Open Society and Its Enemies.* London: Routledge.

Poteat, V. Paul, Ethan Mereish, Marcia Liu, and Sophia Nam. 2011. "Can Friendships Be Bipartisan? The Effects of Political Ideology on Peer Relationships." *Group Processes & Intergroup Relations* 14 (6): 819–34.

Praet, Stiene, Andrew Guess, Joshua Tucker, Richard Bonneau, and Jonathan Nagler. 2022. "What's Not to Like? Facebook Page Likes Reveal Limited Polarization in Lifestyle Preferences." *Political Communication* 39 (3): 311–38.

Program for Public Consultation. 2021. "Common Ground of the American People: Policy Positions Supported by Both Democrats and Republicans." Program for Public Consultation, School of Public Policy, University of Maryland, a project of Voice of the People. Last accessed January 2022. https://vop.org/wp-content/uploads/2021/07/CGOAP_0721.pdf.

Putnam, Robert. 2000. *Bowling Alone: The Collapse and Revival of American Community*. New York: Simon & Schuster.

Quattrone, George, and Edward Jones. 1980. "The Perception of Variability within In-Groups and Out-Groups: Implications for the Law of Small Numbers." *Journal of Personality and Social Psychology* 38 (1): 141–52.

Rainie, Lee, Scott Keeter, and Andrew Perrin. 2019. "Trust and Distrust in America." Pew Research Center report, 22 July. https://www.pewresearch.org/politics/2019/07/22/trust-and-distrust-in-america/.

Ranney, Austin. 1951. "Toward a More Responsible Two-Party System: A Commentary." *American Political Science Review* 45 (2): 488–99.

Redlawsk, David, Andrew Civettini, and Karen Emmerson. 2010. "The Affective Tipping Point: Do Motivated Reasoners Ever 'Get It'?" *Political Psychology* 31 (4): 563–93.

Reid, Anne, and Kay Deaux. 1996. "Relationship Between Social and Personal Identities: Segregation or Integration?" *Journal of Personality and Social Psychology* 71 (6): 1084–91.

Reid, Scott. 2012. "A Self-Categorization Explanation for the Hostile Media Effect." *Journal of Communication* 62 (3): 381–99.

Ripley, Amanda. 2019. "The Least Politically Prejudiced Place in America." *The Atlantic*, 4 March. https://www.theatlantic.com/politics/archive/2019/03/watertown-new-york-tops-scale-political-tolerance/582106/.

Robinson, Robert, Dacher Keltner, Andrew Ward, and Lee Ross. 1995. "Actual Versus Assumed Differences in Construal: 'Naïve Realism' in Intergroup Perception and Conflict." *Journal of Personality and Social Psychology* 68 (3): 404–17.

Rocas, Sonia, and Marilyn Brewer. 2002. "Social Identity Complexity." *Personality and Social Psychology Review* 6 (2): 88–106.

Rogers, Steven. 2016. "National Forces in State Legislative Elections." *The Annals of the American Academy of Political and Social Science* 667 (1): 207–25.

Rogowski, Jon, and Joseph Sutherland. 2016. "How Ideology Fuels Affective Polarization." *Political Behavior* 38 (3): 485–508.

Rosenblum, Nancy. 2008. *On the Side of Angels: An Appreciation of Parties and Partisanship*. Cambridge, MA: Harvard University Press.

———. 2011. "A Political Theory of Partisanship and Independence." In *The State of the Parties: The Changing Role of Contemporary American Parties*, 6th edition, ed. John Green and Daniel Coffey. Lanham, MD: Rowman & Littlefield Publishers.

Rossiter, Erin. 2021. "The Consequences of Interparty Conversation on Outparty Affect and Stereotypes." Unpublished manuscript, Washington University, St. Louis, MO.

Rothbart, Myron, and Oliver John. 1985. "Social Categorization and Behavioral Episodes: A Cognitive Analysis of the Effects of Intergroup Contact." *Journal of Social Issues* 41 (3): 81–104.

Ruggeri, Kai, Bojana Većkalov, Lana Bojanić, Thomas L. Andersen, Sarah Ashcroft-Jones, Nélida Ayacaxli, Paula Barea-Arroyo, et al. 2021. "The General Fault in Our Fault Lines." *Nature Human Behaviour* 5 (10): 1369–80.

Sabl, Andrew. 2005. "Virtues for Pluralists." *Journal of Moral Philosophy* 2 (2): 207–35.

Sanders, Lynn. 1997. "Against Deliberation." *Political Theory* 25 (3): 347–76.

Schaffner, Brian, Stephen Ansolabehere, and Sam Luks. 2021. "Cooperative Election Study Common Content, 2020." Computer file, Harvard Dataverse. https://dataverse.harvard.edu/data set.xhtml?persistentId=doi:10.7910/DVN/E9N6PH.

Schaffner, Brian, and Samantha Luks. 2018. "Misinformation or Expressive Responding? What an Inauguration Crowd Can Tell Us about the Source of Political Misinformation in Surveys." *Public Opinion Quarterly* 82 (1): 135–47.

Schattschneider, Elmer Eric. 1942. *Party Government.* New York: Farrar and Rinehart.

Schildkraut, Deborah. 2010. *Americanism in the 21st Century: Public Opinion in the Age of Immigration.* New York: Cambridge University Press.

Schlozman, Daniel, and Samuel Rosenfeld. 2019. "The Hollow Parties." In *Can America Govern Itself?* ed. Frances Lee and Nolan McCarty. New York: Cambridge University Press.

Schwalbe, Michael, Geoffrey Cohen, and Lee Ross. 2020. "The Objectivity Illusion and Voter Polarization in the 2016 Presidential Election." *Proceedings of the National Academy of Sciences* 117 (35): 21218–29.

Schwarz, Norbert, and Herbert Bless. 1992. "Scandals and the Public's Trust in Politicians: Assimilation and Contrast Effects." *Personality and Social Psychology Bulletin* 18 (5): 574–79.

Sears, David. 1983. "The Person-Positivity Bias." *Journal of Personality and Social Psychology* 44 (2): 233–50.

Settle, Jaime. 2018. *Frenemies: How Social Media Polarizes America.* New York: Cambridge University Press.

Settle, Jaime, and Taylor Carlson. 2019. "Opting Out of Political Discussions." *Political Communication* 36 (3): 476–96.

Shafranek, Richard. 2021. "Political Considerations in Nonpolitical Contexts: A Conjoint Analysis of Roommate Choice." *Political Behavior* 43 (1): 271–300.

Silverman, Alex. 2020. "Demographic Data Shows Which Major Sports Fan Bases Are Most Likely to Support or Reject Social Justice Advocacy." *Morning Consult*, 10 September. https://morningconsult.com/2020/09/10/sports-fan-base-demographic-data/.

Simon, Bernd, and Christopher Schaefer. 2015. "Tolerance as a Function of Disapproval and Respect: The Case of Muslims." *British Journal of Social Psychology* 55 (2): 375–83.

Simonovits, Gabor, Jennifer McCoy, and Levente Littvay. 2022. "Democratic Hypocrisy and Out-Group Threat: Explaining Citizen Support for Democratic Norm Erosion." *Journal of Politics* 84 (3): 1806–11.

Sinclair, Betsy. 2012. *The Social Citizen.* Chicago: University of Chicago Press.

Skitka, Linda, Brittany Hanson, G. Scott Morgan, and Daniel Wisneski. 2021. "The Psychology of Moral Conviction." *Annual Review of Psychology* 72 (1): 347–66.

Skytte, Rasmus. 2021. "Dimensions of Elite Partisan Polarization: Disentangling the Effects of Incivility and Issue Positions." *British Journal of Political Science* 51 (4): 1457–75.

Smith, Rogers. 1983. "The 'American Creed' and American Identity: The Limits of Liberal Citizenship in the United States." *Western Political Quarterly* 41 (2): 225–51.

———. 1997. *Civic Ideals: Conflicting Visions of Citizenship in U.S. History*. New Haven, CT: Yale University Press.

Smith, Rogers, and Desmond King. 2021. "White Protectionism in America." *Perspectives on Politics* 19 (2): 460–78.

Smith, Steven. 2021. *Reclaiming Patriotism in an Age of Extremes*. New Haven, CT: Yale University Press.

Sniderman, Paul, Richard Brody, and Philip Tetlock, eds. 1993. *Reasoning and Choice: Explorations in Political Psychology*. New York: Cambridge University Press.

Sniderman, Paul, and Matthew Levendusky. 2007. "An Institutional Theory of Political Choice." In *The Oxford Handbook of Political Behavior*, ed. Russell Dalton and Hans-Dieter Klingemann. Oxford, UK: Oxford University Press.

Sniderman, Paul, and Edward Stiglitz. 2011. *The Reputational Premium: A Theory of Party Identification and Policy Reasoning*. Princeton, NJ: Princeton University Press.

Sonmez, Felicia, and Rachel Bade. 2019. "'This Is the Agenda of White Nationalists': Four Minority Congresswomen Condemn Trump's Racist Tweet." *Washington Post*, 15 July.

Stanley, Matthew, Alyssa Sinclair, and Paul Seli. 2020. "Intellectual Humility and Perceptions of Political Opponents." *Journal of Personality* 88 (6): 1196–1216.

Stanley, Matthew, Peter Whitehead, Walter Sinnott-Armstrong, and Paul Seli. 2020. "Exposure to Opposing Reasons Reduces Negative Impressions of Ideological Opponents." *Journal of Experimental Social Psychology* 91 (November): 104030.

Sunstein, Cass. 2015. "Partyism." *University of Chicago Legal Forum* 2015, article 2. Last accessed January 2022. Available at https://chicagounbound.uchicago.edu/uclf/vol2015/iss1/2/.

Taber, Charles, and Milton Lodge. 2006. "Motivated Skepticism in the Evaluation of Political Beliefs." *American Journal of Political Science* 50 (3): 755–69.

Tajfel, Henri. 1981. *Human Groups and Social Categories: Studies in Social Psychology*. Cambridge, UK: Cambridge University Press.

Tajfel, Henri, and John Turner. 1979. "An Integrative Theory of Intergroup Conflict." In *The Social Psychology of Intergroup Relations*, ed. W. G. Austin and Stephen Worchel. Monterey, CA: Brooks/Cole.

Tajfel, Henri, and A. L. Wilkes. 1963. "Classification and Quantitative Judgment." *British Journal of Psychology* 54:101–14.

Tamari, Jonathan. 2020. "Donald Trump and Barack Obama Agreed on One Thing in Dueling PA Visits: Win, or It's the Apocalypse." *Philadelphia Inquirer*, 22 August.

Tausanovitch, Chris, and Lynn Vavreck. 2020. Democracy Fund + UCLA Nationscape, Part 1. Computer file, release 1, version 20200814. University of California, Los Angeles. https://www.voterstudygroup.org/nationscape.

Theiss-Morse, Elizabeth. 2009. *Who Counts as an American? The Boundaries of National Identity*. New York: Cambridge University Press.

Thomsen, Danielle. 2017. *Opting Out of Congress: Partisan Polarization and the Decline of Moderate Candidates*. New York: Cambridge University Press.

Timberg, Craig, and Elizabeth Dwoskin. 2020. "Trump Debate Comments Give an Online Boost to a Group Social Media Companies Have Long Struggled Against." *Washington Post*, 30 September.

Transue, John. 2007. "Identity Salience, Identity Acceptance, and Racial Policy Attitudes: American National Identity as a Unifying Force." *American Journal of Political Science* 51 (1): 78–91.

Tropp, Linda, and Thomas Pettigrew. 2005. "Differential Relationships between Intergroup Contact and Affective and Cognitive Dimensions of Prejudice." *Personality and Social Psychology Bulletin* 31 (8): 1145–58.

Tucker, Eric, and Frank Bajak. 2020. "Repudiating Trump, Officials Say Election 'Most Secure.'" *AP News*, 13 November.

Tyson, Alec, and Brian Kennedy. 2020. "Two-Thirds of Americans Think Government Should Do More on Climate." Pew Research Center report, 23 June. https://www.pewresearch.org/science/2020/06/23/two-thirds-of-americans-think-government-should-do-more-on-climate/.

Uscinski, Joseph, Adam Enders, Michelle Seelig, Casey Klofstad, John Funchion, Caleb Everett, Stefan Wuchty, Kamal Premaratne, and Manohar Murthi. 2021. "American Politics in Two Dimensions: Partisan and Ideological Identities versus Anti-Establishment Orientations." *American Journal of Political Science* 65 (4): 877–95.

UVA Center for Politics. 2021. "New Initiative Explores Deep, Persistent Divides Between Biden and Trump Voters." *Sabato's Crystal Ball*, UVA Center for Politics, 30 September. https://centerforpolitics.org/crystalball/articles/new-initiative-explores-deep-persistent-divides-between-biden-and-trump-voters/.

Van Hilvoorde, Ivo, Agnes Elling, and Ruud Stovkis. 2010. "How to Influence National Pride? The Olympic Medal Index as a Unifying Narrative." *International Review for the Sociology of Sport* 45 (1): 87–102.

Van Kleef, Gerben, Florian Wanders, Eftychia Stamkou, and Astrid Homan. 2015. "The Social Dynamics of Breaking the Rules: Antecedents and Consequences of Norm-Violating Behavior." *Current Opinion in Psychology* 6 (December): 25–31.

Van Oudenhoven, Jan Pieter, Jan Tjeerd Groenewoud, and Miles Hewstone. 1996. "Cooperation, Ethnic Salience, and Generalization of Interethnic Attitudes." *European Journal of Social Psychology* 26 (4): 649–61.

Voelkel, Jan, James Chu, Michael Stagnaro, Joseph Mernyk, Chrystal Redekopp, Sophia Pink, James Druckman, David Rand, and Robb Willer. 2021. "Interventions Reducing Affective Polarization Do Not Improve Anti-Democratic Behaviors." Unpublished manuscript, Stanford University.

Voelkel, Jan, Dongning Ren, and Mark Brandt. 2021. "Political Inclusion Reduces Political Prejudice." *Journal of Experimental Social Psychology* 95 (July): 104149.

Voelkel, Jan, Michael N. Stagnaro, James Chu, Sophia Pink, Joseph S. Mernyk, Chrystal Redekopp, Matthew Cashman, Qualifying Strengthening Democracy Challenge Submitters, James N. Druckman, David G. Rand, and Rob Willer. 2022. "Megastudy Identifying Successful Interventions to Strengthen Americans' Democractic Attitudes." Unpublished manuscript: Stanford University.

Wan, Daniel, and Nyla Branscombe. 1993. "Sports Fans: Measuring Degree of Identification with Their Team." *International Journal of Sports Psychology* 24 (1): 1–17.

Wark, Colin, and John Galliher. 2007. "Emory Bogardus and the Origins of the Social Distance Scale." *American Sociologist* 38 (4): 383–95.

Weber, Christopher, and Samara Klar. 2019. "Exploring the Psychological Foundations of Ideological and Social Sorting." *Political Psychology: Advances in Political Psychology* 40 (S1): 215–43.

Webster, Steven. 2020. *American Rage: How Anger Fuels our Politics.* New York: Cambridge University Press.

Webster, Steven, and Alan Abramowitz. 2017. "The Ideological Foundations of Affective Polarization in the U.S. Electorate." *American Politics Research* 45 (4): 621–47.

Wehner, Peter. 2016. "Friendship in the Age of Trump." *New York Times*, 23 April.

Weise, Elizabeth. 2020. "Republican and Democratic Voters Actually Agree on Many Climate Change Fixes. So Why No Action?" *USA Today*, 24 January.

West, Emily, and Shanto Iyengar. 2022. "Partisanship as a Social Identity: Implications for Polarization." *Political Behavior* 44 (2): 807–38.

Westfall, Jacob, Leaf Van Boven, John Chambers, and Charles Judd. 2015. "Perceiving Political Polarization in the United States: Party Identity Strength and Attitude Extremity Exacerbate the Perceived Partisan Divide." *Perspectives on Psychological Science* 10 (2): 145–58.

Westwood, Sean, Erik Peterson, and Yphtach Lelkes. 2019. "Are There Still Limits on Partisan Prejudice?" *Public Opinion Quarterly* 83 (3): 584–97.

White, Ismail, and Chryl Laird. 2020. *Steadfast Democrats: How Social Forces Shape Black Political Behavior*. Princeton, NJ: Princeton University Press.

Wilcox, Clyde, Lee Sigelman, and Elizabeth Cook. 1989. "Some Like It Hot: Individual Differences in Responses to Group Feeling Thermometer Ratings." *Public Opinion Quarterly* 53 (2): 246–57.

Williamson, Kevin. 2021. "The Trump Coup Is Still Raging." *New York Times*, 10 September.

Williamson, Scott, Claire Adida, Adeline Lo, Melina Platas, Lauren Prather, and Seth Werfel. 2021. "Family Matters: How Immigrant Histories Can Promote Inclusion." *American Political Science Review* 115 (2): 686–93.

Wojcieszak, Magdalena, and R. Kelly Garrett. 2018. "Social Identity, Selective Exposure, and Affective Polarization: How Priming National Identity Shapes Attitudes Toward Immigrants via News Selection." *Human Communication Research* 44 (3): 247–73.

Wojcieszak, Magdalena, and Diana Mutz. 2006. "Online Groups and Political Discourse: Do Online Discussion Spaces Facilitate Exposure to Political Discussion?" *Journal of Communication* 59 (1): 40–56.

Wojcieszak, Magdalena, and Benjamin Warner. 2020. "Can Interparty Contact Reduce Affective Polarization? A Systematic Test of Different Forms of Intergroup Contact." *Political Communication* 37 (6): 789–811.

Wojcieszak, Magdalena, Stephan Winter, and Xudong Yu. 2020. "Social Norms and Selectivity: Effects of Norms of Open-Mindedness on Content Selection and Affective Polarization." *Mass Communication and Society* 23 (4): 455–83.

Wolak, Jennifer. 2020. *Compromise in an Age of Party Polarization*. New York: Oxford University Press.

Yeager, David, Jon Krosnick, Linchiat Chang, Harold Javitz, Matthew Levendusky, Alberto Simpser, and Rui Wang. 2011. "Comparing the Accuracy of RDD Telephone Surveys and Internet Surveys Conducted with Probability and Non-Probability Samples." *Public Opinion Quarterly* 75 (4): 709–47.

Yeomans, Michael, Julia Minson, Hanne Collins, Frances Chen, and Francesca Gino. 2020. "Conversational Receptiveness: Improving Engagement with Opposing Views." *Organizational Behavior and Human Decision Processes* 160 (September): 131–48.

Younis, Mohamed. 2019. "Most Americans See American Dream as Achievable." *Gallup News*, 17 July. https://news.gallup.com/poll/260741/americans-american-dream-achievable.aspx.

Yudkin, Daniel, Stephen Hawkins, and Tim Dixon. 2019. "The Perception Gap: How False Impressions Are Pulling Americans Apart." PsyArXiv, 14 September; last updated 8 January 2020. doi:10.31234/osf.io/r3h5q.

Zaller, John. 1992. *The Nature and Origins of Mass Opinion*. New York: Cambridge University Press.

Zeng, Chen. 2021. "A Relational Identity-Based Solution to Group Polarization: Can Priming Parental Identity Reduce the Partisan Gap in Attitudes Toward the COVID-19 Pandemic?" *Science Communication* 43 (6): 687–718.

Index

Note: page numbers followed by *f* refer to figures and by *t* to tables.

Chicago Studies in American Politics

A series edited by Susan Herbst, Lawrence R. Jacobs, Adam J. Berinsky, and Frances Lee; Benjamin I. Page, editor emeritus